Bandage, Sort, and Hustle

Bandage, Sort, and Hustle

AMBULANCE CREWS ON THE FRONT
LINES OF URBAN SUFFERING

Josh Seim

UNIVERSITY OF CALIFORNIA PRESS

University of California Press
Oakland, California

© 2020 by Josh Seim

Cataloging-in-Publication Data is on file at the Library of Congress.

ISBN 978-0-520-30021-7 (cloth : alk. paper)
ISBN 978-0-520-30023-1 (pbk. : alk. paper)
ISBN 978-0-520-97170-7 (ebook)

Library of Congress Control Number: 2019950205

Manufactured in the United States of America

28 27 26 25 24 23 22 21 20
10 9 8 7 6 5 4 3 2 1

Contents

Illustrations

Figure 1. At work. *Note:* Author's photo.

Preface

That's a picture of me driving an ambulance (figure 1). I was somewhere in the dense flatlands of a place in California I call Agonia County. At the time, I was working as one of the nation's many emergency medical technicians (EMTs). My paramedic partner took this photo one hot afternoon in 2016, while we were between 911 calls.

In many ways, the long and winding path that led to this photograph began five years earlier in Oregon. I was in Portland, meeting with James, who, like me, is a white male. Unlike me, though, James has spent much of his adult life in and out of squad cars, courtrooms, probation meetings, jails, prisons, and parole offices. I first met him inside a prison while I was conducting a different study.[1] However, on this particular occasion, we met on the streets, just a few blocks from the transitional housing facility that he moved into after his recent release from prison. James told me that he hated his current living situation. He said residents were frequently stealing from one another, people were often fighting, and the living conditions constantly tempted him with the narcotics he was once addicted to.

Providing me with further evidence of this facility's horrors, James said the ambulance was always there. He told me that ambulance crews were rushing in and out of the building at least twice a week, responding to assaults and other crises. James also mentioned that an ambulance crew had recently discovered a parolee's corpse in the building. Rumor suggested it was a heroin overdose. For James, the ambulance's frequent presence seemed to offer some proof that mayhem defined his living conditions.

After this conversation, I started to notice ambulances a lot more. Not only did they stick out in traffic, they also stuck out in a number of books I was reading. Written in as a background prop and with its workers cast as extras in someone else's drama, the ambulance appears in some of sociology's most influential ethnographies. Careful readers can find it in Elijah Anderson's *Code of the Street*, Mitchell Duneier's *Sidewalk*, and Martín Sánchez-Jankowski's *Cracks in the Pavement*.[2] More recently, it can be found in Matthew Desmond's *Evicted* and Forrest Stuart's *Down, Out, and Under Arrest*.[3] Not unlike James, most of these sociologists seemed to mention the ambulance simply to highlight some disorder or death in their respective field sites.

Suddenly a bit more curious about ambulances, I turned to the scholars who honed their focus on this institution. I found a number of ethnographers who had entered the ambulance to reveal its unique work culture and organizational dynamics.[4] However, these scholars had done very little to detail the ambulance's prevalence or function in poor and nonwhite communities. I also found some statistical research, published mostly in the professional literature on emergency medical services, that demonstrated relatively high ambulance utilization among poor people, people of color, the elderly, and other populations that tend to bear the brunt of suffering in American society.[5] But these studies offered minimal insight into the way ambulance crews were handling such people on the ground. I didn't see these ethnographic and statistical accounts of the ambulance as insignificant. They just didn't really help me understand the role that this institution was playing among those who suffer most in the American city.

Fast-forward four years past my conversation with James. I was shadowing ambulance crews at a firm I call Medical Response and Transport (MRT) and collecting data for the book at hand. MRT is a for-profit 911 ambulance provider that holds contracts throughout the nation. I embedded myself within its operations in Agonia County. There, management generously allowed me to ride along in ambulances and take notes. They even permitted me to observe some managerial activities to get a "bird's-eye" view of the organization. And, as an added bonus to this rare entry, I was able to secure over one hundred thousand deidentified medical records completed by MRT crews.

My ride-along observations brought me seemingly everywhere, from multistoried mansions perched atop steep hills to homeless encampments planted beneath highway overpasses. It nonetheless became very obvious to me after just a few days in the field that, while the ambulance can pop up just about anywhere, it's usually pulled toward impoverished and otherwise disadvantaged territories. This wasn't surprising given my conversation with James and the brief, yet frequent, appearances that ambulance workers were making in urban ethnographies.

What was surprising was the variety of problems that ambulance crews were responding to. As you might imagine, the paramedics and EMTs I shadowed were definitely rushing severely sick and broken bodies to the hospital, and they were disproportionately collecting these patients from poor and nonwhite neighborhoods. However, such "real emergencies" ultimately accounted for a minority of the 911 calls I encountered. Ambulance crews were more commonly mitigating less urgent symptoms of the chronically ill, connecting drugless patients to prescription-writing physicians, and scooping drunk people off the sidewalk.

This book started to come into focus. I was going to break from the popular but limited understanding of the ambulance as an institution for saving and transporting the critically ill and injured. The point was not to forgo this framing entirely, but instead to think of the broader role that the ambulance is also playing in the American city. I started to consider how paramedic and EMT labor contributed to what sociologists were more or less synonymously calling a "regulation," "management," or "governance" of those populations that suffer most in the economically and racially polarized metropolis.[6] By concentrating on the *labor* of ambulance crews, I was also poised to build upon a rich scholarly tradition that focuses on the frontline workers who tend to handle such populations (e.g., welfare caseworkers, police officers, and emergency department nurses).[7]

This labor-centric analysis proved fruitful for three reasons. First, in carefully documenting what paramedic and EMT work involved, I was able to unpack social relations *inside* the ambulance. Beyond underlining the fact that it's heavily the poor, the nonwhite, and otherwise vulnerable populations that ambulance crews are working on, an analysis of the ambulance as a worksite clarified a general outcome of ambulance labor. I started to more clearly see paramedicine as an institution that offers rapid but generally superficial and very specific aid to suffering bodies. Second, this focus on labor also helped me locate the ambulance *between* two other institutions that tend to handle poorer and darker-skinned bodies in urban America: the hospital emergency department and the police squad car. I quickly noted how crews regularly shared the subjects of their labor with other frontline workers like nurses and cops. These cross-institutional interactions between workers structured not only life inside the ambulance but also the manner in which people were distributed across institutions. Third, my labor-centric analysis inspired me to consider how the ambulance is situated *underneath* a series of political and economic forces that control and coordinate crew labor. I learned that said forces help set the possibilities for the street-level relations between crews and their patients on the one hand and crews and other frontline workers on the other. I saw how MRT's pursuit of profit rests on the efficiency and flexibility of crew labor. This helped explain why the people who most rely on ambulance services regularly encounter exhausted and frustrated providers.

In short, I found the key to this book during my ride-along observations. I was going to rethink the ambulance as an institution for regulating urban suffering and I was going to deploy a labor-centric framework to do this. There was a clear novelty to this approach and I figured it could help social scientists understand other institutions that tend to handle relatively poor and powerless populations at ground level. A hunch to study the ambulance years earlier was finally paying off. The plan was so simple.

Until it wasn't. After nearly a year of doing fieldwork, my wife abruptly lost her job. Suddenly, the research fellowships that funded my research were not going to cut it. It was during this time that Grant, a field supervisor at MRT and one of my closest subjects, encouraged me to apply to MRT. He recommended I work as an EMT, which is the lower-paid position on the standard paramedic-EMT crew. According to Grant, I'd be like a "caddie" to paramedics who would lead the administration of care while I would mostly drive them around in the ambulance and prep their equipment. He reasoned this would be a great way to make some extra money and learn about ambulances. I asked several workers and managers what they thought of this. The response was overwhelmingly positive. "Finally," one paramedic said with a smirk, "You won't be just standing around with your hands in your pockets." Another noted that this would give me a taste of what ambulance work was *really* like.

So, I began an unanticipated transition from ride-along to EMT. It helped that I completed a six-week intensive EMT training after my conversation with James but before I ever stepped foot into an MRT ambulance. I initially did this training to introduce myself to ambulance work and to network with people in the industry. To actually become employable, though, I had to clear a few more hurdles at MRT headquarters. These included a fitness and agility trial, a mannequin-based skills exam, and a fifty-question multiple-choice test covering anatomy and physiology, prehospital emergency procedures, and other topics.

I was eventually hired at MRT for pennies above the county's living wage. Following two additional months of company-based training, I was then seated behind the steering wheel of the ambulance to assist better-trained paramedics. Indeed, it's the paramedics, not the EMTs, who inject needles into veins, slide tubes down throats, and administer effectively all medications in the ambulance. On rare occasion, I was tasked with leading the administration of care for low-acuity calls that involved no medical interventions beyond some simple first aid and the construction of a written medical record.

That said, I found that EMT work forced me to confront human suffering in a way far more challenging than what I had done previously. As a ride-along, I was occasionally asked to assist crews when "shit hit the fan." This usually meant manually stabilizing an injury or collecting information from a bystander. Otherwise, I stepped back and jotted notes. But there was no stepping back as an EMT. I was thrown deeper than a ride-along, but not as deep as a paramedic, into the tangles of 911 ambulance encounters. This work was far more exhausting than observing crews.

However, working as an EMT was also enlightening. The job forced me to put pen and paper down. It needed my hands to steer the ambulance and lift the gurney. This was more than a fair trade because I learned so much about ambulance work by actually working. Beyond deepening my knowledge of various work procedures, this experience revealed a number of taken-for-granted assumptions about the job. It unearthed seemingly trivial but actually important elements of ambulance operations. Still committed to understanding the ambulance as an institution for governing urban suffering, this experience also helped me better understand workers' frustrations, joys, and indifferences when handling the bodies that carry the brunt of misery in the American city.

I focused on being the best EMT I could be. While that focus was easy to lose toward the end of my twelve-hour shift or when the occasional "spitter" was trying to get me, I took my job seriously. Among other things, this meant that I couldn't write detailed notes like I did as a ride-along. But this didn't mean that I forgot what initially brought me into the ambulance: a curiosity to understand this institution amid urban suffering. I also never forgot what awaited me once my family's finances were in order: a book on the ambulance.

So, from home, I journaled every shift I worked. At first, I thought of this as a kind of "post-fieldwork" exercise that could help me clarify what I had already learned inside the ambulance as a ride-along. Over time, though, the particular lessons I learned as a rookie EMT became too significant to ignore. Working on the ambulance fundamentally influenced my understanding of paramedicine. Even if I hadn't journaled my shifts, I would have still felt obligated to confront my experiences as an EMT when writing this book.

Whether or not my time as an ambulance worker constituted "research" in the same way as my attempts to mimic a fly-on-the-wall observer is somewhat beside the point. This experience yielded *empirical knowledge,* a knowledge acquired through my direct engagement with the world. It just so happens that this knowledge concerns the very corner of the world that this book sets out to describe and explain. Failure to integrate my insight as an EMT into the analysis that follows would be reckless and, I argue, impossible.[8]

I'm not so naïve as to assume that my nine-month stint as an EMT makes me the ultimate ambulance insider, nor do I think this experience should eclipse what I learned through a year of ride-along observations. But a simple fact remains. My unexpected time as an EMT roots a particular viewpoint that shapes every chapter that follows this preface.

Author's Note

This book uses fictitious names for the studied county, company, and people. Let me explain why.[1]

During the beginning of this project, I promised labor and management at the private ambulance firm that I studied that I wouldn't publish their real names. I made this commitment under the assumption that they would speak more candidly and act more "natural" if they trusted me not to print their identities. I obviously don't know how the alternative would have played out, but I think this was a fair assumption to start with. I also was, and continue to be, skeptical that any of the potential benefits of unmasking workers and managers' identities would have outweighed the potential costs of doing so (e.g., the increased risk of embarrassing particular individuals).

My decision to conceal the identities of patients, nurses, cops, firefighters, doctors, bystanders, and other individuals was much easier. While my primary focus was on ambulance crews, I couldn't ignore their interactions with these other people. But at no time did I feel like I could ask these individuals to consent to my use of their real names. Such requests would have been impractical and could have potentially interfered with emergency services.

Still, it's one thing to print fictitious names for individuals and something else to mystify a place. There are obviously fewer counties in California than there are ambulance workers, patients, nurses, cops, and so on. I accept that many readers will probably correctly guess where this book takes place. Even so, I think many of those correct guesses would be somewhat lucky. There are many counties that run ambulance operations in a way similar to what's detailed in this text. I should also note that there are multiple counties where it would have been more or less equally "convenient" for me to conduct this study. Ultimately, my goal is to leave you a little confused as to where exactly this book takes place.

This, of course, raises the question as to why I would want to confuse you at all. The main reason I don't print the county's real name is because I want to obscure the specific ambulance company I studied. As is the case for the county in this book, local governments that rely on privatized 911 ambulance operations typically hold contracts with one ambulance firm at a time. Thus, if I explicitly named the county, I might as well name the company. And that option seemed to be a bit distasteful to management. A number of managers claimed they liked the idea of me not printing the firm's name. They said this helped separate me from some of the journalists who liked to write "hit pieces" on the organization. That seemed like a reasonable point to me, even if it was only articulated by a few people in the firm's leadership. Plus, if I were to explicitly name the county and by extension the company, I would only be making it easier for curious readers to deidentify the small number of upper- and mid-level managers who appear in this book. So, as part of my commitment to use a pseudonym for the company, and also as part of my efforts to mask the identities of individual managers, I simply don't name the county.

Please trust that I did not hide the real names of people, places, or organizations in an effort to conceal methodological flaws, nor did I do so as a thoughtless commitment to customs in my discipline.

Acknowledgments

I owe a lot of thanks to a lot of people. First and foremost, I am grateful to labor and management at the studied ambulance firm for letting me poke my head around and get my hands dirty. I can never truly repay the people who appear in the pages that follow but writing a book that neither glorifies nor demonizes their world seems like a good start.

This text is based on my doctoral research at the University of California, Berkeley. My dissertation advisor, Michael Burawoy, was a tireless coach. I can't imagine where I might be without his support. For years, Michael has offered rich commentary on my work and has remained genuinely committed to this project. The other members of my dissertation committee, Dave Harding, Seth Holmes, and Armando Lara-Millán, were also incredible mentors.

Additionally, my comrades in Michael's legendary dissertation group—Zachary Levenson, Benjamin Shestakofsky, Emine Fidan Elcioglu, Andy Chang, Herbert Docena, Andrew Jaeger, Shannon Ikebe, Aya Fabros, Thomas Peng, and Shelly Steward—all offered extensive feedback on many of the arguments presented in this book. Workshopping my writing with these brilliant people over dinner, drinks, and dessert in Michael's condo will forever remain one of the highlights of my academic life.

I was also very lucky to receive feedback from other great scholars at various stages during this project: Cybelle Fox, Margaret Weir, Martín Sánchez-Jankowski, Loïc Wacquant, Claude Fischer, Chris Herring, David Showalter, Lindsay Berkowitz, Alex Barnard, Zawadi Rucks-Ahidiana, Michaela Simons, Esther Cho, Seth Leibson, Bill Hayes, Vikas Gumbhir, Deborah Gordon, Adam Reich, Peter Moskos, Denise Herd, David Brady, Megan Comfort, and Steve Viscelli. Additionally, my wonderful colleagues in the Sociology Department at the University of Southern California—especially Ann Owens, Jody Vallejo, and Paul Lichterman—provided me with much needed advice and encouragement as I approached the finish line.

All of this was added to the more technical but nevertheless critical support I received from Carl Mason, Patty Frontiera, Karl Sporer, Melody Glenn, Joshua English, Tarak Trivedi, and others. I'm also very thankful for the beautiful cover art done by Glynnis Koike, the sharp copyediting done by Robert Demke, and the thorough indexing done by PJHeim.

This book extends, and at times replicates, my writing in "The Ambulance: Toward a Labor Theory of Poverty Governance," *American Sociological Review* 82 (3): 451–75. I'm indebted to the reviewers and editors at this journal for their invaluable feedback during a critical stage in this project's development.

Likewise, I greatly appreciate the hardworking people at University of California Press. Naomi Schneider was a very supportive editor at all stages in this book's development. Benjy Malings, Kate Hoffman, Summer Farah, and Chris Sosa Loomis were always quick to answer the naïve questions of a first-time book author. The reviewers recruited by the press also provided excellent notes that shaped the final product.

More than anyone else, though, I am grateful to Brenna Seim. She's my wife, my best friend, and the single most important advisor I have. She read every page of this book and provided excellent editing advice. But that's just the tip of the iceberg. She's my biggest advocate and has been so since I was a GED-holding community college student who daydreamed about becoming a sociologist. There's no way I can summarize the many ways Brenna has supported me throughout the years, but without her I simply wouldn't be publishing a book. That much is clear to me.

Finally, I want to acknowledge the many fellowships and grants that funded my research and writing. The Graduate Division at Berkeley provided me with a number of financial packages: the University of California Dissertation-Year Fellowship, the Doctoral Completion Fellowship, the Mentored Research Award, and a couple summer research grants. Berkeley's Department of Sociology funded portions of this research through small research grants and the Leo Lowenthal Fellowship. The Dana and David Dornsife College of Letters, Arts, and Science at the University of Southern California also provided funding for the completion of this book.

Introduction

I remember my first day of fieldwork at Medical Response and Transport (MRT) very well. A few minutes before 5:00 AM, I walked into the firm's headquarters, sometimes referred to as the "barn." Inside a small office, I met Eric, a white man in his early forties. As one of the company's dozen or so field supervisors, Eric's primary task for the day was to monitor the largest segment of MRT's 911 ambulance fleet, the portion servicing the urban core of what I call Agonia County. However, he also agreed to a secondary task: taking me on a sightseeing journey of sorts. Per the recommmendation of upper management, this day with Eric was partially meant to introduce me to MRT before I actually started jotting notes from the backs of ambulances. It also didn't hurt that all supervisors are experienced paramedics, meaning Eric could provide insight beyond his current position as a middle manager. After exchanging a few pleasantries about the weather and my research, we walked out of the barn and headed toward a company-issued SUV known more informally as a supervisor rig.

As we prepared to depart from MRT's headquarters for the day, I took a mental note of Eric's appearance: stocky build, veiny arms, and a high-

1

and-tight haircut. I thought he looked a lot like law enforcement in his
company uniform, which included a shiny supervisor badge. Either due to
coincidence or Eric's secret ability to read minds, he told me that he looks
especially cop-like when he wears a bulletproof vest under his shirt. He
wasn't wearing the vest on this particular day though. It's hot and bulky,
but he promised his wife he'd at least put it on during night shifts. Before
leaving the barn for the day, Eric told me he'd show me some of the reasons why he protects himself with a vest from time to time.

He drove me through some "ghettos" and "hoods." I'd later learn that
these are terms MRT workers and supervisors casually and interchange-
ably use to identify poor neighborhoods, which are disproportionately
occupied by Agonia County's black and Latino residents. Eric first took me
to the "killing fields," a predominately black neighborhood with a high
homicide rate. From there, we cruised into some nearby "barrios" before
we made our way to see some "projects."

Inside the supervisor rig, Eric provided a verbal commentary for the
sights outside our window. "There're usually prostitutes here, but not at this
time," he said. It was 8:00 AM. I found this to be an odd summary for an
avenue that seemed to be better defined by its "Cash for Gold" signs, fast
food restaurants, liquor stores, and pay-day loan centers, but I appreciated
Eric's spontaneous description of place. In addition to prostitutes, he told
me there are lots of "bangers" on these streets. But again, he insisted we
wouldn't find such characters at this hour. The wicked evidently rest.

After driving up and down the streets of these neighborhoods, waving to
the ambulance crews we saw in the process, we eventually paused at a red
light. An older black man in torn clothes lumbered across the street, passing the front of our vehicle. Eric lowered his voice, adding an extra assur-
ance of privacy, "There's a zombie." I chuckled nervously and asked, "What's
that mean?" "He's an alcoholic. You can see it in the yellowing of his eyes,"
he said, describing some jaundice that *could* be associated with liver problems and apparently by extension with the problematic consumptions of
this man whom we never actually spoke to. I soon learned that Eric's zombies also include people who use heroin and other "downers," and are distinct from his more animated "tweakers," "crack heads," and "meth heads."

As the tour continued, I asked Eric to tell me about the types of calls his
crews run. He didn't know where to begin and, in retrospect, I don't blame

him. I didn't know it at the time, but the hundreds of calls I saw in the months following the tour covered just about every inch and layer of the human body, from the head down to the toe and from the skin into the marrow.

Eric grabbed a protocol book he keeps in the supervisor rig and tossed it into my lap. I skimmed through it as he continued to drive somewhat aimlessly through busy streets. The book is a thick manual, but it fits perfectly in the side pocket of an EMT or paramedic's cargo pants. Almost biblical in its authority, this book is published by Agonia County Emergency Medical Services (EMS), the public agency that oversees MRT's contract with the local government. It outlines a number of protocols from how to manage grieving bystanders to how to work with police during an active shooter event, but it mostly covers treatment procedures for a variety of medical problems. Among other things, these include cardiac emergencies, overdoses, psychiatric crises, pregnancy complications, respiratory issues, strokes, seizures, and trauma (i.e., physical injury).

Of course, some calls are more severe than others. Eric explained to me how county dispatchers classify ambulance responses not only according to the type of emergency (e.g., chest pain, headache, and stab wound), but also by the presumed urgency of the problem. In reverse alphabetical order, and from the most acute to the least, there are five primary levels of severity determined by dispatchers: "echo," "delta," "charlie," "bravo," and "alpha." Echo responses include things like cardiac arrests while alpha responses include things like flu-like symptoms. The main point of these classifications is to set guidelines for how fast an ambulance crew should arrive at the scene of a call. For example, crews are supposed to arrive within eight minutes and thirty seconds to most echo responses while they usually have thirty minutes to show up to an alpha response.

Eric warned that these dispatcher-determined triages are usually "good guesses" but they can be misleading. For him and essentially everyone I spent time with at MRT, there is a more informal but a more important distinction in severity. It's determined on 911 scenes and in the backs of ambulances by crews who can see, touch, and speak to patients directly.

There are "legit" calls and then there are "bullshit" calls. Legit calls are the so-called real emergencies that necessitate and justify the craft of paramedicine. These are typically the cases that have crews exercising the skills that they were taught: intubating breathless airways, compressing lifeless chests, plugging bleeding wounds, and so on. In contrast, bullshit calls are the so-called nonemergencies that involve little more than a collection of vital signs, a ride to the hospital, and maybe some minor interventions like the icing of a sore joint. As I eventually came to understand this distinction, legit and bullshit are not really binary categories but are instead more like poles on a continuum.

During the tour, Eric offered me his thoughts on legit and bullshit ambulance cases. In teaching me about the latter, he depicted two forms of people, what we might call the "selfish" and the "stupid." Supposedly, selfish people often call 911 because they want a quick painkiller fix, they wish to bypass an emergency department waiting room, or they desire some other convenience provided by the responding ambulance crew. Such people greedily take an ambulance away from a more deserving soul in the area, like a gunshot or heart attack victim. But not everyone who calls for bullshit reasons is seen as selfish. According to Eric, stupid people purportedly call for different reasons. They're not interested in executing some sinister plan for self-reward. Instead, they lack basic problem-solving skills. They call 911 for nonurgent problems because they don't know any better. Or at least that's the impression I gathered from Eric's impromptu lectures on the tragedy of bullshit.

Luckily for him and his crews, the calls are not all trivial. Eric also told me about some of the "good" and "interesting" calls he had run. As an experienced paramedic, he has certainly seen his fair share of legit calls. He told me stories of how he skillfully brought the dead back to life with a mixture of CPR and drugs. He also told me how he cleverly identified cardiac abnormalities through an electrocardiogram. Eric then provided some gruesome accounts of salvaging flesh and bone nearly obliterated by car accidents and other catastrophes.

This man's reflections of past calls eventually led him to some "war stories." As he drove me through more neighborhoods, Eric's voice sometimes shifted to a somber tone. He told me about finding young bodies pumped with bullets, intestines spilled out of abdominal walls, and the maggot-infested corpses of suicide victims. He told me heartbreaking tales of having to inform children that their parents were never waking up and of patients taking their final breaths under his care. Even though

Eric complained a lot about bullshit, it seemed like every few blocks reminded him of the real-life horror shows he was abruptly cast into during their climaxes or epilogues. Still, Eric said, "It's not like the movies." Ambulance operations are not always adrenaline-rushing, and even when they are they can mentally wound providers. Like many of the experienced ambulance workers and supervisors I met, Eric seems to traverse the streets of Agonia with ghosts in tow.

Suddenly, our conversation was interrupted. A short and loud alarm flooded the interior of the SUV. Eric turned up the radio to hear what the dispatcher was assigning him. It was a "GSW," a gunshot wound. As a supervisor, Eric is frequently summoned to high-profile calls like this one for a twenty-four-year-old black man who was shot in the gut.

However, by the time we arrived at the scene, not much remained but some blood that was splattered on concrete and encircled in crime scene tape.[1] We were left in the dust on this call, but it worked out for the tour. Eric had planned on driving me through this area of town anyway. The blood splatter left on the sidewalk was located almost perfectly at the epicenter of what he described as "a little nexus of evil." Along with a couple of other locations in the county, this five-or-so-block area is distinctive not only in its intense marginality, but also in its apparent offensiveness to Eric and many others at MRT.[2] He insisted an open-air drug market was just north of this blood splatter and a homeless encampment was only a few blocks south.

I didn't know it at the time, but I ended up frequenting this "little nexus of evil" a lot during my fieldwork. Beyond encountering people whom Eric would probably consider bangers, zombies, and tweakers, I experienced some memorable "firsts" in this area. This place not only included my first gunshot scene; it also included my first death, my first overdose, and the first time I saw bone cut through skin.

I also encountered plenty of low-priority calls in this particular area of the county: people needing prescription refills, clinically stable people requesting or perhaps even "seeking" pain medication, and people looking to sleep in a bed at a hospital. While in this five-or-so-block area, I frequently shadowed crews who were more or less just "taxiing" people to the emergency department for seemingly nonurgent reasons. And, when I worked as an EMT, I drove those who supposedly misuse the ambulance to the hospital myself. Eric's voice popped into my mind nearly every time I stepped out of an ambulance in this part of Agonia. "This place is a little nexus of evil." I started to think he was sort of right.

But true wickedness probably comes from outside the nexus, from those nefarious human systems that pack suffering into places like this. Eric and I witnessed the aftermath of an attempted murder here, but we may have also witnessed what Friedrich Engels calls "social murder," capitalism's inevitable wasting of human life.[3] The market yields and necessitates exploited (e.g., workers), excluded (e.g., jobless), and precarious (e.g., temporary employed) populations that are all exposed to an array of bodily risks.[4] Systemic racism is also suspect, from the continued legacy of Agonia County's segregated neighborhoods to the casual "color-blind" biases that help maintain white supremacy across market, state, and civil society.[5] Public health scholarship is actually pretty clear on this point: risks for illness and injury increase toward the bottom of the American racial hierarchy.[6]

As such, it's not very surprising that poorer people and people of color are more likely to experience what Eric considers to be "legit" emergencies. This is true not only for things like gun violence, but also for intense traffic accidents and other sources of severe injury.[7] It's also true for heart attacks, strokes, drug overdoses, seizures, breathing difficulties, psychiatric crises, and essentially every emergency listed in Eric's protocol book.[8] For many social scientists, these patterns are indications of a society that concentrates vulnerability on down-and-out populations.[9]

Structural forces seem to also account for all the so-called bullshit that Eric's crews are responding to. Persistent barriers to primary care likely motivate many people to turn to emergency medicine for an array of problems.[10] Changes to the American social safety net during the past couple of decades have probably had an effect as well. A neoliberal shift toward market-based policies has made traditional welfare programming more disciplinary and arguably more stingy for vulnerable populations at a time when their economic and social precarity has increased.[11] One of the effects of this transformation seems to have been a "medicalization" of public aid, meaning people are turning to medical entitlements like public disability benefits and emergency care for more generalized assistance.[12] From this point of view, it's not the selfishness or stupidity of individuals that is to blame. It's the selfishness and stupidity of a society that pressures legions of people in need to turn to one of the few institutions that are promised to them, the ambulance.

Ultimately, an expansive library of sociological thought tells us there's little reason to doubt that my sightseeing tour brought me very far "downstream" in a causal river linking macrostructural conditions to personal hardship. It was never very obvious to me where all these bodies Eric described floated down from, but float they did. My objective is not to follow the stream up, but to make sense of the workers who are waist-deep in the water trying to pull people out. Such an objective, however, necessitates that we first break from some common assumptions of ambulance operations in the United States.

RETHINKING THE AMBULANCE

Thousands of local agencies and organizations form a complex web of 911 ambulance operations in America.[13] In the space between federal regulation and the ambulances that roll past you in traffic, state-level emergency medical services authorities (e.g., California Emergency Medical Services Authority) charge local bureaucracies—often divisions of county health or public safety departments (e.g., Agonia County EMS)—with assuring ambulances to citizens. Some of these agencies deploy 911 ambulances directly, such as in Pittsburgh and New Orleans. However, it's more common for them to delegate these operations in portion or in full to fire departments, such as in Dallas, or to private firms like in San Diego. In California, it's estimated that less than a quarter (22 percent) of ambulance-providing agencies are private, yet over three-fourths (76 percent) of 911 calls are responded to by crews working for private companies.[14]

Buried somewhere in this web, we find MRT. As previously noted, MRT is a large for-profit firm that provides 911 ambulance services in several locations across the United States. I focus on MRT's operations in Agonia County. There, the company employs a few hundred frontline workers and effectively monopolizes ambulance operations through a contract with the local government.[15] MRT primarily secures revenue from ambulance patients and personal health insurance providers (overwhelmingly public ones like Medicare and Medicaid) under a fee-for-service model. In billing people or their insurance providers, MRT is similar to essentially all 911 ambulance operations in the country, be they private or public.[16]

My time at MRT taught me the ambulance is an institution that in many ways fulfills its formally articulated mission to provide timely and consequential care to "anyone." Similar to the emergency department, the ambulance cannot deny services based on a person's ability to pay. As such, the provision of paramedicine cuts across divisions in class, race, citizenship, age, and gender. By and large, people just need to ask for an ambulance or somehow imply that they need one (e.g., by lying unconscious in the street).

In fact, if you're reading this book somewhere in the United States, you can have an ambulance right now if you want one. Just pick up a phone, dial 911, and tell the operator you need some medical aid. The state, at multiple levels, promises you an ambulance in a somewhat timely fashion. More times than not, it will deliver on this promise.

Of course, there are some caveats. While you probably won't get a busy signal when you call, you shouldn't be totally surprised if you do.[17] Still, I'd bet it's more likely you'd have to wait longer than expected for an ambulance because there are few to none currently available in your area.[18] Yet, even this is exceptional. Perhaps there are some legal reasons that make you hesitant to dial 911. The police may very well show up along with ambulance crews, especially if you call for something like an assault, an overdose, or a psychiatric emergency.[19] So, if you want to avoid law enforcement, you've been warned. Maybe it's not so much the police that scare you from calling, but the invoice. You should be scared. Even if you have insurance, you may get stuck with a bill well over a thousand dollars in a few weeks.[20]

With these conditions in mind, concerns over ambulance accessibility for poor people and people of color are certainly reasonable. Indeed, a number of researchers have pointed to help-seeking reluctance and thinned emergency services toward the bottom of class and racial hierarchies in the American city.[21] We must nevertheless be careful not to write the ambulance off as an institution that is absent in oppressed and marginalized communities.

Paramedics and EMTs respond up and down the polarized city and there are people toward the bottom who choose to avoid it, but neither of these facts negate an important feature of the ambulance: it's an institution that's disproportionately utilized by destitute and otherwise vulnerable populations.

This isn't a particularly new pattern either. From the horse-drawn buggies that were run by hospitals after the Civil War to the motorized vehicles that were run by police departments, fire stations, funeral homes, and small companies after World War II, the ambulance has long been present in the lives of the urban poor.[22] Moreover, civil rights activists in the 1960s and beyond helped expand ambulance accessibility to racial minorities, and particularly to blacks in large cities.[23] The ambulance's gravitation toward the bottom of the urban hierarchy held during the national expansion and standardization of paramedicine during the 1970s, the partial federal withdrawal in ambulance operations during the 1980s, and the rise of national ambulance corporations during the 1990s.[24] Today, ambulance crews working for both public and private entities continue to disproportionately treat and transport relatively disadvantaged populations.[25]

What does this look like for MRT specifically? Well, over half the firm's invoices are billed to either uninsured or means-tested Medicaid patients. And, as Eric told us, MRT's crews are disproportionately sent into Agonia County's poorer neighborhoods, where a large share of the county's black and Latino residents dwell. I was able to confirm this not only through my fieldwork, but also through my analysis of several thousand medical records completed by crews.

Figure 2 summarizes the neighborhood-level response rate for MRT in the year 2015, which I have age-adjusted and averaged across poverty concentration deciles. The pattern is clear: ambulances are rolling into poorer neighborhoods at a relatively high rate. Look at the bar farthest to the right, the one with the highest mean rate of MRT responses. It captures the thirty poorest neighborhoods in the company's jurisdiction and includes the "killing fields," "barrios," "projects," "little nexus of evil," and other areas that I encountered during my sightseeing tour with Eric. While not evident in this simple figure, these neighborhoods capture less than a tenth (9 percent) of the people living within MRT's market, but they account for nearly a fifth (19 percent) of the firm's responses. Perhaps unsurprising to most readers, these neighborhoods also contain a high proportion of Agonia County's black and Latino residents (64 percent on

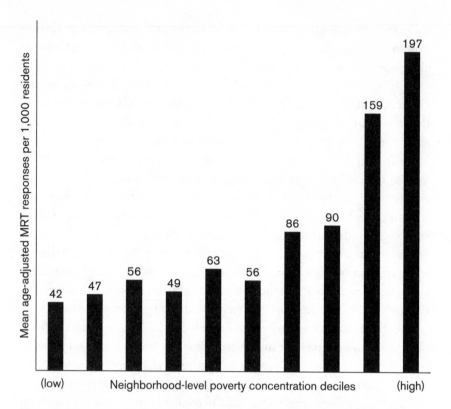

Figure 2. Mean age-adjusted ambulance responses by neighborhood poverty concentration. *Source:* MRT deidentified patient care reports, 2015; American Community Survey Five-Year Estimates, 2011–2015. *Notes:* Observations = 300. Neighborhoods defined as census tracts. Records geocoded by author using QGIS 2.14.6 (92 percent success). Excludes MRT responses to highways and bridges.

average versus 36 percent of MRT's jurisdiction overall). The ambulance is not limited to poor or minority neighborhoods, but something seems to push or pull it toward these areas.

Not long after my introductory tour with Eric, I led a research team that included a couple of emergency room physicians and a paramedic to further examine this association between neighborhood poverty and ambulance responses. Drawing on the same medical records used to construct figure 2, we found evidence suggesting that a ten-percentage-point increase in neighborhood poverty is associated with a 45-percent increase in ambulance responses.[26] We even controlled for geographic patterns in race, gender, age, citizenship, and other factors. This pattern held for all the major call types listed in Eric's protocol book and for what he would probably consider to be both legit and bullshit calls.[27] In a subsequent study, we also found evidence suggesting that MRT ambulances are *not* relatively tardy in poor neighborhoods.[28]

None of this is to suggest that ambulances don't ever "no show" or show up devastatingly late in disadvantaged neighborhoods. They absolutely do. For example, once a crew I shadowed didn't arrive on scene until thirty or so minutes past the time a 911 call was placed. This wasn't particularly unusual except that it was for a preschool-aged girl who was shot during a drive-by. We rolled up to a street corner to find a reasonably angry group of people. "You're too fucking late!" one man yelled before somebody else explained to us that a cop took the girl to a hospital. I don't intend to conceal or trivialize tragedies like this or similar ones published in the news.[29] But, just as we should be careful not to assume the ambulance is an institution that's evenly spread across the polarized metropolis, we should be careful not to conclude that it's absent in poor and nonwhite neighborhoods when the evidence suggesting so is often thin.

URBAN SUFFERING

We know the ambulance is generally a present and busy institution in the oppressed and marginalized territories of urban America. Yet, why and how this institution churns through people in these areas remain somewhat of a mystery. The professional literature on paramedicine offers simple explanations for the heavier utilization of ambulances among down-and-out populations: high rates of morbidity and mortality, detachment from primary care, lack of transportation, and shared misconceptions of emergency.[30] However, this literature tends to ignore the structural conditions of paramedicine and says very little about how ambulance crews are dealing with a disproportionately poor and nonwhite clientele. Meanwhile, the limited sociological research on the ambulance offers some rich insight into crew-patient interactions but says effectively nothing of the ambulance as an institution that manages hardships toward the bottom of the polarized city.[31]

To help solve such a mystery, this book rethinks the ambulance as a frontline institution for governing urban suffering. MRT crews traverse a large and densely populated place I call Agonia County, where plenty of people exist in temporary and enduring agony. Agonia is a playful Spanish-word pseudonym I use for a particular area in California, but it's also a kind of generalized description of urban life in advanced capitalist societies. Of course, urban dwellers, be they in the dense core or the sparse periphery, do not live in absolute misery. But all human settlements contain suffering. It's simply the more agonizing side of urban life that paramedics and EMTs frequent most. From stab wounds to strep throat, ambulance crews are dispatched to handle an array of suffering bodies.

As such, it's not that surprising that ambulance crews tend to work toward the bottom of the economically and racially polarized metropolis. Suffering is certainly not limited to poor people, people of color, or other structurally disadvantaged groups, but it generally intensifies on them.[32] As anthropologist Seth Holmes puts it, suffering is "roughly cumulative from top to bottom."[33] We can see this in the anxiety and torment linked to precarious shelter and so-called bad jobs.[34] We can also see it in the pain associated with high rates of street crime, high school incompletion, and predatory lending. These are all conditions that disproportionately afflict people toward the bottom of a complex urban hierarchy.[35] And, as already detailed, the downward intensification of suffering is also apparent in the concentration of illness and injury among the city's oppressed and marginalized people. In short, suffering tends to obey a kind of social gravity. Something in the cosmos pulls it toward the city's destitute and stigmatized populations.

There are a number of institutions that handle people who carry the brunt of suffering in the American city. Be it by protecting them, punishing them, or simply processing them into objects to know and direct, such institutions essentially "govern," "manage," or "regulate" these populations at ground level. This can be seen in the way welfare offices distribute and withhold cash assistance, food stamps, means-tested health insurance, and related forms of aid.[36] It can be seen in the way criminal justice institutions collect, isolate, and surveil a disproportionate number of poorer and darker-skinned bodies.[37] Nonprofit and for-profit organizations that are contracted and subsidized by governments to deliver public goods and services are also important.[38] And, despite reasonable concerns over access to care, medical institutions must also be included in a discussion of how suffering populations are managed by street-level institutions. Often tasked explicitly by law or contract to aid indigent populations, emergency departments, community clinics, and similar sites constitute some critical front lines for managing the city's most pained people.[39]

We should keep in mind that welfare offices, prisons, hospitals, and related institutions are generally disinterested in eradicating the root causes of suffering.[40] The reasonable assumption here is that oppression and marginality—and the suffering that tends to map onto such conditions—are incurable in a capitalist and racist society like the United States. While the frontline institutions that tend to handle people toward the bottom of the urban hierarchy may certainly alleviate (or even exacerbate) suffering, they are not generally oriented toward abolishing its fundamental causes and indeed they're not really expected to be oriented as such. Thus, we're left with a fragmented, and often a contradictory, mess of institutions for handling suffering populations but not for terminating the root sources of their agony.

The ambulance is somewhere in this mess and probably has been for some time. Paramedicine may never become the quintessential case for understanding how suffering populations are governed at ground level, nor is it an institution that exclusively handles people toward the bottom of the urban hierarchy. Nevertheless, I argue the ambulance is parked at a couple of really important intersections that can help us understand the regulation of urban suffering more generally. On the one hand, it's frequently interacting with two larger institutions that also disproportionately handle poor people and people of color in the United States: the hospital emergency department and the police squad car. As such, the ambulance offers a unique view into the intersections of the welfare state and the penal state. On the other hand, those who control and coordinate ambulance fleets often meet at the intersection of bureaucracy and capital, where public and private distinctions are increasingly blurred by the delegation of governmental functions to third parties. In this regard, the ambulance is not unlike the many "private" for-profit and nonprofit agencies that handle suffering populations on the ground (e.g., transitional housing facilities and corporate security firms). As such, the ambulance is not just a suitable case for studying the street-level governance of urban suffering; it's also a *strategic case* for doing so. However, to make the most of this case, I argue that we need to tweak how we typically see and study the regulation of urban suffering.

ON THE FRONT LINES

Beyond providing some insights into the world of the ambulance, this book develops a broader understanding of how suffering bodies are governed at street level. I advance a labor-centric framework to make sense of how frontline institutions handle a variety of problems that disproportionately torment down-and-out populations.[41] Perhaps the true promise of this framework stems from its ability to illuminate significant blind spots in existing social theories. Next, I briefly detail some of these blind spots before outlining the general theory that organizes this book from start to finish.

Forgetting the Workers

As already noted, social scientists examine a range of institutions when considering how economically and racially oppressed populations are governed. These include institutions that can alleviate, maintain, or exacerbate suffering. To help make sense of this variation, a simplified but useful distinction is sometimes made between the protective and the repressive functions of state power. This is most notably accomplished by Loïc Wacquant, a sociologist who offers an analysis accounting for prisons, welfare offices, and seemingly everything in between.[42] He details a horizontal struggle between the "Left hand" of the state, which steers the welfare institutions that protect and extend life chances, and the "Right hand" of the state, which directs the penal institutions that impair them.[43] According to Wacquant, the state's Left hand is weakening, shrinking, and losing autonomy under neoliberalism. This helps explain why welfare programs like cash assistance for poor parents are often becoming more temporary and parsimonious. Meanwhile, the operations of the state's Right hand are strengthening, broadening, and encroaching on operations traditionally exercised by its Left hand. This is most evident in the United States by a near-simultaneous ascension in criminal justice and in the various welfare reforms that have made public assistance more disciplinary and punitive (e.g., requirements to work in order to receive benefits).[44]

While certainly useful, this kind of framework tends to direct our attention away from the front lines. It glosses over the face-to-face interactions between suffering populations and the workers they interact with in welfare offices, courtrooms, homeless shelters, community clinics, and related spaces. The result is a generally passive and overly macro theory that risks fogging potentially critical activities at ground level. Indeed, people are not passively arrested, hospitalized, or fed by the policies of an ambidextrous state. Others actively arrest, hospitalize, and feed them. People on the front lines do the actual labor of classifying, assisting, and punishing subjects, be they patients, inmates, or some other human category to be processed.

Ignoring the Sides

Luckily, there are scholars who can help us make sense of the front lines and the people who work on them. There's probably no better example of this than Michael Lipsky and his illustrious writings on "street-level bureaucracies."[45] For this political scientist, the policies that most affect disadvantaged populations are "made" at ground level by social workers, police officers, nurses, and other frontline workers.[46] These are the people who execute the delivery of public goods, services, and sanctions, and according to Lipsky they have a fair amount of discretion in doing so (e.g., when a police officer decides to arrest someone or not). Still, these workers don't have absolute agency. Their decisions are hindered and enabled by their relations with management from above and with clientele from below. Ultimately, through examining governance at "street level," Lipsky and his interlocutors reveal the management of vulnerable populations as both a "top-down" and a "bottom-up" process.[47]

Such a basic framework is useful for understanding the institutions that directly handle suffering populations. However, in detailing the vertical relations of policy work, visions of street-level bureaucracy often ignore some important horizontal relations across the front lines. The institutions that handle suffering populations often overlap. For example, parole agencies have long referred and mandated felons to drug counseling, transitional housing, and related third-party programs.[48] The different front lines that contact disadvantaged people also operate in reference to one another. Community colleges, as another example, often set curricula to assure that eligible students can receive welfare funds.[49] Indeed, street-level governance can be "bottom-up as well as top-down, but also 'sideways.'"[50] According to sociologist Megan Comfort and her colleagues, a key feature of this horizontality is irrationality, namely, in the "massive disconnect between institutions" on the ground.[51] While they might share clientele, said institutions are often oriented toward distinct missions that can undermine one another. Ultimately, a number of contradictory institutions govern suffering populations simultaneously, and Lipsky and many of the social scientists who deploy his ideas don't seriously examine this. Such porous conditions likely affect frontline labor by determining whom workers handle and what other actors they have to work with in the process. In other words, interinstitutional horizontality likely affects how frontline workers "make" policies in important ways.

Neglecting the Top

To be clear, I'm not suggesting that no one has seriously examined the interactions between frontline laborers. There are some excellent studies that account for the more "sideways" interactions between workers of contradictory institutions. Consistent with Wacquant's claim that the penal state (Right hand) is encroaching on activities traditionally held by the welfare state (Left hand), Armando Lara-Millán analyzes the daily interactions between nurses and police inside the hospital.[52] His ethnography of an emergency department shows how the labor of medical triage influences, and is influenced by, the interactions between these two parties. Nurses justify the rushing of medical services to criminal arrestees and jail inmates as a form of professional courtesy to the police who accompany these patients. And officers detailed to the inundated emergency department assist nurses by thinning clientele demand (e.g., running occasional background checks on people in the waiting room). Likewise, Kathleen Nolan, another ethnographer, details the relationship between police and educators inside a high school attended by mostly poor and nonwhite youth.[53] She too focuses on moments that could be described as professional courtesy to make sense of how order is established at her studied site. However, she also clearly emphasizes moments of lateral conflict, as police and teachers struggle to determine who has ultimate authority over student discipline.

In focusing on the grounded interactions between different frontline workers, studies like these nevertheless come with their own blind spots. Such research can sometimes sacrifice an analysis of the important vertical conditions that direct frontline labor. In fairness to Lara-Millán and Nolan, they do not outright ignore the top-down forces that influence the workers they study. Both write about the political and legal circumstances that have positioned law enforcement in their field sites, and they mention managerial actors like deans and charge nurses.[54] But, even so, the specifics are pretty thin in comparison to the relations they detail *between* workers. Studies in this vein tend to neglect the intricate forces that influence frontline labor from above.[55] This could be problematic since such forces seem to guide decision-making on the front lines and probably affect interactions between workers.

The Labor Process

I propose an easy solution for the blind spots noted above. We should treat the frontline regulation of urban suffering as a *labor process*. I claim this yields a more comprehensive framework for examining the institutions that tend to handle economically and racially oppressed populations. Key analyses of the labor process span a number of sites that include but are certainly not limited to factories, nursing homes, hotels, casinos, fast food restaurants, department stores, and semi trucks.[56] The versatility of the concept, which can be traced back to the writings of Karl Marx, comes from its simplicity.[57] It merely refers to *how the capacity to labor is translated into productive activity.*[58]

The labor process involves both a *practical* and a *relational* component. The practical component involves a transformation or regulation of the world by the hands and minds of workers utilizing the instruments of production.[59] With respect to the institutions that handle suffering bodies, this can be seen in the sheltering of unhoused people, in the feeding of hungry mouths, and even in the beating of supposedly dangerous subjects. This can also be seen in the way frontline workers process people into, or preserve them as, clients (e.g., patients and inmates) so that other workers can monitor and adjust them. The results may be micro and momentary, but they are transformations and regulations nonetheless. The relational component of this same process concerns the multidirectional associations through which these transformations and regulations occur, namely, the relations workers enter into "with one another and with management."[60] This can be seen in the horizontal relations between frontline workers and in the vertical relations between these workers and the actors who control and coordinate their labor. This dual consideration of the practical and relational components of the labor process is what allows us to respond to the shortcomings in extant scholarship.

The labor-centric approach I advance throughout this book offers a promising and unique framework for examining the frontline governance of urban suffering. It rests on three general claims. First, suffering populations are handled by street-level workers who are embedded in both vertical and horizontal relations of production. These workers' practical interactions with their subjects depend in large part on their interactions with management from above and with fellow workers to their sides. Second, these multidirectional interactions are intersectional and interdependent. Among other things, this implies that we shouldn't examine the horizontality of the front lines without also considering their verticality and vice versa. Third, the life chances of people processed at street level are altered through a vertically and horizontally structured labor process. How frontline workforces are positioned, organized, and activated influences how suffering bodies are assisted, punished, or otherwise treated on the ground.

Ultimately, this book develops a framework that can help us better understand how urban suffering, which tends to intensify near the bottom of the polarized city, is handled by an array of institutions. The point is not to abandon useful scholarship, but instead to add to it through an analysis of the labor process. The implications of doing this, I will argue, extend well beyond ambulance operations in a single county.

MAPMAKER

During my first weeks of working as an EMT, I struggled to navigate Agonia County. The ambulance's navigation system was pretty helpful, but also pretty distracting. Glancing at it before putting the ambulance in drive was one thing but looking at the monitor as I drove through traffic with my lights flashing and siren blaring was nerve-racking to say the least. My paramedic partners helped me out. They'd tell me things like, "Left on X street, then a right on Y street, and it'll be a block south of Z street." They would say these things in a you-should-know-what-I'm-talking-about tone. However, I often didn't know, and I frequently made wrong turns before I got the usual scolding. "Wrong turn! Wrong turn! Wrong turn!" I was embarrassed. At that point, I had spent a year doing ride-along observations and had already been to most of the areas I was driving into as an EMT. It wasn't until I was behind the wheel that I started to realize how difficult navigation could be.

When Lance, one of my trainers, figured out I was struggling to find my way around, he recommended I draw a map of the county. It was around 3:30 AM and we were parked outside a hospital. He turned on the dome light inside the cab of the ambulance, gave me a pen and some scratch paper, and asked me to sketch a simple map of Agonia County. I outlined the county's major highways and noted a few exits. Lance corrected my many errors and then helped me draw a grid for the busiest streets. He had me draw this map again the next night. This was such a simple exercise, but it really helped me distill the county's geography to its essence, or at least to its essence according to a nervous and inexperienced EMT.

In a way, I do something similar in this book. I draw an analytical map to help locate ambulance crews amid an array of social relations (figure 3). This simple illustration summarizes a deeply complicated world of paramedicine. As in any clinical setting, we find a basic hierarchy, with crews positioned above their patients.[61] We can think of this as paramedics and EMTs *working on* their subjects. Ambulance patients can demand (and often refuse) services and some even resist crews by kicking, punching, and spitting. Crews nonetheless coax and coerce mostly obedient subjects. At the same time, ambulance patients often slide between other transient statuses like hospital patient and police subject. This situates ambulance workers between nurses and police. Atop the ambulance we find a

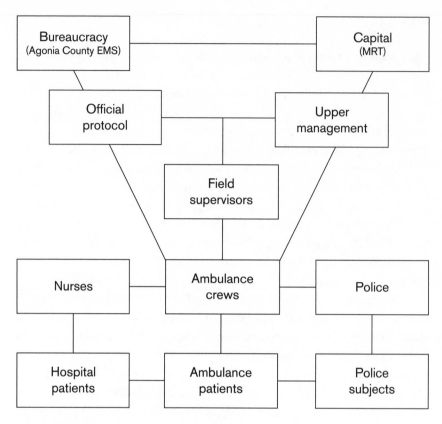

Figure 3. Locating ambulance crews.

proximal trinity of forces: official protocols published by Agonia County EMS, upper management at MRT, and the company's field supervisors. Further up, we find a particular relation between county government and private capital, where the former delegates operations to the latter. The county contracts ambulance operations out to the firm and gives them the right to earn revenue through a fee-for-service model. However, instead of totally hollowing itself out, the state remains present and powerful by setting the conditions, surveilling the activities, and sanctioning the performances of capital via Agonia County EMS.

I cover this map across nine chapters that are evenly divided between three parts. Part 1 takes us *inside* the ambulance. Chapter 1 summarizes ambulance work as a process that involves two material regulations: a transformation of spaces in bodies (e.g., clinical interventions into flesh and bone) and a transformation of bodies in spaces (e.g., moving people from streets and homes into the hospital). These physical adjustments, however, cannot be understood without accounting for the socially produced and realized categories these workers use to navigate their jobs. So, chapter 2 details a central but fuzzy moral distinction that workers make between "legit" and "bullshit" calls. I show that paramedics and EMTs hold a strong sense of duty and purpose when it comes to making critical and deep interventions into the more "legitimately" suffering body (i.e., transforming spaces in bodies). However, much to their frustration, their work seems to involve little more than administering shallow treatments and giving people with "bullshit" problems rides to the hospital (i.e., transforming bodies in spaces). Chapter 3 extends, but also complicates, this analysis by accounting for the emotional aspects of ambulance work. Together, these chapters help demystify a key mechanism for how urban suffering is handled on the front lines: *bandaging bodies*. Like many institutions, the ambulance generally offers superficial solutions for the hardships that heavily afflict destitute and stigmatized populations in the American city. But this cannot be fully understood without accounting for the horizontal and vertical relations that ambulance workers are caught up in on the front lines.

Part 2 locates the ambulance *between* two places that also disproportionately process poor people and people of color: the hospital emergency department and the police squad car. Chapter 4 details the "fix-up" work ambulance crews share with nurses and chapter 5 details the "cleanup" work they share with police. These two chapters make it clear that ambulance crews often work with their police and nurse counterparts without conflict or tension, but conflict and tension are nevertheless frequent. So, chapter 6 details a common form of tension that I call "burden shuffling." This refers to the strategies that workers deploy in an effort to push, or shuffle, undesirable tasks or cases onto other workers. Ultimately, part 2 demystifies another key mechanism for how urban suffering is handled on the front lines: *sorting bodies*. Examining the lateral relations between workers helps us better see how people toward the bottom of the polarized city are distributed across a landscape of often contradictory institutions.

Part 3 locates the ambulance *underneath* a nexus of bureaucratic and capitalistic forces. Chapter 7 takes us into MRT headquarters, "the barn." There, I show how the firm's relationship with Agonia County EMS affects how upper management organizes the ambulance fleet. MRT is essentially forced to service a mostly unprofitable clientele (i.e., uninsured and publicly insured patients) and they respond to this problem by trying to deploy a lean workforce that can efficiently and flexibly complete as many transports as possible. Chapter 8 details a key weapon that management uses to assure such efficiency and flexibility: the field supervisor. We'll return to Eric's and other supervisors' SUVs. However, instead of looking out their windshields to see the common places ambulances are responding to, we'll see how company management more directly negotiates a lean workforce. Chapter 9 brings us back into the ambulance to make sense of how crews are responding to pressures above them. Beyond further contextualizing the relations that influence a bandaging and sorting of bodies, part 3 demystifies another mechanism for how urban suffering is handled on the front lines: *hustling bodies*. Workers hustle clientele along through hurried interventions and this complicates, but does not contradict, claims that people spend much of their time waiting for something to happen on the front lines.

I end this wave of short chapters with a conclusion that looks beyond the ambulance. This final chapter includes a call to bring a labor-centric approach to other front lines of urban suffering like the welfare office and the prison. It also considers the applicability of those key mechanisms revealed through this case study: bandaging, sorting, and hustling bodies. At the very end, I consider some ways to make the ambulance better for both patients and workers.

PART I Bandaging Bodies

INSIDE THE AMBULANCE

This first set of chapters jumps into the ambulance. I cover the manual, mental, and emotional aspects of ambulance labor and detail some of the subtle and not-so-subtle distinctions ambulance crews use to make sense of their work. The point is not to simply demystify what happens within this mobile structure that frequents poor and nonwhite neighborhoods. That's one of my objectives for sure, but I'm also interested in laying the foundation for the horizontal and vertical analyses that follow (parts 2 and 3 respectively).

Life inside the ambulance can be first and foremost summarized as a site of "people work." This work involves a physical regulation of spaces in bodies (e.g., clinical interventions into flesh and bone) and bodies in spaces (e.g., moving people from streets and homes into the hospital). However, ambulance work cannot be reduced to just a manual execution of treatment and transport. This material engagement with the world is interlocked with symbolic transformations, like the basic assemblage of a medical case. Workers' written and verbal articulations of vital signs, diagnostic categories, and other formal classifications are essential to understanding how crews process people into ambulance patients. Yet, there are more informal classifications at play too. Workers' shared distinctions in different kinds of people (e.g., racialized and gendered subjects) shape, and are shaped by, the labor they perform.

Such biases are significant, but I argue that another axis of preference is also at play: the taken-for-granted distinction in "legit" and "bullshit" cases. More pure types on a continuum than binary categories, these folk terms tend to map onto variability in spaces in bodies (more legit work) and bodies in spaces (more bullshit work). Understanding the fuzzy moral order in legit and bullshit cases requires an understanding of ambulance work as a vocation. While a number of workers, especially the more veteran ones, describe themselves as "jaded" and "burnt out," the overwhelming majority of people I met at MRT articulate some generally strong commitments to the craft of paramedicine. They want to "truly help" people by doing what they are primarily trained and equipped to do: salvage bodies in crisis through relatively deep and technical interventions into human flesh. However, to their frustration, much of their day-to-day labor involves not a regulation of spaces in bodies, but the inverse. They're often moving forget-table cases from homes and streets into the hospital for "nonemergency problems" like mild chronic illness exacerbations and empty prescription bottles.

Among other things, this legit-bullshit continuum is intertwined with crews' mechanisms for coping with the particular challenges of ambulance-based people work. I argue that two opposing sets of dispositions are especially important: "being a dick" (apathetic, hostile, and cold) and "having heart" (sympathetic, hospitable, and warm). There are plenty of factors that engender someone's disposition at work, many of which prob-ably extend well beyond the workplace. I don't deny this or intend to sug-gest that some one-dimensional spectrum between being a dick and hav-ing heart captures the entirety of worker temperament. However, the emotional thread I detail helps clarify the pathways through which the immediate conditions of labor influence the interactions between crews and patients. The lows of bullshit work tend to motivate a cold handling of patients and the highs of legit work tend to encourage a warm handling. I link crew-patient struggle to the former and crew-patient solidarity to the latter.

This layering of the physical, mental, and emotional aspects of people work inside the ambulance is no doubt complicated, but it's important. It helps us piece together the practical component of a labor process. Recall that the practical component refers to a transformation or regulation of the world by the hands and minds of workers utilizing the instruments of production. While the effects are often micro and momentary, ambulance workers nevertheless change and maintain the world. They identify and correct abnormalities within people and move those deemed ill and injured into places they're better fit for.

We must not forget that these transformations are unevenly spread across the urban landscape. Neither legit nor bullshit calls are limited to poor or racially oppressed populations, but both call types—and essentially everything in the gray area between—concentrate downward. Morbidity and mortality risks are higher near the floor of the urban hierarchy, and so too are the risks of being excluded from the yolks of medicine, housing, and social security more generally. Crises, the "urgent" or the "nonurgent," the "medical" or the "nonmedical," accumulate in poorer and less white territories. The men and women who labor the ambulance are some of the few people the state dispatches to handle crises and this means much of their work brings them toward the bottom of the polarized city.

In several respects, ambulance labor amounts to *bandaging bodies*. Crews generally offer superficial responses to complex problems. This can be seen not only in the application of gauze and pressure to a bloody gash but also in the movement of a body from the cold concrete into the relatively warm hospital bed. It can be seen in the fentanyl, albuterol, and other medications that crews throw at the chronically ill, just as it can be seen during the forced restraint and transport of drunk or otherwise disordered subjects. Ambulance crews ultimately constitute a reactionary force for stabilizing, but not fundamentally solving, many of the crises that disproportionately plague destitute and stigmatized populations in the American metropolis.[1] This fact isn't lost on crews either. As many put it, much of their job means applying "bandage solutions" to a variety of hardships.

We can learn a lot about the regulation of urban suffering by looking in the back of an ambulance. Representative of the state's quick and temporary responses to crises, the ambulance is a suitable analogy for a number of interventions that mitigate social suffering but rarely target its root causes: emergency housing, short-term cash assistance, expedited food stamps, and so on. We may live in an era of "retrenched" or "disciplinary" welfare, but we also live in an era of *ambulance welfare*.[2] Many of the fragmented programs and policies that disadvantaged populations depend on are not just stingy; they're also superficial.

1 People Work

Paramedics and EMTs work on people. The primary material that's labored by ambulance crews are human beings—their organs, their categorizations, their locations, and so on. Consider five seemingly disparate cases.

Stabbing at a Bar

Paramedic Edward and EMT Morgan arrived at a bar. Police and firefighters were already on scene and directed the crew to John, a white male in his late twenties who works as the bar's bouncer. He was lying in the parking lot. Someone stabbed him multiple times. John's inner left arm was sliced just below the elbow and there was a laceration on the back of his head. There were also deep punctures to his gut, flank, and lower back.

With the help of some firefighters, Edward and Morgan covered John's oozing wounds, loaded him into the ambulance, and gave him some fluid through an intravenous (IV) line. As Morgan drove to the hospital, John screamed through the non-rebreather oxygen mask that Morgan attached to his face. "Fuck," he shouted from the gurney, "Don't let me die! You need to get me to a doctor!" "We're going there right now," responded Edward as he spiked another IV bag. A firefighter also rode in the ambulance and helped Edward control the patient's bleeding. Midway through the transport, John's screams faded to moans before he began to nod off. Edward shook his patient to keep him awake. "Stay with me! Stay with me!" he shouted. It wasn't long until Morgan parked the rig. A trail of blood then connected the ambulance to the emergency department.

After transferring care to a team of trauma specialists inside the hospital, Morgan hosed blood off the gurney as Edward documented details regarding the call in his laptop. In addition to logging John's demographics (e.g., age and gender), Edward noted his "primary impression" of the patient (i.e., his field diagnosis) and listed the interventions he and Morgan performed (e.g., bleeding control, oxygen therapy via a non-rebreather mask, and fluid via IV). Edward uploaded this medical record known as a patient care report to a secure server and printed a copy for hospital staff.

Living Room Death

Paramedic Stacey and EMT Jeremy, along with the assistance of local firefighters and a paramedic supervisor, responded to a "code" (i.e., a cardiac arrest). The victim was a seventy-or-so-year-old black man who lay on the floor of his apartment living room. He was "PEA," meaning the monitor connected to his body via some sticky electrodes indicated "pulseless electrical activity." The man's body was hooked up to a Lucas CPR device, a special machine that delivers automatic sternum compressions.

Firefighters shoved nearby furniture toward the walls to make room for the "pit crew," the resuscitation team of five or so first-responders led by Stacey. While one firefighter paramedic intubated the patient by carefully guiding a plastic tube down the airway, Stacey drilled a hole into the old man's shin to initiate intraosseous infusion (IO). Once an IO was established, Stacey's team periodically administered medications like epinephrine directly into the bone marrow. They paused regularly to shock the patient with a defibrillator. For over thirty minutes, the pit crew attempted to revive the patient through a mixture of compression, ventilation, electrical shock, and drugs.

They eventually "called him" (i.e., determined death) before Stacey even had a chance to learn the patient's name. The paramedic and EMT returned to their ambulance without a body, where Stacey documented some intricate details of the case in her laptop before they responded to another 911 call. Among other things, she had to carefully report the timing of the pit crew's many interventions.

Septic at the Sniff

Paramedic Derrick and EMT Martin responded to a skilled nursing facility or what is colloquially referred to as a "sniff." They were greeted by a certified nursing assistant (CNA), a nurse, and someone from the sniff's management team. Firefighters were also on scene and introduced Derrick and Martin to their patient: Barbara, a seventy-five-or-so-year-old white woman, who lay in bed and mumbled. The firefighters had already collected some baseline vitals indicating a rapid heart rate and low oxygen saturation. The CNA and nurse also informed the crew that Barbra has type-2 diabetes, osteoporosis, and a pressure ulcer (i.e., a bedsore). They also stated that Barbara seemed to experience discomfort upon recent urination.

Derrick placed his gloved hand on Barbara's forehead and noted that she was warm to touch before he checked her blood sugar levels using a glucometer. Derrick also directed Martin to run an electrocardiogram (EKG) while Barbara was still in her sniff bed. In following through with the paramedic's wishes, Martin struggled at first to stick the EKG electrodes to Barbara's skin. It was covered in some sort of lotion. This may have helped thwart new bedsores, but Derrick suspected it was worsening Barbra's fever. After an unremarkable EKG, Derrick and Martin started to transport Barbara to the hospital, suspecting the early stages of sepsis, and Derrick gave her some low-flow oxygen on the way.

During the transport, Derrick typed away on his laptop and periodically checked on Barbara and the monitor that summarized her heart rate, oxygen saturation, and blood pressure. He used paperwork provided to him by the sniff staff to log Barbara's date of birth, medical history, current medications, insurance policy number, and other information.

Drunk and Drowsy in Downtown

Paramedic Rob and EMT Logan were summoned to a downtown side-walk to aid Darrell, a "frequent flyer" known to both ambulance workers by name. It was unclear how this fifty-five-year-old black man got there or why he was leaning against the side of a building with his eyes closed. However, it was clear who called 911: a security guard who roams these business-hugging sidewalks. He was unable to convince Darrell to leave the area on his own, so he reported the seemingly intoxicated person to dispatchers who in turn sent Rob and Logan.

After kicking the bottom of Darrell's shoes and struggling to converse with the slurring man, Rob determined that he was too drunk to leave. So, the crew loaded their patient, who carried a strong smell of alcohol and vomit, into the ambulance, where they then hooked him up to a monitor to collect a baseline set of vitals: blood pressure, heart rate, and blood oxygen saturation. Logan sat on a chair next to the gurney and began a patient care report on the laptop while Rob asked Darrell about his medi-cal history. The workers also ran an EKG before they determined Darrell to be a low-priority case. The man mumbled the name of a hospital across the county, but Rob refused to take him there. Instead, Rob let Darrell chose one of the three closest hospitals. The patient then said the name of a large public hospital a few miles away.

Logan left the back of the ambulance and took the driver's seat. Rob stayed in the back with Darrell. During the transport, Rob continued the medical record started by Logan. The computer program soon forced him to enter a primary impression. He was given some closed-ended options and selected the category that seemed to best summarize his patient's state: "ETOH," an acronym for ethyl alcohol. Rob told Darrell he drinks too much, but Darrell just moaned some incomprehensible speech in response. The crew eventually rolled their patient into an emergency department, where a nurse and physician happened to also know Darrell by name.

Home with a Cold

Paramedic Drew and EMT Marco responded to a house where they found Alicia, a twenty-one-year-old black woman, standing just inside the doorway. Alicia confirmed that she was the person who called for an ambulance and she listed her symptoms: a headache, some generalized body pain, a sore throat, and a nonproductive cough.

The conversation between crew and patient continued inside the ambulance, where Alicia reclined on the gurney. As Drew talked with this patient, Marco placed a pulse oximeter on her finger and a blood pressure cuff around her bicep before he started a medical record. All measured vital signs—heart rate, respiratory rate, blood pressure, and oxygen saturation—were within normal limits. Drew then told Alicia this was "not an emergency," but she still requested a ride to a hospital, and more specifically to the hospital a couple miles from her house. Marco moved to the driver's seat and drove to that facility.

During the short transport, Drew continued the patient care report started by Marco. However, he paused for a moment to tell Alicia she was most likely going to be triaged into the emergency department waiting room. "For real?" asked Alicia, apparently surprised. Drew responded with a smirk, "I bet you thought you'd get in quicker if you called 911, but you won't." Alicia didn't respond and Drew continued to work on his laptop. At the hospital, Drew had Alicia walk in with him through the ambulance entrance without a gurney. Drew spoke to a nurse and recommended a waiting room triage. The nurse concurred.

THE PEOPLE WORKERS

Ambulance workers often say, "no call is the same." The five vignettes above confirm this point in many ways. We find a stabbing, a cardiac arrest, a sepsis alert, an intoxication, and some symptoms of the common cold. These variably urgent problems are scattered across a bar, an apartment, a skilled nursing facility, a sidewalk, and a house. The outcomes of these cases are different too, from a corpse being left on scene to someone being *walked* into the emergency department waiting room. There's also some notable range in the social positioning of patients: white and black, young and old, housed and unhoused, and so on.

Yet, despite all this variation, I hold that we can still offer a generalized description of ambulance labor. Sure, ambulance work can be reasonably labeled as a form of "care work" or "service employment." But, as already noted, I think the productive activities of paramedics and EMTs are best summarized as *people work*. Sociologist Erving Goffman developed this concept to make sense of staff inside "total institutions" like asylums and prisons.[1] The concept nevertheless works in any setting where the primary material of labor, that which is practically transformed through the social relations of production, is people. I'm especially partial to Goffman's concept because it forces a simultaneous consideration of both the material and the classificatory moments involved in production.

Whether laboring living or dead bodies, there is a definite physicality to people work: surgeons cut into flesh, morticians dress corpses, and prison officials feed inmates. Ambulance work is physical too. Crews pry open jaws, stick needles through skin, and compress sternums. They also lift bodies onto gurneys, roll them into ambulances, and drive them across town.

At its essence, ambulance work involves a manual regulation of body and space. We can think of this as unfolding in two ways. On the one hand, ambulance crews regulate *spaces in bodies*. Much of their labor involves them tweaking people as independent structures divided into anatomical and physiological regions. For example, they inject fluid into the veins to lift falling blood pressure, stream oxygen into the airway to counter low oxygen saturation, and cover wounds to prevent blood loss. On the other hand, crews also regulate *bodies in spaces*. They move people from homes, sidewalks, bars, sniffs, and other places to the ambulance and then transport them to hospitals.

Still, people work cannot be reduced to manual labor alone. As several paramedics and EMTs liked to tell me, there's also a "mental aspect" to their work and it's inseparable from a "physical aspect." Paramedics and EMTs are trained to link external symptoms to internal problems (e.g., fever, elevated heart rate, and low oxygen saturation as indications of sepsis) and internal problems to targeted treatments (e.g., countering low oxygen saturation with oxygen therapy). The patient body becomes a text of sorts. It's something to read and interpret. But it's also a text to code and revise. Much of the more mental aspects of ambulance work can be equated to classificatory labor. Crews work to classify suffering.

This classificatory labor is perhaps most visible during documentation. Ambulance crews construct medical records—informative receipts that

summarize assessments and treatments—and they do so by reading people through an institutional-specific scheme that identifies and distinguishes human suffering in a particular way (e.g., diagnostic categories).[2]
They, in a sense, "check a box" and this is intertwined with their physical
interactions with patients. While the five vignettes that opened this chapter certainly involve different classifications in terms of primary impressions, logged vital signs, and level of urgency, none is without some formal
classification. And essentially no cases conclude without some official
record keeping. Ambulance crews even document cases where they interact with potential patients who refuse treatment or transportation. Thus,
in many ways, people work is paperwork.

The remainder of this chapter sets out to describe a few basic features
of ambulance-based people work. I further detail some of the instruments
that crews use to work on people. I then offer a summary of how ambulance calls are generally run, and this provides us with some more insights
into how crews handle their patients. Yet, as I'll continue to make clear,
there's a lot of variation in how calls are run. This is at least partly so
because the material to be labored is not uniform. Crews see different
kinds of people (e.g., racialized and gendered subjects) and this shapes the
productive process in important ways.

TOOLS OF THE TRADE

Nicknamed "rigs," "trucks," and "buses," ambulances can be described as
mini hospital rooms on wheels. They're loaded with instruments for
examining, adjusting, moving, and documenting people. We don't need to
take a full inventory of what's inside, but a quick glance at some of the rig's
equipment will give us a sense of what *can* happen in the ambulance.

Let's start in the back (figure 4). At the center is a gurney, which is easily loaded and unloaded through the back doors. A waterproof—or rather
a blood, vomit, and fecal proof—mattress sits on top and is covered first
with a cloth blanket and then with a paper sheet. The sheet is disposed of
after each transport and the blanket helps crews drag their patients off the
gurney and onto a hospital bed should such a maneuver be necessary. A
portable oxygen tank is also attached near the head of the gurney in case

Figure 4. An open ambulance. *Note:* Author's photo.

a patient happens to require any low- or high-flow oxygen. Additionally, a few pouches are strapped to the gurney and they carry nasal cannulas, spit masks, and other items.

As a ride-along, I usually sat in the captain's seat immediately next to the gurney's head. This provided me with a head-to-toe view of patients while they lay on the gurney or, far more commonly, as they reclined in the semi-Fowler's position (i.e., around a forty-five-degree angle). This seat also offered me a great front-to-back view of the ambulance's main interior.

Cabinets covering the wall to the left of the gurney contain various needles, tubes, masks, drugs, gauze, and other tools. A monitor usually sits on a nearby shelf, but it's frequently moved. When on scene, for example, crews often hook the monitor to the back of the gurney. This boom box shaped device has defibrillation capabilities ("Clear!"). However, as the beginning of this chapter demonstrated, it also includes a number of instruments for "objectively" assessing the body (e.g., blood pressure cuff, pulse oximeter, and EKG electrodes). One of the side pockets of the monitor includes a glucometer and a set of lancets for checking blood sugar.

The wall to the right of the gurney includes a bench that paramedics usually sit on as they examine and treat their patients. A stethoscope and a pair of shears are often nearby if they're not in the paramedic's pocket. Underneath the bench are additional tools, including leather limb restraints, a patient urinal, and some roadside flares. Most paramedics set a few items on the bench for easy access, like a small bin with some IV needles of various gages.

There are some additional shelves near the head of the gurney by the bench. Among other things, they hold a "med bag," which carries a majority of the rig's medications like Benadryl (for allergic reactions), Zofran (for nausea), and Narcan (for opioid overdoses). Drugs requiring more security, like fentanyl (for alleviating pain) and Versed (usually for sedation during severe psychiatric emergencies), are locked in a safe above the shelving that holds the med bag.

A few cabinet doors can be found on the ambulance's exterior. These include more items for moving ill and injured bodies. A stiff spinal board and some cervical collars are included for when a crew needs to immobilize a patient's spine before moving them into the rig. These exterior cabinets also include a "tarp," a heavy-duty plastic sheet with handles that crews can use to lift and drag people on scene.

As already discussed, for essentially every instrument that crews can wield in the back of the ambulance there is a digital echo of sorts inside the crew's laptop. In addition to documenting patient demographics and billing information, crews must use these computers to record vital signs, medical histories, current medications, primary impressions, and treatments performed. In addition to checking boxes and selecting entries from dropdown menus, they must also write short open-ended narratives that summarize key aspects of the labor performed.

And then there's the front cab. In addition to a radio for communicating with dispatchers, the cab includes a series of switches and buttons for controlling the rig's lights and sirens. A second computer, which is installed into the dash, has a touch-screen interface. This computer mainly runs a live map that shows crews where they are and where they should be going. A couple pairs of latex gloves are usually tossed somewhere on the dash, allowing crews to glove-up before they step out onto an emergency scene.

Ultimately, and unsurprisingly, the ambulance contains a variety of tools for treatment and transport. Some are used to examine and regulate spaces in bodies, such as by measuring electrical activity in the heart (EKG via the monitor), lifting low blood pressure (saline via intravenous access), and stimulating bronchodilation for more effective breathing (Albuterol via nebulizer). At the same time, we find tools that are used for regulating bodies in spaces. These include things like the gurney, the tarp, and even the rig itself, which are all used to move people away from a given area and toward a hospital bed. However, these also include instruments for regulating the movements of particular body parts, like limb restraints.

Taking stock of some of these tools is important because they enable, but also constrain, the activities that can unfold inside the ambulance. Such objects are clues into what kinds of problems do, and do not, fall under the scope of paramedical operations. However, rummaging through this rig can only tell us so much. Many of the instruments that can be found in the back of the ambulance lay unused for entire shifts, while others are used on nearly every call. Plus, as we'll soon see, ambulance crews are in many ways ill equipped to handle a number of the problems they confront. In moving toward a better understanding of the people work performed inside and around ambulances, we need to look beyond the instruments that are available to crews and examine what these workers actually do.

RUNNING CALLS

There's a basic pattern and rhythm to most ambulance responses. Before a call "drops," the crew is often in the cab with the EMT in the driver seat and the paramedic in the passenger seat. If they're not departing from a hospital on a previous transport, they're usually "posted" (i.e., parked) at an assigned street intersection waiting for a 911 call or en route to a posting location. Wherever the crew may be, a call will almost certainly drop on them soon.

Per the year of patient care reports I acquired, three-fourths of 911 ambulance dispatches in Agonia County require crews to respond with lights and sirens. As the EMT drives the loud and flashy ambulance through the usually dense city streets, running red lights and sometimes driving in the opposite direction of traffic in the process, the paramedic reads the digital map and provides verbal directions for the EMT. He or she will also typically read the "call notes" that the dispatching office automatically sends to the rig's computer, but these notes usually provide vague and often inaccurate details.

According to the medical records, roughly 52 percent of ambulance contacts occur in residential space (including yards and porches), while 16 percent are located on streets or sidewalks and another 16 percent are in commercial or public buildings. Most of the remaining 16 percent bring crews into skilled nursing facilities (or "sniffs"), rehabilitation centers, assisted living facilities, community clinics, and similar settings.

Crews usually park their rigs on scenes already attended to by firefighters. Somewhere between 70 and 90 percent of 911 calls that firefighters respond to in large American cities do not involve fires but are instead "medical emergencies."[3] In Agonia County, as in many places with private paramedical operations, firefighters are supposed to arrive on scene first and stabilize patients for ambulance transport. All firefighters in the studied county are licensed EMTs and most fire crews include a paramedic called a "fire medic." When extra hands are needed on high-priority calls, the fire medic will enter the ambulance and assist the MRT medic, who is sometimes called a "transport medic." However, this is typically not necessary and most fire crews simply give the ambulance crew a brief oral report and a set of initial vital signs before returning to their station.

With the exception of those who are pronounced dead on scene or those who refuse MRT services, most of the people whom ambulance crews respond to are then transported to the hospital. But first they are typically moved onto the gurney and loaded into the rig. Some calls are time-sensitive and require crews to "load and go." The gurney is quickly locked into the back of the ambulance and the EMT jumps up front and drives to the hospital (sometimes with lights and sirens) while the paramedic attends to the patient in the back. That's what happened, for example, with John, the stabbing victim we met at the beginning of this chapter. However, this is not typically necessary and so most crews do a "stay and play" instead of a "load and go." When this happens, both the paramedic and the EMT will enter the back before heading toward the hospital. The paramedic sits on the bench and talks to the patient. The EMT sits in the captain's seat and begins to construct a patient care report on a laptop. For example, that's what happened when the ambulance crew responded to Darrell, the drunk man found on a downtown sidewalk.

As the EMT types on the computer, the paramedic performs a medical assessment. Often, one of the things he or she does first is determine patient consciousness and the degree to which the subject is "alert and oriented" or "A and O." When in doubt, the crew calculates an A and O score by asking their patient some simple questions: "What's your name?" "What city are you in?" "What day of the week is it?" "Do you remember how you got here?" If the patient answers each of these questions correctly, she or he is classified as "A and O times 4" (often written "A&Ox4"). This indicates that the patient is alert and oriented to person, place, time, and event. Patients with lower A and O scores are usually deemed incapable of making their own medical decisions. Protocol commands that crews treat and transport such people without their verbal approval under the justification of "implied consent." The assumption here is that people who are not alert and oriented would agree to ambulance services if they were lucid.

Regardless, most patients are alert and oriented enough to at least articulate a "chief complaint." For ambulance crews, a chief complaint really just means a *medical* complaint. Consistent with what Michel Foucault calls a "medicine of the sick organs," paramedics usually help their clientele make sense of their suffering in terms of physical problems that can be located *in* the body.[4] The more specific, the better. "Do you have any head, neck, chest, or abdominal pain?" "Any nausea or dizziness?"

As sociologist and physician Howard Waitzkin might argue, these interactions can depoliticize the root causes of suffering and misidentify an etiology of illness in the "physical realm."[5] External causes are certainly considered, but paramedics keep them proximate rather than distal.[6] This often involves a commentary on lifestyle: "Smoking isn't good for your emphysema," "You shouldn't drink so much," and "You gotta find a better man (who doesn't beat you)." Likewise, assessments for "trauma calls" (i.e., physical injury cases) typically involve the paramedic determining the most local mechanics of wounding: "What did you trip over?" "How fast was the other driver going?" "Did he hit you with an object or just his fists?"

The paramedic's "subjective" assessment is coupled with an "objective" one, and for patients unable or unwilling to articulate a chief complaint this is all the crew can rely on. In a way, the objective assessment begins the moment a crew first sees their patient. Is the person ambulatory (i.e., walking)? Is she or he speaking in full sentences (i.e., breathing appropriately)? Is their skin pink, warm, and dry (i.e., not pale, cool, or diaphoretic)? Objective assessments continue in the rig, where patients are set up to the monitor reporting blood pressure, heart rate, and oxygen saturation. Paramedics and EMTs also touch patients during the objective assessment. They press their gloved hands onto the body to check for bone instability, abdominal distension, and fever, and to determine whether or not the patient guards from any pain. If the paramedic suspects a respiratory problem, she or he will often auscultate lung sounds with a stethoscope. His or her sense of smell is also important, as it can detect incontinence, alcohol consumption, infection, and even hyperglycemia (which may present as a "sweet" smelling breath). Indeed, the paramedic's "medical gaze" is, as Foucault originally described it, a "plurisensorial structure."[7]

The assessment leads to a primary impression and this, in turn, guides the crew's intervention. More formalized and objective than chief complaints, primary impressions are essentially field diagnostic categories (e.g., myocardial infarction, tension pneumothorax, and nontraumatic body pain). A "secondary impression" is also possible for people who present with multiple problems (e.g., a skin abrasion secondary to a fainting episode), but all cases must be assigned at least one major field diagnosis. Sometimes described as "checking a box," this process means reducing a person's suffering to one of the medical problems listed in the menu of impressions recognized by county protocols. As noted in the introduction, the protocol book includes several step-by-step guides for paramedical intervention, and these are divided by primary impression categories. Perhaps more than anything else, imposing a primary impression is what transforms citizens of Agonia County into clients of the ambulance. According to Jeffery Prottas, all frontline workers must "simplify and standardize" their subjects in order to process them through their institutions.[8] A patient's chief complaint, the set of assessment findings, and, most of all, the primary impression do precisely that.

Once the paramedic determines a primary impression and performs any immediately necessary interventions, he or she then typically discusses transport options with the patient and the EMT. There are over a dozen emergency departments in the county and protocols require crews to take patients to the "closest" and "most appropriate" hospital. For some calls, this can be an easy decision. Heart attack victims are taken to the closest cardiac center. Stroke patients are taken to the closest stroke center. The severely wounded are taken to the closest trauma center. However, most calls are not so severe, and this gives both crews and patients the ability to select one of the three or so closest emergency departments.

Once a transport decision is made, the EMT will usually drive and the paramedic will remain in the back with the patient. For most transports, this means the paramedic will continue filling out the medical record started by the EMT. Sometimes the roles will reverse and paramedics will drive after "turfing" a low-priority case onto the EMT. "Turfing" simply means transferring the responsibility of care down to the lower-trained worker. However, EMTs still do most of the driving because county protocols limit many forms of turfing. Additionally, paramedics often see driving as more annoying than sitting in the back with a low-priority patient after a stay and play.

According to the year of patient care reports I analyzed, 94 percent of MRT rigs roll into hospital ambulance bays without lights and sirens. Together, the paramedic and EMT unload the patient from the back but keep her or him on the gurney. The Hollywood cliché of crews sprinting into the emergency department while pushing the gurney occurs, but it's rare. The reality is not usually so exciting: crews walk gurneys just inside the rear entrance of an emergency department and stand in line behind other crews who are also transporting relatively stable patients. This time standing in line is often called "holding the wall" and is in stark contrast to those many movie and television scenes where crews rush critically ill or injured cases directly into a hospital room.

As a crew begins to interact with the triage nurse, it becomes clear why paramedics are so concerned with reducing their patients to specific medical problems. Nurses usually begin with a simple question, *"What you got?"* The paramedic's response might include the patient's name or some details on where she or he was picked up, but it always includes a primary impression, a summary of the medical assessment, and details on any interventions made. Crews must simplify and standardize their clientele as sick or injured subjects not only to complete their own paperwork, but also to successfully release them into the administrative machinery of the hospital. Nurses want to know the nature of the problem (e.g., dizziness), its urgency (typically coded in the objective scores for blood pressure, heart rate, respiratory rate, oxygen saturation, blood glucose, and an A and O score), and any interventions that were made to address the problem or correct any abnormalities in vital signs (e.g., oxygen via nasal cannula at a rate of four liters per minute).

At some hospitals, the nurses send very low-priority patients to the waiting room as we saw with Alicia, but usually they triage them to a bed where the paramedic and EMT roll the gurney. After wishing the patient luck, the paramedic has the nurse sign the medical report using a touch screen on the crew's laptop. This signature officially transfers care to the hospital.

The crew will then return to the rig in the ambulance bay, where more work awaits. The EMT will clean the gurney and retuck it with a new paper sheet before replacing and prepping any equipment that may have been used on the previous call. Meanwhile, the paramedic will complete his or her paperwork, which by now usually means writing the short open-ended narrative I previously mentioned.

At this point, an informal break is typically squeezed in. Like many paramedical providers today, MRT does not operate ambulance stations. The firm instead runs on a "dynamic posting" system, which means they assign crews particular street intersections to park at and wait for their next call. Hospital ambulance bays are some of the few places workers can rest during their shifts. By waiting an extra ten or so minutes after cleaning their rig and finishing their paperwork, but before officially returning to 911 service, workers are able to use the hospital restroom uninterrupted and maybe even run to the cafeteria.

Following this break and before driving out of the ambulance bay, the EMT will announce their availability to the dispatcher. The voice on the other end assigns them a post or immediately gives them a new 911 call, should one be pending. Either way, more people work awaits.

KINDS OF PEOPLE

People work is complicated by the fact that the subjects to be labored do not enter into the worksite as uniform material. Instead, people come in with a number of physical variations, many of which are technically irrelevant for the procedures outlined above. Yet, technical irrelevance does not equal practical irrelevance. Ambulance crews collectively render otherwise clinically insignificant physical features as meaningful information. They see different *kinds of people*.

We encountered some of this during Eric's tour in the introduction. There, the paramedic-turned-supervisor told us about "zombies," "bangers," and other caricatures. Labels like these are not uncommon or unimportant, but there are some more general distinctions that inform ambulance-based people work. Select physical features of patients, like their size and color, influence how ambulance work is performed. Crews often subtly rely on their shared understandings of such characteristics when determining the intensity and authenticity of their patients' suffering.

For example, the weight of patients is perhaps one of the most obvious physical features that shape crews' opinions. While in the field, I quickly learned that "fat fucks" and "heavy hitters" are generally considered to be pains in the ass. From the standpoint of workers, such bodies often force them to put their careers on the line. It only takes one "bad lift" of these substantial bodies to permanently damage a worker's back. Yet, raw weight in pounds doesn't fully account for their distaste. I learned that a very heavy, but tall and muscular, body is more forgivable than a short and lumpy one of the same weight. A language of deservingness mixes into workers' discussion of obese patients. But, in my experience, this isn't so much about deservingness of care as it is about deservingness of suffering. These "fat asses" supposedly bring it on themselves through a gluttonous and lethargic lifestyle. Worker pity seems to be a bit thinner when thicker people are involved.

A patient's age is another important feature. With reasons justified by paramedical textbooks and county protocols, crews understand vulnerability to be intensified toward the beginnings and ends of long lives. Ambulance workers tend to look at babies, toddlers, children, and elderly people with somewhat looser standards for detecting authentic suffering. Such hypersensitivity for the very young and the very old yields a relative hyposensitivity for working-age people.[9] The baseline assumption here is that these kinds of people are more likely to be medically stable. What might be seen as a critical symptom for babies and the elderly (e.g., a fever) might seem trivial for those between these stages in the life course. In addition to this, workers tend to see nonelderly adults as being more lucid and thus more scheming. Crews seem quicker to assume that such people are seeking medication by faking or exaggerating their pain. And, when punches are thrown, crews are generally more forgiving of elderly patients. Old people's punches are generally softer and the minds behind them are presumably much more senile.

The cleanliness of people, detected through both sight and smell, also shapes the perceptions and actions of workers. Several workers told me that street slumberers—or "bums"—have leathery skin that is often caked in filth. Such skin can make it difficult for crews to perform a medical assessment, because many instruments assume a clean body. Electrodes from the EKG, for example, can fail to stick to sweaty and greasy chests. Much of this can be solved, though, with a sanitary wipe and some gloved-handed fanning. Crews are more concerned about the stench and residue that can accompany extreme deprivation. Early into my employment as an EMT, my trainer, Lance, taught me how to "burrito" smelly people with soiled clothes. It's a simple and common procedure, but it can't be found in textbooks: wrap a water-repellant sheet, which is intended to shield patients from raindrops outside the ambulance, around these people in an effort minimize cleanup. In addition to containing the odors that sometimes watered our eyes and had us gagging in the confined space of the ambulance, this method helped minimize any leakage of bodily fluid onto the gurney. Thus, crews often hope to minimize the exposure of dirty flesh.

The consequences can be tragic. On a night I wasn't in the field, a crew picked up a man lying in a park. The patient was supposedly an unhoused person who often slept on grass and pavement. Like many people in the field, I heard this story secondhand. The responding crew apparently believed the man was in a drunken slumber. However, as physicians and nurses would later surmise, this man was probably assaulted and knocked unconscious. As one paramedic told me he heard, the crew didn't "get their hands dirty" and they subsequently missed a large hematoma underneath the patient's knotted hair. Protocols clearly state that when a subject is unconscious for unknown reasons, the crew must perform a head-to-toe trauma assessment. They should feel for injuries and abnormalities by running their gloved hands across the entire body. As the rumor went, the crew simply didn't do this, or they did it carelessly. They transported the patient as just any "ordinary drunk" they tend to encounter on a daily basis. As such, the man remained in ambulance triage at the hospital for over thirty minutes as an assumed low-priority intoxication case. He reportedly died. For weeks, his case became an awful example of what can go wrong when crews don't properly assess and *touch* their leper-like patients. Many of the workers I talked to about this expressed remorse and heartbreak even though they didn't work this particular case. They feared this scenario could happen to them if they didn't just suck it up and do a proper assessment.

People's skin color also matters. Paramedics and EMTs, who are much whiter than their clientele, were quick to tell me that racial categories didn't influence their care.[10] Several insisted it was like they didn't even see skin color beyond what was necessary for a medical assessment (e.g., identifying pale skin as an indication of sickness). Of course, they *did* see race. In ambulance bays, they frequently talked to one another about their "homeboy," "esé," and "white trash" patients. And, while muddied by perceptions of class and citizenship, a particular vision of race was clearly important.

Over time, I learned that crews generally look upon darker-skinned patients more suspiciously. This suspiciousness comes in two general forms, and while neither is limited to black or Latino bodies they do intensify on them. First, there is often a suspicion that such people are 911 abusers and this includes the so-called seekers looking to score a high off ambulance pain medication. Second, there is a suspicion that black and Latino people are evasive and are therefore criminals trying to hide something from crews (e.g., providing a fake narrative for their injury to avoid the police). Indeed, these are like ambulance versions of Ronald Reagan's welfare queen (blackness linked to welfare abuse) and George H. W. Bush's Willie Horton (blackness linked to criminality).

Like perceptions of bodily cleanliness, visions of race may produce dev-
astating outcomes. This became especially obvious to me once I started
working as an EMT. Like most novice ambulance workers, I eventually
became accustomed to the term "Hispanic Panic." It's the idea that many
Latino patients—especially older women who immigrated to the United
States—exaggerate their agony or get unnecessarily carried away with
grief. I like to tell myself that I am above such language, but this is a lie.
While I still don't think I ever uttered the term at work, I nevertheless
learned to hear this as code for insignificant suffering.

This became especially worrisome when paramedic Matt and I responded
to a high school near some of the "barrios" that Eric drove me through
months earlier. We found a teenage girl sprawled on the ground outside,
surrounded by students, teachers, and firefighters. As I lowered the gurney,
a firefighter whispered his suspicion into my ear. He figured this could be
just a case of "HP," a common abbreviation for Hispanic Panic. In other
words, this was probably not a real, let alone a severe, emergency. It wasn't
until we were in the ambulance, when I rubbed my knuckle into this girl's
sternum, that Matt and I realized something was wrong. She didn't respond
to my painful stimulus, which I was trained to use as an easy way to detect
the level and authenticity of unconsciousness. I remember thinking to
myself, "Why the fuck didn't fire figure this out on scene?" It was only then,
after double-checking a test the firefighters should have done, that Matt and
I started to take this girl's problem seriously. We ended up rushing her to the
hospital with lights and sirens, suspecting a brain bleed. It's certainly possible that we would have assumed the girl was "faking it" if she was not
Latina or if the firefighter didn't tell us he suspected Hispanic Panic.
However, more than any other call, this one taught me how racialized
visions of clientele can be mixed with perceptions of authentic suffering.

The gender of clientele also matters independently of these other factors. Just as race relations in the ambulance are shaped by the fact that
crews are disproportionately white in reference to their clientele, gender
relations are shaped by the fact that crews are disproportionately male.[11]
As a kind of people to work on, women occasionally come with some
uncomfortable material to labor according to many workers. A number of
men told me they generally don't like calls "involving the vagina" (e.g.,
pregnancy emergencies, miscarriages, and certain cases of sexual assault).

To be clear, these workers don't prefer penis calls either, but there's something about female genitalia in a clinical space that they find especially distasteful. Additionally, many paramedics and EMTs told me they find women's breasts to be mildly awkward material to work with, especially if they need to lift one in order to place an electrode for an EKG. It's impossible to say for sure, but this might help explain why the medical records I examined show that women who encounter the ambulance for chest pain have lower odds of receiving an EKG screening.[12]

At the same time there are cases in which the adult female body is desired, especially if it's young, clean, and thin. Some male workers told me about their excitement in "stripping and flipping" attractive women (e.g., removing or cutting their clothes to check for trauma). However, there are some fine moral boundaries here. The strip and flip needs to be necessary and justified or else fellow ambulance workers, nurses, and even the patient may accuse the scissor-wielding ambulance worker of being a creep. But even beyond this specific procedure, my colleagues frequently exchanged stories of the beautiful women they worked on. Simply talking to such people seemed to bring them pleasure.

LABOR OF REGULATION

Ambulance crews work on an array of people who concentrate toward the bottom of the urban hierarchy. All workers transform the world in some way and ambulance workers are no different. Their labor, however, focuses on transforming relative abnormality into relative normality. At its core, ambulance-based people work involves a *labor of regulation*.

On the one hand, crews identify and mitigate problems located inside the human body. Using a number of tools and techniques, they peer into people as anatomically and physiologically divided structures. They look for irregularities and then work to correct them with more tools and techniques. Among other things, these workers lift falling blood pressures, ventilate breathless airways, and alleviate pain. The point is to help restore some order to people who are disordered from within.

On the other hand, crews also labor to restore some order to the disorders that exist outside individual structures of flesh and bone. They carry ill and injured bodies from streets, homes, and other places into the hospital. In this way, they temporarily cleanse certain sections of the world of certain abnormal bodies. Crews pipeline the sick from spaces they're ill fit for and into the clinical spaces that more or less welcome them.

Both of these regulations—of spaces in bodies and of bodies in spaces—can be dramatic, such as when a crew shoves tubing down a patient's throat or when they drag an unconscious and bloody body off the street. However, these regulations need not be so extreme. This is obvious when a crew simply gives a patient a Zofran pill for nausea relief or when they're summoned to transport a nonurgent patient from home to the emergency department.

Regardless of its intensity, this labor of regulation is complicated by the basic material that crews must work on: people. As Goffman tells us, this material is peculiar for a number of reasons, including its many protections under mutable notions of "humane treatment" and its variable appeal to frontline workers' empathy.[13] I hold that people are also hard to labor because they're differentiated by certain physical differences that workers collectively render as meaningful distinctions (e.g., thin/fat, young/old, clean/dirty, white/black, and male/female). In other words, people workers understand there to be different kinds of people and this can affect the labor they perform. My fieldwork convinces me that these distinctions, which are intermixed with broader social divisions that exist outside the worksite, can establish the possibilities for biases in examination and treatment. The next chapter, however, points to another axis of distinction that is also critical for understanding what's happening inside the ambulance: the gradient between "legit" cases and "bullshit" cases.

2 Ditch Doctors and Taxi Drivers

During my year of shadowing ambulance crews, most shifts began with workers hoping I'd "catch something good." Later, as an employee, I learned that this is a somewhat common thing to say to ride-alongs, like the EMT students and resident physicians who occasionally accompany MRT crews. Paramedics and EMTs generally hope that their guests get to see the craft of paramedicine in action. In theory, there are plenty of possibilities. The crew might plug a gunshot wound. They may even administer some naloxone, the miracle drug that can bring people overdosed on opioids back to life. Or maybe—*just maybe*—they'll run a "code." That's the holy grail for many crews, the cardiac arrest call where a resuscitation effort is made through chest compression, airway intubation, and other interventions.

Several paramedics and EMTs said they hoped, as we departed from headquarters for the day or night, that I wouldn't be a "white cloud" or bring the "curse of the ride-along." Such clouds and curses might be the reason why I wouldn't see "legit" calls, the so-called real emergencies that necessitate and justify the craft of paramedicine. These are the cases that task crews with exercising relatively deep and timely clinical interventions in an effort to salvage bodies. Legit calls have crews compressing lifeless chests, splinting broken bones, and ventilating breathless airways. They can be contrasted with "bullshit" calls. The latter are the so-called nonemergencies and the cases that seem to be generally misplaced inside the ambulance. Unlike legit calls, bullshit calls don't typically involve much of an intervention into the body. They are mundane at best and insulting at worst.

Needless to say, crews want calls that are more legit than bullshit. But it's not up to them. It's up to the "ambulance gods," the special deities of chance that grant rewards and punishments to workers. Mere mortal paramedics and EMTs can't really hope to forecast what the ambulance gods will grant them, but they can guess. Some night crews joked that the moon would be a curious predictor. A full one can supposedly summon a bizarre brutality in the city. More seriously, many workers told me that weather plays a role. Apparently, when it's hot outside people will be more likely to booze and brawl and that can increase the likelihood of legit cases. That's the assumption at least.

A number of crews also emphasized a myth that legit calls can peak on the first and fifteenth days of the month. This was easy to disconfirm in the patient care reports (as were the predictions for both lunar and temperature effects), but the underlying intuition behind this claim is nevertheless telling.[1] Workers who articulated such a belief said that legit calls can peak on the first and the fifteenth because that's when welfare checks are issued. Seemingly oblivious to the fact that neither cash benefits nor food stamps are distributed on these particular dates, several crews speculated that partying and violence were likely to increase when the dole was allocated. Among other things, I was told that "junkies" like to get super high on the days that Uncle Sam pays them.

However, the real junkies might actually be the crews themselves. Eddie Palmer, another ambulance ethnographer, describes paramedics and EMTs as "trauma junkies."[2] Arguing that these workers realize "role validation" through "advanced lifesaving, rescue, and medical skills," he notes that severe trauma calls in particular become like an "occupational drug" and can lead to a "psychological high" for crews. There's a degree of truth to this assessment, but Palmer misses the mark a bit. The ambulance worker's drug of choice is not trauma (i.e., physical injury). It's any "legitimate" medical emergency that the crew is equipped to treat.

CATCHING SOMETHING GOOD

Consider a legit call. Per witnesses and victims, a twenty-or-so-year-old Latino man named Saul got into an argument with a couple of "bad dudes" in the parking lot of his apartment complex. He lives in the general area that Eric referred to as "the killing fields." It's never clear why the men were fighting there, but at some point the dudes struck Saul several times with a metal pipe.

Saul's father, Manuel, heard the beating from the second floor of the apartment building and ran downstairs to defend his son. In return, one of these men drew a pistol, but not before Manuel could lift Saul from the ground. The father-son duo ran back toward their apartment. As they retreated up the exterior stairs of the building, their gun-wielding enemy aimed high and squeezed the trigger. He sent a bullet upward, through Manuel's groin and into his guts. Saul and his dad crawled into their apartment and the other men fled the scene.

Shortly thereafter, two ambulance crews, a supervisor, and I as a notebook-toting observer showed up. We entered the apartment shortly after police and firefighters to find a bloodied and dazed Saul vomiting in the kitchen (a sign of severe head trauma). Manuel was on the living room couch, soaking the cushions with blood.

Both of these men were separately transported to a local trauma center, and Manuel was driven with lights and sirens. While a paramedic was able to plug the wound and prevent more blood from *spilling outside* of Manuel's body, he couldn't control the blood that was *spilling inside* him. Luckily, this paramedic was able to "challenge" a corresponding drop in blood pressure by administering saline via IV therapy.

After Saul and Manuel were dropped on hospital beds, the two crews, the supervisor, and I convened in the hospital's ambulance bay. Despite the grim circumstances of the call, everyone was smiling and laughing. In some ways, it seemed like a strange celebration of violence. The crews shared opinions on the event and told other coworkers in the bay about the call. Spirits were high because the call was good. From the standpoint of crews, cases like this one confirm the value of ambulance work.

Call legitimacy, however, is not limited to such cases of severe trauma (i.e., physical injury). Good nontraumatic "medical calls," like those for diabetic emergencies, strokes, or even legitimate pain management cases, are also welcome. And they don't necessarily have to require such swift interventions. While riding around in ambulances and talking with crews, I quickly realized that a "legit call" simply means an event that necessitates ambulance response as a form of medical intervention, ideally beyond a simple transport to the hospital. A legit call does not necessarily mean a life-threatening emergency or a blood-splattered scene. It also doesn't mean the call needs to be very memorable. Ambulance crews simply desire patients who have what Howard Becker calls "real physical pathologies."[3] They want to treat crises made legible to the craft of paramedicine.

Calls that are more legit often also lead to moments of solidarity between crews and patients. It's a solidarity of interdependence, where both parties essentially need each other. Patients not only need crews, in some cases to live, but crews in a way need patients with legit complaints to realize a sense of honor and purpose at the worksite. Saul and his father were writhing in pain, but legit calls with more lucid patients often include moments of desperation and gratitude. Patients beg their crews to mitigate their suffering and, in some cases, to keep them alive ("Don't let me die!"). They often thank their crews, sometimes for "saving" them. Meanwhile, crews, usually hungry for a legit call, "need something good." As Palmer might put it, they need "their fix."[4] Legit cases allow crews to realize their craft. But while there are plenty of so-called legit calls, there are many more of the opposite variety.

DEALING WITH SOMETHING ELSE

On another shift, I shadow Mark and Danny. This veteran crew has been working together for well over a decade. Both are men in their fifties, but Mark is white and Danny is Latino. Danny, however, told me that most people see him as white. Mark, the paramedic, entered his current profession after years of "boring office work," and Danny entered after leaving a truck-driving gig.

Mark and Danny were summoned to an apartment complex a few miles from where Saul's father was shot. They both groaned when they read the specific address they were summoned to. "Oh fuck!" exclaimed Danny,

"Again?" They were called to a person who summons the ambulance a lot, a "frequently flyer." After he parked the ambulance at this location, Danny told me they will not need the gurney. "She's walking," he said in a frustrated tone that made it sound like he was going to vengefully *make her walk*. We headed up some steps of the apartment building. Danny pointed to one of the steps. "See that, Josh?" he asked. It was an electrode sticker that matched what MRT crews use to run EKGs. Danny suspected it was from the last time an ambulance crew was responding to this "regular." "That's the kind of shit we gotta deal with," said Danny, "But you know, though. You've seen shit like that before, huh? It's ridiculous."

When we walked up to the apartment door, we were greeted by a woman who told us that her sister was the one who requested an ambulance. "Oh yeah, we know," said Danny through a sigh. The patient was Denise, a black woman in her early fifties. "What's wrong?" Mark asked her as she walked toward the front door of the apartment. "I got this burning on my insides. It's burning me inside and out." Mark was unimpressed with this woman who stood in the doorway with her purse in hand. As he later said to me, she was standing there "ready for a taxi ride." Danny responded to the woman's complaint of internal burning, "So you want to go to the hospital?" Denise said, "Yeah, that's where you go when you're sick, right? You go to the hospital when you're sick." "OK," conceded Danny, "Let's go." At this point, Denise's sister pulled me to the side and told me she thought Denise was off her "psych meds." When I whispered this information to Mark on our way back to the rig, he simply shrugged.

Denise followed us to the ambulance. She stepped inside and sat on the gurney. Where the crews on the call for Saul and his father did a "load and go," Denise's crew did a "stay and play." Mark performed the usual assessment. All objective signs suggested there was no emergency here and Danny later explained to me that the woman couldn't have been "in that much pain" given her behavior and speech pattern. Mark asked his patient, "Do you think it's heartburn?" "I don't know what it is. It's burning all over," responded Denise. Mark eventually turfed this call to the lesser-trained Danny before he jumped out of the back of the ambulance and drove us toward the hospital.

During the commute, Danny and Denise argued. Danny was frustrated that his patient refused to score her pain on a scale of one to ten, which is required for the medical record. "Come on," said Danny, "I know you've had to answer questions like this before. Why are you making it difficult?" Danny later told me that Denise was abusing 911, but he wasn't sure why. Denise's actions didn't quite fit the profile of a "seeker." It is often assumed that suspected pain med seekers provide a ten out of ten or "higher" score (e.g., "a thousand out of ten!"). Frustration seemed to flow in both directions though. Denise mumbled something I couldn't hear, but Danny later told me it was "the race card." And if there's one thing that's almost guaranteed to annoy a paramedic or EMT, it's that damn race card. He snapped back, "Don't bring up race. You did this last time. This has nothing to do with race." Danny seemed to stop just before telling her what this probably had to do with in his opinion: Denise was wasting his time with a bullshit call.

We eventually found our way into the hospital. While holding the wall and waiting for triage, Mark turned to Denise. He gave her the lecture Danny seemed tempted to give. He said, "You know, I'm about the same age as you. Do you know how many times I've been to the ER (emergency room)?" Denise, who then lay on the ambulance gurney in a hospital hallway, didn't respond. "Twice," he said, "That's it. Twice." "I didn't make myself sick," said Denise. "But why don't you take care of yourself?" asked Mark. Denise responded, "You don't know what I've been through. You would be shocked if you've seen the things I've seen." Mark didn't like this answer and responded, "You would be more shocked if you've seen the things *I've* seen on a given day. Trust me." I think Mark was implying that he knows true suffering because he encounters it daily at work among emergencies he considers to be more legit. "I'm a good person," said Denise, "I don't want to be sick anymore. What do you want me to do?" "Call your doctor," said Mark. "Don't call 911." "But I hurt now," asserted Denise. "Call your doctor," repeated Mark. "What am I supposed to do when I'm burning at home?" asked his patient. *"Call. Your. Doctor."*

Once Denise was given a room, she complained to a nurse that Mark just wants her to die. Upon hearing this, Mark whispered in my ear as we left the room, "She'd be doing us all a favor." We stepped into the ambulance bay and I helped Mark clean the rig while Danny completed his patient care report. Mark told me he hoped his conversation with Denise would be a "teachable moment." "Do you think it worked?" I asked. "Nope. Not today."

Crews often associate regulars like Denise with bullshit, but it's important to note that *people* are not classified as bullshit or legit. Instead, *cases* are categorized as such. Indeed, there are some regulars that slide between the legit and bullshit poles, depending on how "truly" sick or injured they are during a given ambulance encounter. For example, a woman a few miles away from Denise's apartment calls frequently for breathing difficulties. It's usually for low-severity problems, but it's also well known among the fleet that on a couple of occasions crews needed to provide aggressive airway management for this woman and she had recently been "tubed" (intubated) at the hospital.

Of course, like legit calls, bullshit calls take many forms. Consider some other scenarios. A young man called 911 for what the crew described as a "papercut" after a knife fight. Someone called for COPD exacerbation and felt better after they sat up and were given a bit of oxygen. A man missed his curfew at a transitional housing facility and then used a payphone to dial 911: he decided then and there that he wanted to go to the hospital for a leg injury he sustained weeks earlier. A young girl apparently faked a seizure for "attention" while at school. A worried mother called for her toddler's moderate fever.

Crews may visualize some significant problem with many of these cases. For example, Mark told me Denise does have a "real psych" issue. But these are problems that ambulance crews generally believe they cannot reasonably address. The corresponding solutions exist somewhere outside the ambulance. Some paramedics and EMTs told me their patients need housing, food, and cash. But many crews tended to locate the root problem in the lifestyles and behaviors of their clientele. They need to find employment, stop drinking, and do a better job taking care of themselves. But, perhaps above all, they need to stop requesting the ambulance for problems this institution is not equipped to handle.

LEGIT AND BULLSHIT WORK

Ambulance crews work in ostensibly wild places. They step onto scenes made of dismembered flesh, broken glass, and hysterical bystanders. Even in less dramatic circumstances, they're summoned to provide some order to disorder, such as when they're called to temper someone's rapid breathing or when they're tasked with removing an intoxicated body off the sidewalk. In addition to this, they're frequently encountering people who verbalize multiple hardships interwoven into convoluted narratives of personal suffering.

A significant portion of ambulance work involves these men and women *making sense* of the world. They must decipher the wilderness if they hope to work in it. In addition to translating clientele problems into a primary impression category that is made legible to protocol ("checking a box"), crews mentally carve the world into informal classifications. These include shared understandings of categories like "ghetto" and "junkie" and even more particular labels like Eric's "little nexus of evil" and "zombies" discussed in the introduction. These also include the "kinds of people" that crews distinguish by skin color, cleanliness, weight, and other physical features covered in the previous chapter.

However, there is another meaning-making scheme at play inside the ambulance and it's evident in the cases of Saul, Manuel, and Denise. It concerns the informal distinction that workers make between "legit" and "bullshit" work. This distinction is a reflection of not just how crews see their suffering patients but also how they see themselves. Both paramedics and EMTs generally understand ambulance work to be a craft, albeit a low-paid and underrecognized one. At the same time, they frequently highlight how this craft—what they "signed up for"—is frequently denied to them on the jobsite. What they want to do doesn't typically match what they actually do. They want to be "ditch doctors" who handle legit medical emergencies by performing relatively deep, technical, and timely interventions into the human body. However, they are more typically cast to act like "taxi drivers" who do little more than transport bullshit cases to the hospital.

This basic distinction in cases seems to be as old as the modern ambulance. Dorothy Douglas's groundbreaking ethnography of paramedicine in the 1960s offers a distinction between a "good load" and a "bad load," with the former capturing the so-called real emergency.[5] Likewise, Donald Metz, writing more than a decade later, distinguishes between "good runs" and "shit calls" before he cuts the latter into some more specific types: "walkers," "regulars," "fakers," and "drunks."[6] Comparable divisions can also be found in the ambulance ethnographies by Eddie Palmer in the

1980s, James Mannon in the 1990s, and Michael Corman in the new millennium.[7]

When reading my study along with these previous inquiries, it seems as if the so-called bullshit calls are more common today. That's certainly a pattern that would be consistent with some of the recent changes in welfare and medicine discussed in the introduction. As noted there, social scientists have suggested that a more disciplinary and stingy welfare regime has led many people to turn to the emergency department to treat suffering that can often seem trivial to hospital staff.[8] Indeed, there seems to be a starker contrast today between the demands of patients and the mission of emergency medicine.

I hold that legit and bullshit are best understood as two poles on a continuum. Most cases fall somewhere between the purified versions of these classifications, but crews generally locate their cases closer to one end over the other. Instead of saying a call was "totally legit" or "totally bullshit," I found that paramedics and EMTs were more likely to say a call was "pretty legit" or "mostly bullshit" and sometimes they even said a call was in a "gray area" on this continuum.

Table 1 further distinguishes the legit and bullshit categories. Legit calls tend to correspond with a regulation of spaces in bodies. These are cases where crews locate a legitimate problem inside their patient's flesh and then take efforts to correct that problem, such as when a paramedic injected saline into Manuel's veins to lift his falling blood pressure. It can also be seen in the way crews administer albuterol to compensate respiratory distress, push antiarrhythmic drugs to fix an abnormal cardiac rhythm, or perform any other intervention that targets specific structures and processes within the body. Bullshit calls tend to correspond to the inverse regulation. These cases are defined less by an adjustment to spaces in bodies and more by an adjustment to bodies in spaces, such as when they transport a so-called stable 911 caller like Denise to the hospital. These are ambulance cases that are defined more by transportation than by treatment. While the correspondence is not perfect, ambulance crews generally associate good work and legitimacy with deep clinical interventions and bad work and bullshit with shallow clinical interventions. Again, they want to be "ditch doctors" for patients like Saul and Manuel and not "taxi drivers" for patients like Denise.

Table 1   Legit Calls and Bullshit Calls

	Legit Calls	*Bullshit Calls*
Regulation	Spaces in bodies	Bodies in spaces
Vocation	Realized	Denied
Solidarity w/Patient	Relatively high	Relatively low
Struggle w/Patient	Relatively low	Relatively high

Another distinction is thus important. Legit calls and the laboring of spaces in bodies correspond to ambulance work as a vocation and bullshit calls and the laboring of bodies in spaces do not. While legit calls are more obviously associated with the skillset of paramedics (who lead clinical interventions) and bullshit calls are more obviously associated with the skillset of EMTs (who do most of the driving), it's important to note that both paramedics and EMTs prefer legit calls.[9] Denise's EMT, Danny, seemed to be just as frustrated as her paramedic, Mark.

The "goodness" of legit calls can be detected not only in the enthusiastic summaries provided by workers but also in the interaction between crews and their patients. While I wouldn't necessarily conclude that most legit calls are associated with crew-patient solidarity or that most bullshit calls are associated with crew-patient struggle, I'm confident that solidarity is relatively high for legit calls and struggle is relatively high for bullshit calls. As already noted, such calls frequently lead to moments of solidarity, where not only do clientele need crews (sometimes to live) but crews also need clientele with legit complaints to realize a sense of honor and purpose at the worksite. Bullshit calls, on the other hand, frequently lead to moments of verbal struggle where crews blame their patients for abusing ambulance services and clientele accuse crews of being assholes who don't care about them, their problems, or their communities.

There is, however, another important distinction not captured in figure 1. Most calls are toward the bullshit end of the continuum, but not dramatically so. Evidence for this can be demonstrated in the patient care reports. While crews obviously do not provide a legit/bullshit score, protocol mandates them to report the medical interventions they made in somewhat

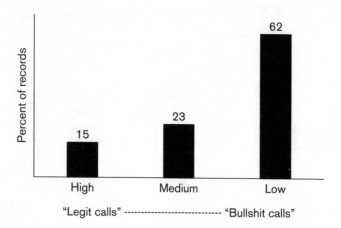

Figure 5. Intervention severity. *Source:* MRT deidentified patient care reports, 2015. *Note:* Observations = 107,089.

granular detail. Previous research on intervention severity can help us make sense of these records. Originating from a focus group study that asked paramedics to rank interventions in terms of their severity, this scholarship offers a three-level ranking system that generally maps onto an ethnographically detected continuum in legit and bullshit cases.[10] Under this framework, higher-severity calls involve more depth into the patient's body: intubation, bronchodilators, defibrillation, antiarrhythmic drugs, and so on. Lower-severity calls involve comparably shallow interventions and don't involve much beyond some low-flow oxygen, an icepack, or a simple transport to the hospital. The middle category approximates a middle depth: pain medication, high-flow oxygen, antinausea medication, and so on.[11] As evident in figure 5, most calls involve shallow rather than deep interventions. Put another way, most are better characterized as bullshit than as legit.

It's also important to note that cases across this legit-bullshit continuum concentrate in poorer neighborhoods, which of course disproportionately hold the county's black and Latino residents. If we somehow diverted cases like Denise's burning sensation away from the ambulance, paramedics and EMTs would still be rushing toward the bottom of the urban hierarchy to aid cases like those of Saul and Manuel.[12] Suffering, in the multiple forms that ambulance crews encounter it on the streets, gravitates toward destitute and stigmatized bodies.

But, of course, suffering is not exclusive to down-and-out populations. And neither is its variation. People in wealthier and whiter neighborhoods summon ambulances for both legit and bullshit reasons too, but, as noted in the introduction, the overall volume of ambulance responses is generally lower in those areas.[13] The most typical (or at least the modal) call for MRT crews involves low-severity interventions with a patient collected near the bottom of the class or racial hierarchy. Instead of approximating the caricature of the "ditch doctor" who aids an entire county during clinically relevant crises, crews are usually closer to embodying the image of a "taxi driver" who tends to work in the county's ghettos and hoods.

AMBIGUOUS MOMENTS

I have little doubt that most of the crews I spent time with would consider Saul and Manuel's case to be legit and Denise's case to be bullshit. However, there are some more obvious gray area cases and they too can help clarify this distinction in legit and bullshit calls. Consider another example, one that the responding crew loosely considered to be legit even if the interventions were not very deep or time-sensitive.

I was riding with paramedic Mason, a Latino man in his late thirties, and EMT Rocky, also a Latino man around the same age. I spent the night with these men awake in the ambulance, from 6:30 PM Saturday to 6:30 AM Sunday. Our first call of the night brought us near but not quite inside Eric's "little nexus of evil." We entered an apartment to find Barry, a black man in his late fifties. He was sitting on his couch and talking to firefighters. Barry was wincing and seemed unnecessarily sweaty given the temperature of the room. A fire medic told us they had just arrived to the apartment but he had already done some of the work of classifying the event for Mason. "Looks like abdominal pain," he said before he and the other firefighters in his unit departed the scene.

Mason and Rocky helped Barry inside the ambulance, which was still parked outside his apartment. Unlike the crews on the call for Saul and his father but like Denise's crew, Barry's paramedic and EMT did a "stay and play." Meanwhile, Barry's wife and her friend sat in a car nearby. They planned to follow us to the hospital. In my experience, situations like this typically frustrate and annoy ambulance crews. Many told me they believe that friends and family with a working car should just drive the patient to the hospital themselves rather than waste 911 resources. However, Mason didn't express this sentiment for Barry's case and he later told me that Barry would have had to unnecessarily suffer in the hospital waiting room on a busy Saturday night if he didn't go by ambulance. He said, "It's a pain management call, straight up. It's legitimate though. His wife could have drove him, but he gets medication quicker in the ambulance."

Inside the parked rig, Rocky began a patient care report on the laptop and Mason asked Barry a series of questions while collecting vitals via the monitor. Barry explained that he has a history of hernia pain. "Oh, that's why your abdomen is so extended," said Mason as he triangulated a subjective complaint with an objective observation. Barry, who was still wincing and clenching, explained in a pained voice that he also has a history of high blood pressure and cysts on his liver and kidneys. There was a lot going on *in there*—inside Barry's body—and Mason had no doubt that there was a real physical pathology to explain the man's suffering. Mason's assessment continued by asking Barry to rank the intensity of his pain on a scale of one to ten, to which Barry responded, "It was a ten at first, but it's like a nine now." He explained he was going to wait to see his primary care physician, but the pain had become too unbearable to wait for an appointment. Mason seemed to genuinely sympathize with Barry as the patient told the paramedic he had to "work through the pain" today while at his low-level job at a nursing facility.

Rocky drove us to the hospital and I sat in the back with Mason and his patient. His intervention into Barry's body was mild, but for the paramedic it was justified and valuable. He pierced Barry's arm with an eighteen-gauge needle to "access" a vein. In withdrawing the metal needle, Mason left a tiny catheter hanging out of the patient's limb. He then connected the catheter to a "saline lock," a couple inches of exterior tubing that he then taped to Barry's arm. Mason is skilled and was able to accomplish this delicate procedure in a moving ambulance on the first attempt. He then used a syringe to push fentanyl, a pain medication, into a port on the saline lock. After a few minutes, Barry's posture and face relaxed. "I can feel this pain med," he said. "Yeah, it works good, huh?" responded

Mason as he continued to type the medical record Rocky had started. "Thank you," said a relieved Barry. "No problem, man."

Calls like this one are not particularly exciting or the "most legit." Using the intervention-based severity scheme I imposed on the patient care reports, this would be a "medium" call, in a gray area between high/legit and low/bullshit. But Mason was clear: this call was legit, even if not very thrilling. It's not one that you would find crews bragging to one another about in ambulance bays or the type of call they might hope their ride-alongs witness. Nonetheless, Mason saw Barry's suffering as a legitimate crisis and one that he had the tools and skills to mitigate. It was a "real" pain management call and one the paramedic seemed to find some sense of duty in treating through a moderate intervention into the bloodstream. The crews I shadowed were not just "trauma junkies" as Eddie Palmer insists. The fleet is not made up of blood-craving adrenaline fiends. These workers typically characterized themselves as emergency care profession-als, as "ditch doctors," who are broadly equipped to aid a variety of crises whether "traumatic" (injury) or "medical" (illness) in nature.

There's also something to be said about the similarities and differences between Denise's internal burning and Barry's abdominal pain. While these cases involved different genders and unique crews, I suspect most paramed-ics and EMTs would classify Denise's case as bullshit and Barry's case as closer to legit or at least in a gray area. The latter is more clearly linked to Howard Becker's "real physical pathology" and is rendered more visible through Michel Foucault's "medical gaze." But while Foucault is right to claim that the medical examination today asks patients to locate suffering in the body through a central question—"Where does it hurt?"—that question is often not sufficient. In order to be best transformed into what Jeffrey Prottas calls a "client" inside the ambulance, alert and oriented patients need to provide some additional answers, which Barry gave but Denise did not (e.g., pain score and relevant medical history).[14] Perhaps more impor-tantly, subjective pain should also correspond to some objective sympto-mology (e.g., Barry's distention, sweating, and clenching versus Denise's relatively "symptomless" presentation on scene and in the ambulance).

The words "legit" and "bullshit" are part of the lexicon, but, as already noted, these are pure types. When prompted, most workers had difficulty stating if a call was totally bullshit or absolutely legit. As previously mentioned, phrases like "mostly bullshit" and "mostly legit" were common. They accounted for some admitted doubt: a mostly bullshit case could have some latent legitimacy and some seemingly legitimate cases may secretly carry some inauthenticity.

There are also some more obvious moments of ambiguity. Many death cases are examples of this. Some deceased people are initially "worked up" with compression, intubation, injection, and other interventions before they're "called" (i.e., pronounced dead in the field). We saw this in the last chapter. Despite a deep intervention into the body (likely the deepest of the month for a fulltime paramedic), crews do not consider such death cases desirable at the conclusion of the call, given the grim outcome.[15] Other deceased bodies are not even worked up because the crew identifies rigor mortis or other obvious signs of death when they first see the subject. Still, crews do not consider such cases to be bullshit because the case *was* recently linked to a legit bodily crisis that concluded with a violent, surprising, or "natural" passing.

Additionally, there are scenarios where a call is *too legit* but not necessarily fatal. These are "nightmare calls" that are so grotesque and haunting they cannot clearly be considered to be good according to crews. Paramedics and EMTs often noted how the mutilated and limp bodies of children and babies were especially chilling. Even if the outcome is desirable in terms of a "real save," the dark circumstances of some legit calls, such as responses to rape, can overshadow the rewarding aspects of the case.

In short, there is no shortage of examples that can be used to complicate the legit-bullshit distinction that I insist is so important for understanding ambulance work. However, those cases that seem to fall in a gray area or somehow beyond the continuum (e.g., nightmare calls) are nevertheless generally interpreted with some distinctions between legit and bullshit in mind. Crews may shrug some calls off as not quite bullshit but not quite legit and recognize others as so legit that they become undesirable, but they nevertheless make sense of such ambiguity relative to a shared schema that significantly organizes their perceptions of good and bad work. The existence of ambiguity doesn't threaten the validity of the proposed distinction. Rather, it helps clarify the boundaries.

THE MORAL ORDER OF CASES

Ambulance work is as much mental as it is manual. In addition to physically adjusting the world, ambulance crews symbolically tweak it. They convert people into patients, transforming citizens into clients. In doing this, crews impose a series of formal classifications (e.g., determining a primary impression, logging a set of vital signs, and documenting a medical history) that help make their subjects legible to emergency medicine. They also impose informal classifications like "bum" and "Hispanic Panic" to make sense of their work from beyond the earshot of patients and bystanders.

Another informal classification concerns a distinction between "legit" and "bullshit" calls. This moral distinction shapes, and is shaped by, crews' material adjustments of the world, with legit calls usually involving a deep regulation of spaces in bodies and bullshit calls usually involving little more than a regulation of bodies in spaces. It's not only a retrospective estimation of a call's value; it's also a triaging device for determining how to handle particular cases. This distinction is perhaps best understood as a form of vision, as a lens through which these workers see the very world they transform.

Although flexible and fuzzy, crews' general preferences for legit cases help clarify ambulance work as a vocation. From their point of view, responding to so-called real medical emergencies is an end in itself. Compression, intubation, and other deep clinical interventions into the failing body add up to something greater than just a job. Indeed, ambulance crews appear to be driven by what Max Weber calls an "inward calling."[16] They're passionately devoted to working legit cases and this is especially obvious when they articulate a relative distain for bullshit cases (i.e., the denial of vocation).

For Weber, such a subjective calling must correspond to some objective circumstances. Three complementary conditions seem to root and nourish a shared taste for legit cases among workers. First, this bias is crystalized in pedagogy. EMTs and paramedics are first and foremost taught to treat severe bodily crises. Training inculcates within them a technical knowledge that is simply oriented toward the legit end of the continuum.

Second, crews' preferences for legit cases are in many ways supported by both the physical and the procedural infrastructures of the ambulance. Most of the rig's instruments are directed toward the treatment of legit emergencies, and official protocols frequently emphasize the importance of "severe" cases. Third, recognition from peers is linked to cases that are more legit than bullshit. While never guaranteed, some glory can be won through legit calls. This is evident in the hospital ambulance bay where the mixed chatter of praising and bragging voices can often be heard after legit runs. Ultimately, paramedicine, like any vocation, comes with what Weber calls a "strange intoxication," a vision made hazy by the context-specific passions of those gripped by their craft.

Understanding the moral order that workers impose on their work will be essential for deciphering both the horizontal and the vertical social relations through which ambulance operations occur. Perhaps the most important takeaway from this chapter is best stated as a question and an answer. The question: Why do ambulance crews generally prefer legit calls over bullshit calls if they're more physically, mentally, and emotionally exhausting? As already demonstrated, legit calls tend to require more tiring movements (e.g., rapid extraction), include relatively stressful procedures (e.g., complicated paperwork), and come with an increased risk of emotional depletion (e.g., coping with a patient dying in the ambulance). The short answer: They're committed to ambulance work as a craft. Legit calls provide an opportunity to realize paramedicine as a vocation, while bullshit calls typically offer a recurring reminder that the dream of "real ambulance work" is dead, is dying, or was weak to begin with.

I end this chapter with a couple of reminders. First, as you read the rest of this book, remember that legit-bullshit distinctions are not clear labels imposed onto persons. Instead, they're fuzzy categories imposed onto problems. This distinction is a worker-made scheme in *kinds of cases*, not kinds of people. Individuals can slide across the legit-bullshit continuum. Also, remember that legit and bullshit are best described as pure types. There's a lot of ambiguity and uncertainty on the front lines. Rather than branding their cases as totally legit or totally bullshit, crews tend to see the problems they confront as "mostly legit" or "mostly bullshit."

Second, while I suggest that this distinction in kinds of cases is often more fundamental than the distinctions workers make in kinds of people (e.g., race and gender), it's important to remember that I don't intend to suggest that the latter are irrelevant. As I detailed in the previous chapter, there is little doubt that the socially significant physical features of patients shape the labor process and, in a partial break from Erving Goffman, I suggest this is a key feature of so-called people work.[17] Yet, the moral classification I detail in this chapter transcends the other divisions of human material in important ways. Crews would generally prefer to work a legit fatty than a "better"-shaped body with a bullshit problem. They'd usually rather aid a seriously ill working-age adult than a "false alarm" geriatric patient. These workers would often rather assist a dirty body with a legit problem than a clean one with a bullshit problem. Crews would overwhelmingly prefer to treat a gunshot or cardiac arrest patient who is black than a white patient with a nonurgent complaint. And while the female body offers some complications—some push and pull in terms of appeal— the central distinction in desirability concerns whether or not the body, however it's gendered, presents as a more legit or a more bullshit case. The kinds of people matter in shaping perceptions of authentic suffering, but the kinds of cases sorted on a legit-bullshit continuum often matter more.

The next chapter continues an effort to detail life inside the ambulance by examining a dimension only briefly discussed so far: emotion. In better explaining the previously noted link between legit calls and solidarity and bullshit calls and struggle, I'll illustrate how legit and bullshit calls correspond to two interactional styles linked to the affectual experiences of labor. I call one style "being a dick" and the other "having heart." The former is an apathetic and hostile disposition while the latter is a sympathetic and hospitable one. I argue that both orientations, which I learned firsthand as a novice EMT, are linked to experiences with legit and bullshit calls in complicated but nevertheless patterned ways. Ambulance patients are variably handled by both warm and cold hands and to understand this we must consider not only what crews see but also what they feel.

3 Feeling the Ambulance

Maybe due to morbid curiosity or a general concern for my emotional well-being, my friends and family often asked me a question that paramedics and EMTs seem to universally hate, "What's the worst thing you've seen?" With minimal details, I'd offer brief visual descriptions that only seemed to exacerbate their concern: slit throats, exposed muscle, and bloated corpses. This was usually enough to sour their expression before I'd add something like, "It's not that bad overall, though. We get a lot of low-priority calls." As the previous chapter made clear, ambulance work is neither an endless horror show nor a perpetual adrenaline rush. I found the job could in fact be somewhat boring at times. In addition to lots of driving around without lights and sirens and holding the walls of hospitals, most so-called bullshit and even gray area calls were simply not very stimulating or memorable.

My vague and contradictory descriptions of ambulance work for friends and family outside the trade attempted to capture a complexity that's important for understanding how crews handle their clientele. Ambulance work is indeed stressful and horrifying and those closest to me were right to worry. Even knowing what I know now, I too worry about my EMT and paramedic friends still in the field. Given their somewhat frequent exposure to death and danger, it's not surprising that ambulance crews suffer posttraumatic stress disorder at high rates and face relatively high chances of suicide and suicidal thoughts.[1] This matters for patients too, as the grotesque and otherwise stressful aspects of the job can mentally exhaust workers, desensitize them to misery, and generally chill their perceptions of patients.[2] While no doubt significant, the emotional wounding that many workers experience on the job is just part of the experience of doing people work inside the ambulance. Bullshit calls, while not as stressful, can bring their own emotional trials. Most crews handle multiple bullshit cases a day and this frustrating denial of vocation, as I've already suggested, is often coupled with verbal struggles between crews and patients.

But the emotional aspects of the job are even more complicated because ambulance work is not defined by trauma and frustration alone. As an EMT, I found that there was a lot to enjoy about my work. Not only did I like spending time with my paramedic partners between calls, I learned to appreciate many of my interactions with patients. There was both a rush and a reward to doing the work. Legit calls often led to moments of solidarity between workers and patients and I was not immune to this. It generally felt good to be part of a consequential institution that mitigated suffering in the city. I was deployed far downstream to manage a plethora of problems and I did so mainly as an assistant to better-trained paramedics. But the alternative I also lived as an insulated academic stuck at a desk often felt less admirable. I may have embodied the stereotype of a white ivory tower descendent trying to rescue people on the urban flatlands, but I simply didn't care when my partners and I were rushing to cardiac arrests, diabetic comas, and other so-called legit calls. Moreover, the bullshit calls were not always frustrating. Many of my partners and I found transporting people to the hospital for a prescription refill or just a bed to sleep on for the night to be a rewarding task in its own right. We were sort of like untrained and ill-equipped social workers, and when we thought of it that way we could often salvage some good vibes from these "misuses" of the ambulance.

Thus, as an EMT, I learned that the emotional complexities of my job oriented, and were oriented by, my relations with patients. My partners and I interacted with patients not as fully rational actors, but instead as temperamental creatures whose moods and opinions shifted in patterned ways. Sometimes we handled our patients with *cold hands*. Linked to our more apathetic and hostile visions of clientele, we treated and transported people bluntly, technically, and sometimes coercively. However, we often also handled them with *warm hands*. We treated and transported people in a caring manner that reinforced our more sympathetic (sometimes empathetic) and hospitable visions of patients. With the goal of better understanding the practical relations between ambulance crews and the subjects of their labor, this chapter maps my cold and warm handling of patients as an EMT. It does so by detailing the dispositions I adopted to cope with a central dilemma of ambulance work.

COPING DOWNSTREAM

The mixed emotions of ambulance work, and their implications for crews' handling of patients, are partially rooted in a central problem that ambulance workers confront daily. This was a problem that wasn't very clear to me until I faced it with my paramedic partners as an EMT. *How could I cope with the pressures of mitigating suffering that was as seemingly endless as it was varied?*

My colleagues taught me that I needed to have the right "attitudes," "mind-sets," and "senses" to weather the infinite wave of 911 callers.[3] I soon cultivated not one but two general sets of dispositions and they loosely map onto a distinction in apathetic and sympathetic people work. On the one hand, I became a "dick." I developed a somewhat cold and aggressive style for interacting with patients. However, I also learned to "have heart." I developed a warm and friendly style.[4] These were patterned acquisitions linked to both the material circumstances of my job and the meanings my peers and I collectively attached to these circumstances. And, where being a dick corresponded with moments of struggle with clientele, having heart corresponded with moments of solidarity.

In reflecting on my experience as a novice EMT, I suggest that crews' visions of both legit and bullshit calls can motivate apathetic and sympathetic orientations. However, there are some general patterns I observed when making sense of my new job. Legit calls can usually mean a *realization* of vocation, but they can also be haunting. I learned to tolerate the *grim* aspects of dealing with blood, guts, and broken bones. This helped maintain my commitment to the job, but it also developed my apathy toward clientele, whom I began to see as "meat and bone." And while bullshit calls are usually frustrating and countervocational—the basic pieces of a daily *grind*—some of my colleagues showed me ways to *rearticulate* the vocation. Bullshit calls were almost never preferred, but they occasionally became opportunities to practice a type of ambulance-based social work and there were virtues to this. These calls could indeed involve and develop sympathy.

BEING A DICK

As a rookie EMT I embodied a common strategy of thought, speech, and action to cope with the emotional hazards of my job. Against my previously held standards of proper and professional etiquette, I adopted cold and coercive sentiments to navigate the jobsite. For lack of a better word, I became a *dick*. There are likely many reasons why I often evoked a no-nonsense and apathetic temperament at work, but two forces seem especially suspect: legit calls that were "grim" and the regular "grind" of bullshit calls.

Along with police, firefighters, and coroners, ambulance crews are often dispatched to disturbing circumstances that can "fuck with" or "shake" a person. These are the nightmare calls I mentioned briefly in the previous chapter. Fatal car accidents, vicious crime scenes, suicide discoveries, miscarriages, and child abuse responses are standard examples used by crews, but each person seems to have their own triggers. I did not witness as many brutalities as most of my peers, but I saw plenty of terrible things: a young man dying from multiple gunshot wounds, more than one corpse gripped by rigor mortis, and a raped woman with severe facial trauma gasping for breath. This last call was so horrific I quit my EMT job a bit earlier than expected. I planned on leaving MRT anyway, but after this particular encounter I stopped picking up shifts and I called out sick for the remainder of my final schedule. Certainly, I felt sick. The thought of returning to the ambulance, even for one more shift, was nauseating. I came to terms with the fact that I was probably weaker—and a "bigger pussy"—than most of my peers in the ambulance. I tapped out before giving the job a chance to more permanently shake me.

When they weren't motivating my exit from the field, calls like these dispirited me and drained much of my perhaps naïve faith in human decency. As one of my partners accurately predicted, this job would often have me seeing people as "meat and bone." I came to understand this less as a technical gaze (e.g., a way to see the body as ill or injured) and more as a lens to dull the colors of human agony. The job significantly, and perhaps necessarily, desensitized me to bleeding, weeping, and choking bodies. And where the very thought of touching a dead person once nauseated me, I eventually found myself carelessly eating lunch minutes after I had handled a corpse.

My newfound meat and bone vision of the world was an apathetic one in that it helped me imagine a rupture in person and flesh. It was a reductionist and essentially dehumanizing point of view that kept me from dwelling on the misery of leaking, disfigured, and expiring bodies. However, this newfound vision also narrowed my definition of suffering. Like Mark and other workers who get frustrated with bullshit cases, I too found myself downplaying the pain of many people relative to the "real emergency" cases I had witnessed. In knowing that "it could be a lot worse," I often found myself justifying my general lack of sympathy for less urgent cases. "She'll live," I remember telling myself as a relatively stable woman sobbed on my gurney.

I'm confident such a perception of the world, spawned at least in part by a repeated exposure to the grim circumstances of ambulance work, fueled my cold interactions with clientele. In a tone that deliberately expressed my frustration, I frequently said things like "you're OK" and "oh, chill out" to discount the suffering of others. And, when people were more "truly" suffering, I could in some ways perceptually reduce them to meat and bone. I realize this may be read as a weak justification for my dickish behavior, but many of my colleagues nonetheless helped me make sense of the world this way. My newly harsh and bitter approach to the world, according to veteran workers, could be partially blamed on the grim aspects of ambulance labor.

However, my decreasing sympathy for clientele seemed to be more deeply rooted in the relatively mundane aspects of EMT work. It seemed like every shift my partners and I were getting our "asses kicked" as we ran between so-called bullshit. While not as emotionally shocking as grim scenes, the daily grind of these calls was nonetheless exhausting.

Consider a lesson I learned on the job, midway through one of my shifts with Lance and Vince. You remember Lance. He helped me draw a map, as I mentioned in the introduction. He's that EMT that served as my "field training officer." Vince is his paramedic partner. It was usually around this time, circa 1:00 AM, that these two men liked to offer me grand but informal lessons on how to do my new job.

"You're so green it's cute," said Vince, a white man in his late thirties, as he watched me clean the gurney just outside our ambulance. "You gotta be a dick sometimes." We agreed that Penny, the seventy-something-year-old white woman we had just transported to the hospital from her trailer, was a "pain in the ass." She called 911 for a fever and anxiety before she spent the better part of forty-five minutes yelling at us and hospital staff. Her main complaint was rather simple and potentially accurate: she believed no one was taking her anguish seriously. She chastised us for not believing she had a fever, yelled at nurses for not triaging her quickly, and scolded doctors for walking past her gurney without acknowledging her misery. Penny was, as Lance put it, "fucking annoying." I nervously attempted to calm her down while holding the wall in triage. "I took your temperature twice, ma'am, you don't have a fever. . . . They're (hospital staff) really busy right now, but they'll get you a bed soon. . . . A doctor will see you when you get a bed." I failed. She continued to scream, convinced I was not adequately helping her.

Vince said, "You did your best trying to keep her quiet, talking all soft to her and shit, but it wasn't really working, was it?" I shook my head and he continued, "I'm telling you, man, you gotta be a dick sometimes." Before I could respond, Vince hedged a bit, "I mean don't be a real dick, but don't be extra nice either. Otherwise, people will walk all over you. Get what I'm saying?" I lied and responded, "I think so." "It will get easier," he said, "You see, you still got your soul, but give it time and these people will suck the soul out of you. Me and Lance lost our souls a long time ago. You'll lose yours soon enough." He continued, "It's the harsh truth, but with all the bullshit we run, what do you expect?"

Along with my trainers and our patient, I was caught in a double mismatch in aspiration and action. On the one hand, bullshit calls like the one just described and the ones Vince generally warned of are formed by a *mismatch in vocation and labor*. Instead of performing deep and timely interventions to "save lives" and "really help people," my colleagues and I were more often just taxiing people into the emergency department. To our frustration, much of the day-to-day consequence of our work was the movement of bodies rather than the valorized labor of salvaging them. Penny was one such frustrating call. According to the patient care report, we did little more than collect a set of vital signs and transport her without lights and sirens to the hospital.

On the other hand, calls like this often captured a *mismatch in clientele expectation and worker capabilities*. I learned to accept that I was unable to treat many of the problems that I saw as structural and that many of my partners saw as moral: substance abuse, homelessness, interpersonal violence, and other ostensibly nonmedical problems. I also accepted that many of the more clearly "medical" cases were likely misplaced in the ambulance as well. From chronic pain to mild nausea, a mostly "stable" clientele would often summon the ambulance only to be transferred to an emergency department and *maybe* get some fentanyl for pain or some Zofran for nausea on the way. While many of our frequent flyers seemed to also accept our true potential, less familiar patients would often become frustrated when my partners and I were unable to significantly treat their suffering. This seemed to be a common cause for patient outbursts. On a somewhat routine basis, patients shouted at me and my partners for "not giving a shit" and "not helping." Their expectations usually seemed to be greater than our capabilities.

I hold that these dual mismatches encouraged a rough and forbidding presentation of self. A generally denied vocation was frustrating on its own, but my irritation was usually compounded when patients insisted that we were unwilling (rather than incapable) of aiding them. I soon learned that Vince was right. These bullshit cases seemed to suck my soul.

When soft speech failed to calm irked subjects, I became a dick. My female colleagues often referred to this as "being a bitch." In later shifts I would speak firmly and authoritatively to clients. Short of telling patients to "Shut the fuck up!" (which I often wanted to do), I became accustomed to shouting things like "Stop!" "That's enough!" and "Be quiet!" In a way I had never done before in my life, I yelled commands at people throughout my shifts ("Hold still!") and I occasionally issued threats ("If you keep acting up, we're going to restrain you. Do you understand me?").

I take responsibility for the cold ways I handled many people inside the ambulance. But this is neither a confession nor an excuse. It's a self-analysis that seeks to offer some limited but useful insight into the subjective experiences of ambulance work. My short time as an EMT showed me just how emotionally challenging the job can be. As a ride-along, I found it easy to silently judge crews for being rude to patients. My opinions changed once I started working at MRT. The ride-along shifts were emotionally exhausting in their own right, but actually doing the work intensified my exhaustion. Lifting a screaming and mutilated body off the ground is different than watching others do it. Likewise, getting scolded, kicked, and spit on by patients is different than witnessing these interactions from the sidelines. The job also clarified new frustrations that were difficult to comprehend as a more passive observer. I may not have bled ambulance work like some of my more hardcore colleagues, but I too got caught up in the vocation. I too got a little high off legit calls and this made the lows of bullshit work even more irritating. I hated hearing the dispatcher drop a nearby gunshot or a cardiac arrest call on another crew while my partners and I were stuck dealing with somebody's less urgent complaint. And I too got pissed when patients were so seemingly quick to accuse me of not giving a shit. Still, I can understand why they thought this. On many occasions, I was simply a dick.

HAVING HEART

Luckily for those around me, I wasn't a dick all the time. I like to think I was mostly boring and forgettable. Indeed, it was my paramedic partners who interacted with patients the most. I was more or less assisting them by hooking up *their* patient to the monitor, preparing equipment, and constructing a medical record on the computer. For the most part, my partners weren't presenting themselves as apathetic or hostile either. Monotony best defined our daily grind. We were yawning far more than we were yelling.

Still, flashes of passion occurred inside the ambulance. Scolding patients was just one extreme. I often genuinely sympathized with clientele, despite the somewhat jaded perceptions I adopted over the course of my fieldwork. In addition to learning how to be a dick from time to time, I developed another strategy of thought, speech, and action to cope with the pressures of mitigating endless and varied suffering inside the ambulance. I learned to "have heart."

While "being a dick" and its synonyms were terms frequently used on the jobsite, having heart is a phrase I impose to make sense of my workplace dispositions that countered my apathetic orientations. It nevertheless refers to a shared conception of "truly caring" and an authentically sympathetic stance toward patients. Like being a dick, having heart is less a spontaneous response than an organized and patterned style of interaction. Just as being a dick did not give me the liberty to hit patients, having heart did not give me the freedom to weep with them. But that does not mean we should assume that having heart was a bogus or even a carefully articulated presentation of self. As I felt it, having heart was as genuine as being a dick. It refers to a sincerely friendly and caring demeanor, and it's distinct from the "managed heart" that sociologists insist steers an inauthentic presentation of self.

For sure, I learned what Arlie Hochschild might call the "feeling rules" of MRT.[5] I knew to interact with patients with a forced smile and "good bedside manner," especially when supervisors were around. I also knew to *act* compassionate as a strategy to manage some of our clientele. Patients were less likely, I reasoned, to fight me if I killed them with kindness. I wasn't alone in reasoning this either. On many occasions, my partners told me they feigned a caring presentation of self to help assure that their subjects didn't "lose their shit" or "go over the edge." Patients were not always oblivious to this either and I was called out on a few occasions for "just pretending" to care.

I don't deny that there were moments in which I offered up a phony kindness, but for the most part such an act didn't seem necessary. Management rarely supervised my direct interactions with patients and patients rarely complained about crew behavior to supervisors. Moreover, most of the patients I encountered were not "on the edge," so faking or exaggerating sympathy to avoid a fight was generally rare.

Like being a dick, there are probably many reasons why I adopted an authentically warm and sympathetic temperament for handling clientele, but two conditions specific to the worksite seem likely: legit calls where my partners and I realized the vocation and bullshit calls where we rearticulated it.

More legitimate calls, by their very definition, are seen by crews as more valid forms of suffering. In labeling a call as "legit" paramedics and EMTs are always recognizing some significant degree of "real" hardship. I learned that people couldn't, or at least shouldn't, be totally reduced to meat and bone. This was because seeing and touching people in pain were always somewhat painful experiences. The sting was never crippling, but it hurt to see the mutilated flesh of an assault victim, to feel the fevered skin of a septic body, and to hear the slurred speech of stroke patient. Calls like these occasionally formed a lump in my throat. They sometimes led me into the hospital restroom, where I'd splash my face with cold water in an effort to cool my flushed cheeks and regain focus.

These moments of sympathy weren't always limited to private reflection. Following a legit call, my partners and I would often calibrate a sympathetic, even if fairly shallow, understanding of the patient. Shaking our wincing faces as we departed the hospital, we'd say things like "poor dude" and "that lady was really hurting" before turning our attention to the next call.

While sympathetic moments during legit cases could understandably lead to depressing feelings, I found that they were mostly coupled with a sentiment of good will. They seemed to motivate a caring interactional style with patients. It genuinely felt good to comfort and aid people who appeared to be truly suffering. As an EMT, I never administered fentanyl or any of the medications that somewhat obviously relieved people, but I iced sores, wiped blood, and held hands. I also "talked patients down" from their pain and coached people to slow their breathing as paramedics performed interventions that some saw as frightening (e.g., starting an IV). These were generally rewarding experiences.

Establishing moments of solidarity with patients came easy under these emotional circumstances. This was a solidarity of interdependence. As noted in the previous chapter, patients with legit complaints often need crews to live and crews often need such patients to realize a sense of honor and purpose at the worksite. My partners and I certainly argued with legit patients, especially if they were making decisions we believed threatened their well-being (e.g., refusing to go the hospital), and we sometimes physically wrestled with these individuals (e.g., during "legitimate" psychiatric breaks). In general, though, we struck peaceful and compassionate relations rooted in a sympathetic, even if a somewhat specific, vision of true suffering.

But, just as being a dick is not limited to bullshit calls, having heart is not limited to legit calls. We didn't always discount bullshit cases as obnoxious or infuriating. Even in classifying people's problems as bullshit, and therefore as a relatively wasteful use of time and ambulance resources, there's room for sympathy. Penny didn't get much, but a guy who thanked me profusely for taking him out of a prison-like board and care facility and to an emergency department for a night of relative peace did. Likewise, frequent flyers frustrated me and my partners for sure, but they too yielded our compassion from time to time. In many ways, I found it pretty easy to at least mildly sympathize with bullshit cases attached to docile, grateful, and familiar people.

Moreover, we weren't totally chilled to the fact that patients with bullshit complaints face "real problems" like barriers to primary care, precarious employment, housing insecurity, social isolation, and limited transportation options. We sometimes articulated our sympathy regarding these conditions with patients and with one another. For many of my colleagues and I, the response to this realization was to simply grind through the calls and submit to our specialization: we're just paramedics and EMTs. What could we do?

Some paramedics, though, taught me there are some narrow opportunities to rearticulate the vocation as a kind of social work on wheels. From time to time, I consciously broadened my understanding of what the ambulance can, and perhaps should, do as an urban safety net institution. I learned to draw some emotional reward from taking bullshit cases to the hospital for a prescription refill, a bed to sleep on, and a meal to eat. I wasn't alone either. A few of my colleagues liked to give out company blankets to people on the streets and they often did so against the explicit wishes of management. And, on a couple of occasions, my partners and I checked the blood pressure and glucose levels of people who walked up to the ambulance and asked us to do so. We did this under the radar so the "walk up" wouldn't get billed and we were generally happy to help these chronically ill people monitor their vital signs. Sometimes, while at the hospital, we would go out of our way to request an actual social worker on behalf of our patient, to help connect her or him to housing programs, substance abuse treatment programs, and other resources. While not as exhilarating as realizing the vocation through legit cases, accepting bullshit as an opportunity to do some amateur social work could bring its own emotional rewards.

During my ride-along observations, paramedics and EMTs frequently told me they liked their job because it felt like they were "making a difference" and "giving back to society." As a cynical observer, I found it hard not to roll my eyes when I heard such things. But as an EMT I began to understand what these workers meant. Beneath these corny mantras of benevolence was a kernel of truth I never quite understood until I did the work. The realized vocation, the moments in which workplace aspiration matched workplace action, simply felt good. I learned that running legit calls, and therefore "truly helping" people through assisting paramedics' relatively deep interventions into the body, was something to live for in and of itself. Yet having heart was not totally limited to legit calls. While the very definition of bullshit calls suggests a relative lack of worker sympathy, I nevertheless learned to sympathize with such clientele from time to time. This was especially true when my partners and I could momentarily rearticulate the vocation and our commitments to mitigating a varied and endless wave of suffering bodies.

LOOKING INSIDE

Erving Goffman reminds us that the materials people workers handle "are almost always considered to be ends in themselves."[6] For him, much of this is accounted for by the exogenous but largely unspecified forces that hold an institution accountable to some "broad moral principles." This is where things like general standards for "humane treatment" enter the picture.

I don't deny that such conditions are important or intend to disparage Goffman's contribution. Still, as I've argued, workers see some people to be *more* ends in themselves than others. Crews overwhelmingly see those suffering from legit medical emergencies as ones worth their effort, and in many ways they crave these cases. The same cannot be said about bullshit calls, which are typically seen as just part of a "job." Yet, in order to understand this variation in a sort of taste for patient problems, we must account for an endogenous force that Goffman generally neglects: workers' sense of vocation (i.e., their commitments to a craft).

In several respects, crews' emotional highs and lows are linked to the realization and denial of this sense. Thus, the physical, cognitive, and affectual dimensions of people work are intertwined in complex ways. I'm less concerned with trying to unravel this knot and locate its thickest strand and am more interested in demonstrating its existence and pieces. My goal in writing this chapter in particular has been to locate those emotional threads of ambulance-based people work and to show how they're tangled with both the manual and the mental aspects of that same work.

To sum up, ambulance crews handle suffering bodies with both cold and warm hands. My personal experiences as a novice EMT have taught me that the practical component of ambulance work is not a purely calculated, let alone a fully lucid, engagement. Instead, this labor is heated and cooled by the emotional circumstances of people work and this is significant for understanding how interactions between frontline workers and clientele develop into moments of solidarity or struggle. I have identified two opposing sets of dispositions: the apathetic orientation of "being a dick" and the sympathetic orientation of "having heart." These are general styles of coping with the pressures of mitigating suffering downstream and they further complicate the distinction in legit and bullshit cases. Having heart is linked firstly to a realized vocation through legit work and secondly to a rearticulated vocation through bullshit work, whereas being a dick is linked firstly to the grind of bullshit work and secondly to the grim aspects of legit work.

In wrapping up part 1, we see how ambulance-based people work essentially adds up to a bandaging of bodies. When we look inside the ambulance, we find crews providing generally superficial responses to suffering that concentrates toward the bottom of the urban hierarchy. This bandaging involves more than a manual application of field medicine or a quick transport to the hospital. It's a process enabled and constrained by a series of mental tasks, from imposing official classifications required by protocol (e.g., primary impressions) to articulating informal distinctions linked to the craft of paramedicine (e.g., legit and bullshit calls). Bandaging is also an activity that influences, and is influenced by, the emotional circumstances of people work. Both cold and warm hands are wrapping people in gauze inside the ambulance and this variability shapes moments of struggle and solidarity between ambulance crews and the people they work on.

The analysis can't stop here. In order to understand what's happening inside the ambulance, we must consider some forces outside of it. At the same time, we should consider how the internal dynamics detailed in part 1 react to and affect those external forces. The ambulance cannot be reduced to the practical interaction between crews and their patients. We must consider the relational component of a labor process; we have to account for the social relations through which a bandaging of bodies is made possible.

Hence the remainder of this book. Part 2 accounts for the *horizontal* relations between ambulance workers and workers of different institutions. Particular attention is given to the interactions between crews and their nurse and police counterparts. We'll locate the ambulance between the protective Left hand (i.e., welfare operations) and the repressive Right hand (i.e., penal operations) of the state. Part 3 then accounts for the *vertical* relations between ambulance workers and those who attempt to control and coordinate their labor from above. For MRT crews, and other frontline workers throughout the delegated state, this means positioning the ambulance underneath a nexus of bureaucratic and capitalistic forces. It will become clear, through both of these endeavors, why an internal analysis of the ambulance was necessary and why such an analysis came first.

PART II Sorting Bodies

THE AMBULANCE BETWEEN HOSPITALS AND SQUAD CARS

While on the job, my partners and I often said that we "worked the streets." This had different meanings beyond the obvious fact that we spent much of our time traversing asphalt. It meant we did work that was distinct from those who were seemingly stuck in offices, like upper managers and county dispatchers. For paramedics, street work also meant practicing medicine beyond the walls of the relatively insulated and sanitized hospital. It meant performing CPR on sidewalks and starting IVs on moving ambulances. Saying that we worked the streets also invoked an image of doing work that was a bit exotic. Our work brought us into *the* streets, into the so-called ghettos and hoods that were otherwise invisible to most of us.

However, as a sociologist, I thought of working the streets a bit differently. I watched as ambulance crews worked alongside other frontline workers. They labored next to nurses, police officers, firefighters, skilled nursing facility staff, security guards, and others whose work also gravitated toward the bottom of the urban hierarchy. These relations with other workers seemed to shape, and be shaped by, the ways ambulance crews were handling the subjects of their labor. I quickly figured that if we hoped to understand how ambulance crews were processing suffering populations, then we must examine these "street-level" associations between crews and other frontline workers.

Part 2 does this by focusing on the relations between ambulance crews and their nurse and police counterparts. Firefighters and others will pop in from time to time, but the daily interactions crews have with nurses and law enforcement are particularly revelatory. They help us locate the ambulance between two polar sites that also disproportionately handle poor people and people of color: the protective emergency department and the repressive squad car.

As discussed in the introduction, relatively poor and powerless populations in the American city are governed across a laterally fragmented and an often contradictory regime. This is perhaps most obvious at street level, where we see a series of institutions managing disadvantaged populations simultaneously and in intersection: welfare offices, hospitals, courts, jails, prisons, and so on. There are plenty of factors that separate and position these institutions on the ground, but a left-right, or a welfare-penality, axis proves useful.[1] The next three chapters extend this line of inquiry.

I begin by detailing the relationship between ambulance crews and emergency department nurses. Rather than frame these parties as insulated workers occupying distinct worksites, I connect them by the work that they share. Together, they fix up people with medication, rides, shelter, and other aid. This all hinges, however, on their ability to coproduce patients, a special category of people that follows a dual exercise of manual and mental labor. Still, we must be careful not to assume that those who become patients are passive in this process. Most articulate medical problems in the form of "chief complaints." They nominate themselves for an ambulance trip to the hospital. Being caught by the safety net of emergency medicine often depends on them doing so. It's a safety net made of gauze and one that's labored by ambulance crews, nurses, and other frontline workers in and out of the hospital (e.g., firefighters, physicians, and emergency room social workers).

Ambulance crews also frequently work with the police. While paramedics and EMTs do a kind of fix-up work with nurses, they do a kind of cleanup work with law enforcement. Crews and cops often converge on scenes that need to be temporarily cleansed of an out-of-place body. For some cases this means that paramedics and EMTs remove wounded bodies from the traumatic scenes that both parties share (e.g., car accidents, gunshot wounds, and multi-casualty incidents). However, far more commonly, this usually means cleansing public spaces of drunk, drugged, or otherwise disordered bodies. Many of these cases involve the police forcing ambulance crews to transport people by writing seventy-two-hour involuntary psychiatric holds. Yet, similar to people shared by crews and nurses, those shared by crews and cops are not totally passive in this process. They're more acquiescent overall, but some challenge the coercive powers of the police by articulating a medical chief complaint, redirecting their immediate trajectory (e.g., from jail to hospital). Together, crews and cops successfully labor a kind of public sanitation machine that sweeps the streets of select bodies deemed out of place.

Further analysis reveals that these relations between ambulance crews and their nurse and police counterparts are not always harmonious. Indeed, there's a fair amount of tension between these parties. This seems to stem from the fact that life on the front lines isn't so peachy. For crews, nurses, and police, the hours are long and the cases are endless. And, to top it off, most of the work is not vocationally fulfilling. Just as crews complain about a lack of legit calls, law enforcement officers complain about a lack of "real police work" and nurses gripe about their departments' inundation with low-priority cases. There seems to be a near-universal frustration with so-called bullshit.

As such, it's perhaps not surprising that the tense interactions I observed most, and later participated in, concern what I call "burden shuffling." The point of burden shuffling is to make one's shift easier by strategically pushing an undesirable case or task onto another worker. Such a strategy is both hindered and enabled by protocols. Hence, the primary patterns of shuffling detailed in this book: cops typically shuffle burdensome cases onto crews due to state-level regulations for involuntary psychiatric holds and crews typically shuffle burdensome cases onto particular nurses due to federal regulations in emergency department accessibility. Many frontline workers are able to cunningly navigate a complicated terrain of rules to benefit themselves against the interests of their counterparts in different uniforms. This may motivate more behind-your-back shit-talking than in-your-face confrontation, but the result for clientele is more or less the same: they're frequently shuffled across the front lines by self-interested workers.

Ultimately, part 2 helps clarify the relational component of a labor process. More specifically, it details the social relations between workers of different organizations. I hold that we cannot understand what's happening inside the ambulance without accounting for the labor its crews share with other frontline workers. Paramedics and EMTs doubly regulate spaces in bodies and bodies in spaces and they often do so through their interactions with nurses and cops. Much, but certainly not all, of these productive relations are defined by tension and conflict.

Regardless, the labor shared across the front lines of emergency response helps clarify another key mechanism for how urban suffering is handled on the frontlines: *sorting bodies.* Crews, nurses, and police work with and against one another to distribute cases across a landscape of often contradictory institutions.

Labor power is an essential factor in the sorting of people across medical and penal institutions. Forces beyond the front lines, like official definitions of sickness and criminality, are no doubt important but mainly so in their ability to guide the workers who process people in and out of particular institutions. And, as noted throughout this book, such workers are imperfectly guided. They have significant discretionary power, and this influences the exact sorting observed in the field, from whether someone goes to jail or the hospital to the specific emergency department a patient is transported to. There's a lot that drives discretionary action, but an interest to avoid so-called bullshit seems to be a prominent motivation. Workers across the board want to improve their shifts by reducing the amount of vocationally unfulfilling tasks they have to complete and this often means trying to strategically shuffle undesirable work onto others.

As with the bandaging of bodies, the sorting of bodies can often seem inconsequential. Workers distribute people across institutions that offer generally superficial responses to an array of complex problems. Yet, there are some respective differences for the subjects being sorted. Relative to the emergency department, the jail severs life chances. And, relative to the jail, the emergency department protects and extends life chances. Few would argue that getting arrested, incarcerated, and fined is better than getting transported, hospitalized, and billed. The former comes with more stigma, further disruption, and a higher risk of injury. The specific hospitals that ambulance crews sort people into are not equal either. Some are closer to patients' homes, some have more social workers on the clock, and some have more private rooms to offer patients.

How people are sorted also clearly matters for workers. It can mean the difference in a relatively busier or slower shift. It can also mean the difference in ending a shift on time and having to work an extra hour or two. How people are sorted across the front lines can also mean the difference between avoiding and confronting a shouting and punching subject. Again, the differences can appear inconsequential from a distance, but on the front lines they're often seen as very significant. Many workers at least see them as important enough to motivate their efforts to struggle with both clientele and fellow workers.

4 The Fix-Up Workers

With few exceptions, such as when death is determined on scene or when someone calls 911 but then refuses transport, ambulance encounters conclude with crews transferring their patients to an emergency department (figure 6). Ambulance personnel don't typically see the hospital as a place that offers permanent solutions to clientele problems. Instead, they generally understand it to be a place for stabilizing legit cases and pacifying bullshit ones. It's a place where surgery is performed but also where prescriptions are refilled (or rather rewritten). It's a place where comatose bodies perish but also where intoxicated ones sober up. It's a place where nurses and physicians *fix up* patients not just with bandages and drugs, but also with a few hours of shelter and a meal or two.

However, paramedics and EMTs don't just dump raw materials on the doormats of hospitals. They don't simply unload unprocessed bodies to be fixed up by emergency department staff. Instead, ambulance crews fix up these bodies a bit themselves. Sometimes this is referred to as "working up" the patient. Crews bring in bodies wrapped in gauze, gripped by cervical collars, and decorated with other medical artifacts. Even if they don't do much of an intervention beyond a hospital transport, paramedics and EMTs bring in subjects who are at least fixed up with a field assessment.

Figure 6. A paramedic rings a doorbell for hospital access. *Note:* Author's photo.

They bring in a medicalized body, one reduced to a primary impression (i.e., a field diagnosis) and one that's linked to a set of vital signs (e.g., blood pressure, blood oxygen saturation, respiratory rate) and other medically relevant data (e.g., narrative of problem, medical history, current prescriptions). They purposively fix up the subjects of their labor into cases that are made legible to, and therefore processable by, the administrative machinery of the hospital.

MAKING PATIENTS

In order to release someone into the hospital, ambulance crews must make them into a patient. Such a transformation involves both a material and a classificatory moment.

This process is most obvious during so-called legit calls. Consider what happens when ambulance crews transport a cardiac arrest victim—a *code*—to the hospital. Crews usually arrive on scene to discover a warm yet pulseless body. Typically working with firefighters, the crew compresses the chest, intubates the airway, and administers drugs like epinephrine via IV access, occasionally pausing to "shock" the patient with a defibrillator.

If they "get pulses back"—known more formerly as the "return of spontaneous circulation"—then the ambulance crew rushes the patient to the hospital. Typically, a fire medic will assist the MRT paramedic in the back while the EMT drives. The EMT contacts a nurse at the receiving hospital on the radio while she drives with lights and sirens. She provides a "ring down," a brief summary of the patient's condition, the interventions made, and the estimated time of arrival. The main function of the ring down during a cardiac arrest is to "activate" a team of nurses, physicians, and other workers to prepare for such a high-severity case.

By the time the crew arrives, emergency department staff have usually prepared a room where doctors, nurses, and other hospital workers wait. The crew rushes into the emergency department with a limp body partially encased and infused in medical artifacts: tubes, drugs, and so on. The hospital team helps the crew move the body from the gurney to the hospital bed. During this transfer, the paramedic offers a "turnover report," an updated and more detailed version of the EMT's ring down. As such, ambulance crews bring hospital staff a body that is already physically and symbolically fixed up into a medical case.

While more obvious and dramatic during legit cases like a cardiac arrest, fixing up so-called bullshit cases for the hospital is also a mental and manual process. They too involve an imposition of a primary impression, a collection of vital signs, and an assembly of pertinent medical information. These "less legitimate" cases also involve a verbal flow of information from ambulance to hospital through the labor of the ring down and the turnover report; they're just not so detailed because there're fewer interventions and less remarkable vital signs to speak of. Moreover, even on cases where few interventions are logged into the patient care report, crews use their hands a lot as they attach instruments to the body to collect vitals and they frequently touch their subjects as part of their examination (e.g., feeling the skin to detect a fever).

For many calls that crews see as bullshit, paramedics are often starting IVs as a courtesy to nurses. While they see such calls as not "real emergencies" and as general misuses of ambulance resources, they'll start an IV and simply apply a saline lock and nothing more. In other words, they'll go through the motions of piercing the skin with a needle and accessing the vein, but they won't administer any fluids or drugs. They do it simply as a favor to nurses.

Regardless of severity, every person brought into the hospital via ambulance is "fixed up" a bit first. Crews assign everyone they bring into the emergency department a primary impression, and this is limited to classifications specified in the county protocols and paperwork that crews must complete after each transport. As already noted, these categories include, but are not limited to, problems like shortness of breath, chest pain, sepsis, cardiac arrest, myocardial infarction (heart attack), tib-fib (lower-leg fracture), radius-ulna (lower-arm fracture), nausea, stroke, altered level of consciousness, GSW (gunshot wound), asthma exacerbation, seizure, abdominal pain, general weakness, and ETOH (alcohol intoxication).

Triage nurses who deal with crews at the hospital expect their paramedic or EMT counterparts not only to offer a primary impression but also to justify the impression (e.g., noting vital signs consistent with the category) and the management of that impression (e.g., noting which interventions were performed). For example, if a crew is going to classify a patient as septic, then the nurse is going to expect some evidence that at least two of the following three conditions are met: (a) the body is either hyper- or hypothermic, (b) the heart rate is greater than ninety beats per minute, and (c) the patient is taking more than twenty breaths per minute. He or she is also going to expect that the crew made the appropriate interventions before arriving at the hospital (e.g., administered fluid via IV treatment, especially if systolic blood pressure was less than ninety mmHg).

This flow of information usually occurs at a standing desk in the triage bay, where the nurse begins an emergency department record for the patient. Assuming the case is not so severe that it requires hospital treatment right away (like a cardiac arrest), patients must lie on the gurney and wait until a bed is available. As noted in chapter 1, this moment is sometimes called "holding the wall." When it's his turn, the paramedic will usually then stand next to the nurse, open his laptop, and then rattle off information that he and his EMT partner have already documented on their end: primary impression, vital signs, interventions made, name, social security number, date of birth, and insurance status. Meanwhile, the EMT usually stands next to the patient, sometimes remeasuring their vital signs and casually conversing with them about a variety of topics from children and pets to movies and presidential politics. Sometimes this means the EMT must "babysit" the patient, covering them with a blanket if they're cold and occasionally using a firm paternalistic voice to keep them from shouting out their frustrations or sobbing too loud. We saw a bit of this in chapter 3 as I struggled to keep Penny from screaming. Eventually, the nurse assigns a bed where the crew drops the patient off before collecting a nurse's signature for their paperwork and returning to the ambulance.

In short, when ambulance crews bring people into one of the many hospitals in the county, they must first make these people into patients. This involves more than just medicalization (i.e., the imposition of a medical definition). It also involves manual labor in the form of examination and treatment. Nurses then continue the labor of fixing up. They too must classify and treat their subjects and they lean heavily on the assessments and interventions that crews perform in the field. As fix-up workers, crews and triage nurses labor to push their patients deeper into the emergency department, where they will most likely spend a few hours before they're fixed up a bit more by other medical workers and then discharged.

THE CHIEF COMPLAINERS

The people whom ambulance crews bring into the hospital are far from passive. Indeed, a majority of ambulance contacts are "voluntary," meaning that patients consent to treatment and transport and many summon ambulances themselves by dialing 911. Most request that ambulance crews transport them to the hospital.

In order for such a request to be successful, the 911 caller must articulate what official protocols recognize as a "chief complaint." This is usually understood as the answer someone offers when a crew greets them and asks, "What's going on?" or "Why did you call 911?" It's a subjective problem that is at least imagined to be medical. The answers can vary in specificity, from "I have a sharp pain in the stomach" to "I just don't feel right."

Chief complaints shape the interactions between crews and nurses by informing how crews fix people up for the emergency department. Seemingly obvious to most callers, a person must articulate a *medical* problem in order to enter the hospital by way of ambulance. If a crew finds someone who is unconscious or is struggling to speak, then they infer such an articulation under the protocols of "implied consent." Most people who encounter the ambulance, though, are relatively lucid and do in fact verbalize a chief complaint. Indeed, most people must self-medicalize their problems if they hope to get an ambulance ride.

One late night, Charles, an older black man, dialed 911 on a payphone and requested an ambulance. He was wheelchair-bound at the time and his leg was casted from a fracture he sustained weeks earlier. At first, Charles asked ambulance personnel to take him to his mother's house. His request was met with laughter by both the ambulance crew and a field supervisor who happened to show up. "No way, man," said the EMT before explaining that they can only transport people to an emergency department.

Charles then said he'd like to go to the hospital because "it's cold out" and he missed the curfew at his transitional housing facility. Grant, the supervisor whom I was shadowing at the time, was clearly unimpressed with this answer and asked, "But what's the *medical* problem?" Charles then pointed to his cast and said, "my leg," before insisting that someone at a hospital check it out. The ambulance crew conceded and loaded Charles into the ambulance before collecting his vitals and transporting him with a primary impression of "leg pain."

On another night, while I was working as an EMT, Austin and I were summoned to a shopping center. We responded to Johnny, a Latino man in his late twenties. I don't remember seeing this person before, but Austin told me he'd run into him a couple of times. Apparently, the police regularly place this man on involuntary psychiatric holds, but on this particular night he had summoned the ambulance himself.

Johnny greeted us in the parking lot outside a Target retail store and articulated a clear medical problem: he said he had difficulty breathing. However, Austin wasn't buying it. Both he and I counted the "rise and fall" of Johnny's chest and estimated a normal rate (around sixteen breathes per minute) and his oxygen saturation was normal per our rig's monitor. Austin later told me he thought Johnny was seeking shelter and had articulated a medical complaint to force us to take him to the hospital. Whether this was a correct assumption about Johnny's intentions or not, Austin and I were obligated to make him into a patient with at least a documented medical complaint and a collection of vital signs.

Crews cannot take people to the hospital who cannot be reasonably classified as ill or injured. As noted in part 1, even their paperwork requires them to impose a medical classification. No hospital transport can be done without crews selecting at least one primary impression category on the computer, and "shelter" is simply not an available category. And once someone articulates a medical problem, such as when Charles said that his leg hurt or when Johnny said he was struggling to breathe, it can be very challenging to then negotiate a demedicalization of the complaint. Leaving the scene without the person in question would be difficult because it would require the would-be patient to sign a form releasing the crew of liability. It's easier, or at least legally less risky, to just take people like Charles and Johnny to the hospital at that point.

Emergency department nurses know that protocols force crews to take many so-called bullshit cases to the hospital. It's not unlike their own federal requirements to screen anybody who walks into the emergency department. They also know that protocols force crews to fix up all transported subjects into "patients." Still, through informal exchanges not captured in official records, crews will often tell nurses if they think the case is not very "medical" or "urgent" at its core.

For example, Vince and I once brought in an older white female named Martha to an emergency department. Martha is a "frequent flyer" who spends many of her nights on the streets. Like Johnny, she complained of shortness of breath but all "objective" evidence suggested otherwise. The triage nurse at the hospital, upon recognizing Martha, asked us in a frustrated tone, "What now?" Vince jokingly responded, "She's cold," implying she's looking for temporary shelter before he quickly self-corrected in a blatantly sarcastic tone, "I mean she has shortness of breath." Martha, lying on the gurney in the triage bay, heard this and yelled, "I can't fucking breathe! I need help!" "Oh yeah, Martha, I told them," said Vince.

GREASING THE REVOLVING DOOR

One day, while sitting in the ambulance bay at one of the many hospitals in Agonia County, I seemed to witness about as many people exiting the emergency department as I saw entering it. This probably wasn't just my imagination either. The Center for Disease Control estimates that about nine out of ten people who enter the emergency department are discharged directly from that department.[1] Very few die there and only a minority of emergency department patients are transferred to another hospital or "admitted" deeper into the facility (e.g., into the intensive care unit). Sometimes, my partners and I would even notice people exiting the hospital whom either we or one of our colleagues had brought in just a few hours earlier. Indeed, most emergency department patients are fixed up a bit and then released.

Sometimes, those who are discharged from the hospital don't make it very far before an ambulance crew encounters them. Crews frequently find people who have just been released from the hospital and they occasionally note this in their patient care reports. For example, one paramedic's narrative reads, "Pt [patient] still wearing the ID wrist band [hospital identification] and tape marks from previous venous punctures [from IV]." Another record notes, "Pt has some dx [diagnostic] paperwork and discharge [paperwork] from [hospital]." Similarly, one MRT worker wrote the following sentence, "Pt states that he was discharged from [hospital] several hours ago. . . . Pt stated that he just took the bus to his current location [sidewalk] and was too weak and uncomfortable to ambulate [walk] any further." In my experience, cases like these are almost always brought back to an emergency department.

For example, Martha, the frequent flyer Vince and I brought in officially for shortness of breath but unofficially for shelter, had a hospital band on her wrist when we found her. She was discharged only a few hours before we met her outside a grocery store that was a couple blocks from the hospital. We simply brought her back.

However, sometimes recently discharged patients request a different hospital, usually because they're unsatisfied with the facility they just left. On another call, paramedic Mark and EMT Danny picked up Rob, a black man around forty-five years of age. Like Martha, Rob was sporting a hospital band. Mark and Danny found Rob sleeping on the sidewalk a few blocks from the county's flagship public hospital. Apparently, someone called 911 for a "man down."

Surprised to encounter an ambulance crew, Rob nevertheless asked to go to a hospital. However, he didn't want to go to the emergency department he was recently discharged from, the facility that was only a short walk away. At first, Rob said he had had a seizure, but upon further questioning from Mark and learning that this chief complaint would limit which hospital he could go to, he then said he did not have a seizure. Mark never told me how he classified the call, but he agreed to take Rob to a smaller hospital in a neighboring city of Agonia County. As he later told me, this was at least partially a strategy to get his and Danny's ambulance out of the busy ghetto where they found Rob.

In some respects, this particular transport was a win-win for those in the ambulance. Not only did this transport bring the crew to a somewhat slower area of the county that they preferred to work in; it also brought Rob to an emergency department that he preferred. When Danny and Mark pulled Rob's gurney from the rig and began to roll him toward the emergency department doors, Rob began to nod in approval. "One thing's for sure," he said, "Your damn ass will get a bed here." The last emergency department that discharged him is a "sorry ass place," where getting a bed is less likely and the meals are of worse quality. At least that's Rob's opinion.

Ambulance crews seem to be greasing a revolving door of emergency medicine. They bring back a number of people who have already been processed and discharged by emergency department personnel. Sometimes they bring them back to the same facility but they're also frequently taking them to different ones.

This isn't just a pattern for so-called frequent flyers or even those whom crews find with hospital wristbands, EKG electrodes, and other emergency department materials still attached to their flesh. Ambulance crews are often bringing in people who have visited the emergency department in the past month or two. It's not uncommon for crews to draw on the history of these previous encounters to make their patients. For example, they frequently use discharge paperwork and other documentation held by the patient to help them fill out their own reports. EMTs often copy demographic information, insurance policy numbers, and active prescription lists printed on these forms when starting the paperwork for the case on their computer.

While they constitute a minority of calls, these revolving-door cases are illustrative of a more general relation between the ambulance and the hospital. Crews do not typically encounter raw material untouched by medical labor. Instead, they more often collect bodies that have already been examined and classified in some significant way. For example, they often forge patients out of people who have already been diagnosed with an acute or chronic illness and people who are already under some regimens (e.g., prescribed drugs and lifestyle recommendations). Through their conversations with patients or with people familiar with patients, paramedics and EMTs collect details on pertinent medical histories and current medications. These data points structure their processing of clientele by honing their examinations (e.g., known diabetics get their blood sugar checked while others may not) narrowing their primary impressions (e.g., linking shortness of breath to COPD exacerbation), and focusing their turnover reports (e.g., emphasizing whether someone is compliant with their prescription drugs). Ambulance crews also bring in a number of people who "know their symptoms," meaning people who convincingly link their chief complaints to medical categories (e.g., people who make sense of their wheezing as an asthma attack). As such, they often bring in people who have been preprocessed for the emergency department in some significant way.

A SAFETY NET MADE OF GAUZE

Throughout their shifts, ambulance crews are in recurrent contact with hospital staff and nurses in particular. They regularly bring people from homes and streets into one of the largest and most overwhelmed institutions of the American welfare state: the emergency department.

Be they public or private, essentially all emergency departments are required to assess and aid anyone, regardless of their ability to pay. This is thanks in large part to the Emergency Medical Treatment and Labor Act (EMTALA).[2] Enacted in 1986, this policy basically requires all emergency departments receiving Medicare payments to screen and stabilize anyone who seeks their services. The result of this policy, combined with the retrenchment of other forms of assistance for vulnerable populations, has been an inundation of destitute and stigmatized people seeking emergency medical aid for an array of sufferings.[3]

A combination of federal, state, and county policies assure access and assistance through the ambulance as well, and across the United States people are generally given the right to demand transport to the hospital by way of ambulance. Paramedics and EMTs are often forced by protocols to take people to the hospital and to fix them up into patients in the process. For the most part, people summon the ambulance with a relatively clear medical complaint, but it's not uncommon for some to at least ostensibly request an ambulance trip to the hospital for other reasons like transportation, shelter, or food. Similar to the emergency department, the ambulance exists as a sort of fee-based entitlement program (however paradoxical that might sound) for anyone who presents as ill or injured.

Thus, together, ambulance crews and nurses labor a safety net. While thin and worn, this net is strung across Agonia County. It's made of several hospitals, but its breadth is really made possible by the many more ambulances that can be essentially dispatched anywhere. Still, it's not a net that will catch just anyone. It's limited to those with medical problems. In other words, it's limited to those who can be fixed up as patients. This net is made of medical instruments and processes. It's a net made of gauze.

While not so obvious in this particular case study, we should keep in mind that this net of gauze extends beyond the boundaries of emergency medicine. As medical anthropologist Helena Hansen and her colleagues note, there's been an "increasing medicalization of public support for the poor" in the wake of welfare reform in the 1990s.[4] For her and her team, this is evident in how access to public benefits for people with diagnosed disabilities has become a primary strategy of poverty relief in the United States. As such, cash assistance has become significantly limited to those indigent bodies that can be successfully made into patients. Indeed, to be poor and deserving in twenty-first-century America increasingly means to be poor and sick.

It's within this larger context that we find ambulance crews delivering a variety of suffering bodies to the hospital. Heavily dispatched to aid populations toward the bottom of the urban hierarchy, paramedics and EMTs are processing people into patients and carrying them leftward into the hands of nurses and other hospital workers. They, in turn, usually discharge these people after a quick medical fix-up.

Still, ambulance crews work with more people than just the frontline workers of the emergency department. As detailed in the next chapter, paramedics and EMTs are also in recurrent contact with law enforcement. The safety net of gauze is often knotted with metal chains.

5 The Cleanup Workers

While on the streets, MRT crews frequently interact with police officers from over a dozen law enforcement agencies. Ambulance crews are not interacting with cops as much as they're interacting with nurses, but I estimate that roughly a fifth of MRT calls involve the police.[1] Crews and cops often share a number of "scenes," from those involving gunshot victims and traffic accidents to those involving sidewalk slumberers and drunk wanderers. Just as ambulance crews fix up people for entry into the emergency department, the police frequently usher people off the streets and into the ambulance. Together, crews and cops share a common task: temporarily cleaning up public spaces of the wounded, the nuisance, and the belligerent.

MATTER OUT OF PLACE

The relationship between paramedicine and policing is complicated. Given what we know about the geography of ambulance responses and police surveillance, it's perhaps surprising to many readers that I found little to indicate that ambulance responses in poorer and less white neighborhoods are more likely to involve law enforcement. Instead, when coupled with the ethnographic data, the year of medical records I acquired suggests that cops and crews frequently converge in areas where out-of-place bodies are frequently identified for removal.

Consider what I discovered when I examined the patient care reports in particular. I turned to these crew-produced documents to ask a simple question. What neighborhood-level features predict crew-cop interactions?[2] I found evidence suggesting that, when accounting for population size and density, neighborhood poverty predicts a small increase in the overall share of ambulance runs involving the police. However, my analysis also suggested that this association is weak and not statistically significant when adding in a variable for race. I also did not find convincing evidence that residential racial composition predicts crew-cop interactions when accounting for these other conditions.

This doesn't mean that neighborhood conditions are irrelevant. I discovered that, even when controlling for the factors just mentioned, neighborhoods with metropolitan train stations and neighborhoods with jails or municipal police headquarters (which often include detention facilities) are both positively associated with the percentage of MRT calls involving the police. Jails and similar settings make sense. The police will sometimes request an ambulance crew to transport one of their arrestees/inmates to the hospital for medical evaluation. But why is the presence of a train station positively associated with the rate of crew-cop interactions at the neighborhood level?

I learned early in my fieldwork that train stations are relatively common areas that police officers struggle to clear of drunk or otherwise disorderly people who loiter, panhandle, or slumber in the area. In my experience, train station staff often request the police to respond to a disorderly body and the police frequently determine these bodies to be too sick (e.g., "mentally ill" or "intoxicated") to either jail or release. So, they summon an ambulance crew to take their subject to the hospital. It's not just train stations either. Shopping centers, fast-food restaurants, hotel lobbies, and other commercial spaces stage similar interactions. Employees at these establishments occasionally dial 911 to have the state remove a person from the premises who is not appropriately using the area (e.g., not shopping or eating).

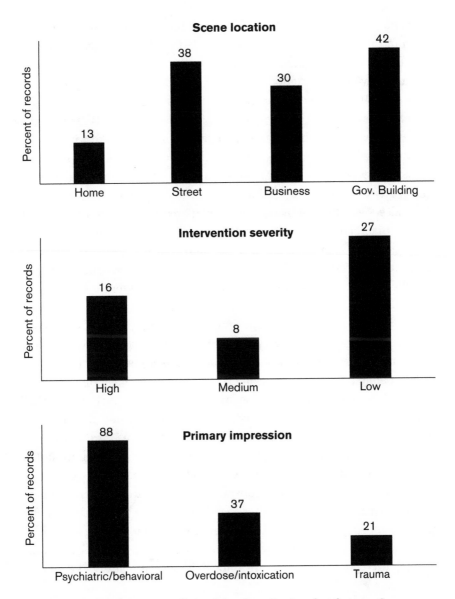

Figure 7. Share of ambulance calls involving the police by select features. *Source:* MRT deidentified patient care reports, 2015. *Notes:* Observations = 107,208 (107,089 for intervention severity). p < .05 (chi- squared).

When I disaggregated these data from the neighborhood level back down to the level of the individual report, I found three notable patterns regarding crew-cop interactions (figure 7). First, there is a lower proportion of crew-cop interactions inside homes than in public spaces like streets, businesses, and government buildings (e.g., jails and schools).[3] Second, there is a higher proportion of crew-cop interactions on calls involving low-severity interventions.[4] High-priority cases like critical gunshot wounds, brutal traffic accidents, and severe overdoses certainly draw crews and cops to the same scenes, but crew-cop interactions claim a higher share of so-called bullshit calls. Third, ambulance cases involving the police are patterned by call type. Compared to less than a quarter of records that do not mention the police, over two-thirds of the records that do are classified in one of three primary impression categories: psychiatric/behavioral, overdose/intoxication, or trauma. Across these categories specifically, crew-cop interactions account for nearly nine-tenths of psychiatric/behavioral calls, over a third of overdoses/intoxication calls, and more than a fifth of trauma calls.[5] Crews and cops are simply more likely to converge in public spaces where they often deal with low-priority medical problems that involve drunk, drugged, or otherwise disordered people.

Ultimately, ambulance crews and police frequently meet on cases that must be cleaned up. They cleanse spaces of seemingly dirty flesh, what anthropologist Mary Douglas might consider "matter out of place" and essential disorder that must be eliminated in a "positive effort to organize the environment."[6] During legit calls, this often means moving wounded bodies from scenes of gun violence, car collisions, and other spaces that crews and cops share. During bullshit calls, which are more common in general and far more common for cases involving the police, this usually means removing an intoxicated or otherwise disorderly body from out of public view. And, it's usually the poor, the racially oppressed, and otherwise marginalized populations that are going to be seen as matter out of place.

GREEN SHEETING

There is perhaps one finding that really sticks out in the analysis above. Nearly half of the patient care reports that indicate a crew-cop interaction are classified as psychiatric or behavioral emergencies. My fieldwork suggests that an overwhelming majority of these cases involve the police placing people under seventy-two-hour involuntary psychiatric holds known as "fifty-one fifties."

Written "5150," the term refers to the hold's numerical reference in the California Welfare and Institutions Code. It's become a number familiar to many beyond the worlds of law enforcement and emergency medicine. For example, Van Halen and Eazy-E, both from California, titled albums after the code.[7] Yet, despite the popularity of the term, few seem to understand how 5150s are actually imposed on many people.

Cops, usually in their response to a disruptive person in a public space, will frequently place their subjects on 5150 holds by filling out a "green sheet." The green sheet, which actually varies in color depending on which police department is issuing the hold, includes a closed-ended item that reads, "Based upon the above information, there is probable cause to believe that said person is, as a result of mental health disorder: [ ] A danger to himself/herself. [ ] A danger to others. [ ] Gravely disabled adult. [ ] Gravely disabled minor." By checking one of these boxes, the officer essentially medicalizes the case and mandates an ambulance crew to transport the subject to a hospital for mental health screening and treatment.

From the standpoint of ambulance crews, there are certainly "legit 5150s." Crews told me there are people who *need* to be placed on these holds, often because they are violent or seem to be on the brink of violence. For example, early into my employment as an EMT, I, along with my field training officer, Lance, and our paramedic partner, Megan, responded to one of our county's train stations. We arrived to find a black man around thirty years old sitting on the ground just inside the station with his hands cuffed behind his back. Police told us they were placing him on a 5150 for yelling unspecified threats at people in the station. We greeted the man, but he refused to tell us his name or anything about his medical history.

Lance decided early on that we were going to restrain this person to the gurney using leather restraints (figure 8). It's a decision consistent with a lesson he taught me weeks before this call and one echoed by many veteran ambulance workers: "If cops, who have guns and pepper spray, decide it's a good idea to cuff someone, then we should restrain them." As cops uncuffed the man, Lance and I used leather restraints to tie his wrists and

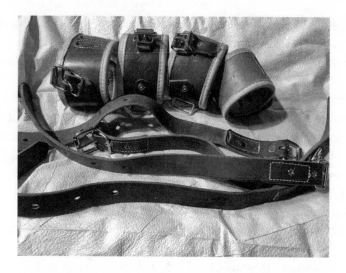

Figure 8. Leather limb restraints. *Note:* Author's photo.

ankles to the gurney. It was during this transition from metal cuffs to leather restraints that this guy became difficult.

The man suddenly pulled his wrist away from me and tried to bite my arm. "Watch out, Josh! Don't get bit!" shouted Lance. At this point, Megan decided to stick the patient with Versed, a sedative. With police helping us hold the man in place and with at least one cellphone camera pointed in our direction, Megan injected Versed into the man's arm against his will. "I ain't getting no fucking shot!" he shouted just before the needle pierced his arm. With the added muscle of law enforcement, Lance and I were finally able to tie the man down to the gurney and load him into the ambulance, where the sedative eventually mellowed him during the transport to a nearby emergency department.

So-called legit 5150s typically involve both some wrestling and some sedation. However, most 5150s don't play out like this. The administration of Versed via syringe and needle happens on a minority of cases. And, while physical restraints are sometimes placed on docile patients as a precaution, most 5150 calls do not involve a physical struggle.

Indeed, ambulance crews often see 5150s as quintessential bullshit. When I'd ask crews in the field to tell me about bullshit calls in general, the go-to answer, along with the archetypal 911 abuser, was the 5150 patient. Most said that the green sheet was a very convenient tool for the police to medicalize undesirable subjects into the ambulance. On several occasions, the police used personal history of mental illness (e.g., "She says she's bipolar" or "We've placed him on a 5150 before") to warrant the hold even if the event seemed to weakly justify the checking of one of the four boxes on the sheet (i.e., danger to self, danger to others, gravely disabled adult, or gravely disabled minor). For example, during one of my ride-along shifts, police placed a suspected shoplifter on a 5150 and justified it because the man had an unspecified history of mental illness and 5150 holds.

On another call I worked as an EMT, the police justified a 5150 hold because Miles, their forty-or-so-year-old black male subject, was walking in his neighborhood with a knife. One of the cops on scene explained that Miles, who later told me he had recently finished three forty-ounce bottles of beer, was somehow disrupting people in the area. Apparently, Miles could not simply return to his home, which was in eyesight, because he had just gotten into a verbal altercation with his mother.

Or something like that. Thoroughly confused, I asked the officer if he found Miles *holding* a knife. "No," said the cop, "It was in his pocket. Says it was for his protection, but he's threatened to kill himself before." "Did he tonight?" I asked. The cop, seemingly irritated with my questioning, said in a firm voice, "I've determined him to be a danger to himself given the circumstances tonight." "It's cool," I said, "I got you. The nurse is just gonna ask me. I just wanna make sure I get the full story." The officer seemed to cheer up a bit, "Oh yeah, I know how it is." "He been cool with you guys?" I then asked. "Sort of," said the officer, "He gave us a little trouble when we put him in the back [of the squad car]."

Austin, my paramedic partner, insisted that we tie Miles's wrists to the gurney. "Those are the kind of guys that will get you." I nodded, but I wasn't sure what he meant. After we restrained Miles to the gurney and loaded him into the ambulance, he pleaded with us to let him out of our rig. "We don't write the 5150s," I said, "You gotta go, man." After explaining that Austin and I had no choice but to take him to the hospital, I said, "My hands are tied." I realized, almost instantly, that this was a bit of a rude thing to say to someone whose hands were literally tied down to the side rails of a gurney.

Austin and I decided not to take Miles to the "nut house," the small and overwhelmed county psychiatric hospital that MRT crews take many 5150 subjects to. Because Miles said he consumed a significant amount of alcohol, we could justify taking him to the closest emergency department instead. While we could have justified transporting the partially inebriated patient to the dedicated psychiatric facility, Austin insisted that a local hospital made more sense for Miles. He assumed out loud that someone at the hospital could hypothetically lift the 5150 hold and discharge the patient closer to his residence. This wasn't the first time I heard a paramedic make such an assumption, and I had no reason to doubt Austin. Miles, still tied to the gurney, chimed in and told us he liked this plan too.

When we eventually arrived at the hospital, the triage nurse called Miles's case "bullshit" before she even asked me any questions about the event. She simply glanced at the green sheet I handed her. "For *past* suicide intentions?" she said, quoting the cop's handwritten narrative. I responded, "Yeah, I pushed him [the cop] on it a bit, but he was set on it." Clearly frustrated, the nurse shook her head, but she seemed more irritated with the green sheet's author than with me.

I'm not sure what happened to Miles. If Austin was right, someone with the power to do so released him from the hospital a few hours later. However, I no longer trust this prediction. Many months after I quit my job as an EMT, a couple of emergency department physicians told me that Austin's forecast was unlikely. They guessed that someone like Miles would have most likely been transferred to the psychiatric facility anyway. Even if staff at the hospital could hypothetically lift the hold that night (and that's a big if), they may not have wanted to risk releasing someone deemed dangerous by the police. Thus, it's possible that Austin and I inadvertently made Miles's life more difficult by increasing the duration of his hold and the cost of his treatment.

We should pause for a moment to consider the structural and historical context in which "green sheeting" unfolds in Agonia County. Law enforcement's daily interaction with people deemed mentally ill is not new or novel.[8] As the American penal state ballooned in the latter half of the twentieth century, more and more cops started to encounter people suffering with mental illness during their shifts.[9] This was not, however, just the result of expanding police coverage. As psychiatrist Richard Lamb and his colleagues insist, the police have become "frontline professionals" for managing mentally ill populations post deinstitutionalization.[10] The massive closure of mental health hospitals in the mid-century seems to have increased demand for police responses to psychiatric and behavioral crises. This historical trend has reasonably led scholars and journalists alike to write about the "criminalization" of mental illness.[11]

However, the reality on the ground—or at least in the streets—seems to be a bit more complicated. There's no doubt that there's a disproportionate number of people with diagnosed mental illness behind bars.[12] It's also worth noting that the three largest psychiatric inpatient facilities in the United States today are all jails.[13] Still, it's not clear that police officers are more likely to arrest people whom they themselves classify as mentally ill. Law enforcement today might be casting a wide arrest net and somewhat "inadvertently" capturing people with mental health problems that are then more formally recognized in jail or prison. In other words, it's not obvious that police read (or at least document) people's behavior as a sign of mental illness and then discriminatorily arrest them. In fact, as criminologists Robin Shepard Engel and Eric Silver demonstrate, there's actually strong evidence to suggest that "police are *not* more likely to arrest mentally disordered suspects."[14]

My time on the ambulance and around "green sheeting" taught me why this might be the case. Police officers across multiple departments in Agonia County regularly confront people with behavioral patterns that can be loosely defined as signs of mental illness. When faced with such subjects, cops seem more likely to recommend a hospital trip for these people than arrest them. Why arrest someone when you can more easily place them on a seventy-two-hour psychiatric hold and have an ambulance crew handle the case? More on this in the next chapter, but first we should consider a different (albeit a less common) way people drift between the squad car and the ambulance.

INCARCERITIS

Just as the fix-up work that crews share with nurses is made complicated by lucid subjects, so too is the cleanup work crews share with the police. With the exception of those who are unconscious, the subjects whom crews and cops share are not entirely passive in how they are swept up. This is often true even for those who experience crews and cops in their most coercive and violent forms. For example, the cuffed man at the train station who Lance, Megan, and I had to transport on a 5150 offered both verbal and physical resistance. He didn't take the limb restraints without a fight and this shaped the way we and law enforcement handled him.

The power of cleaned-up subjects is perhaps best seen during cases of "incarceritis." This occurs when crews and cops assume that an arrestee or inmate feigns a medical symptom in an effort to evade or delay jail. As one paramedic writer in the *Journal of Emergency Medical Services* puts it, incarceritis occurs "when a patient intentionally falsifies or grossly exaggerates symptoms of illness or trauma in order to avoid incarceration."[15] This usually unfolds inside a squad car or a jail cell and common symptoms include difficulty breathing, chest pain, abdominal pain, unconsciousness, and suicidal thoughts.

Of course, these symptoms can be seen as legitimate. During one of my ride-along shifts, the crew I was shadowing responded to an unconscious and likely overdosed man inside the county jail. He was unresponsive not only to verbal stimuli (the paramedic's shouting) but also to painful stimuli (the paramedic's pinch). As ambulance workers explained to me at the end of the call, this particular man was "real unconscious" (i.e., legit) and not "jail unconscious" (i.e., bullshit). Still, most people who provide a medical complaint from inside a squad car or jail cell are met with suspicion by both crews and cops.

For example, on a 5150 my partner and I encountered, the responding officer told us they caught Mia, a black woman in her mid-thirties, shoplifting. Mia had a couple of outstanding warrants. The cop told me, in an exacerbated tone, "Once we told her she's under arrest she started screaming that she was going to kill herself. . . . I explained to her that this is just delaying the inevitable [jail] but she's still screaming that she wants to kill herself." It was assumed that Mia knew how to force the cop's hand to place her on a 5150.

On another call I observed, police arrested a man they claimed was driving a stolen vehicle. According to them, after the man was cuffed and placed in the back of the squad car he immediately suggested he was having trouble breathing. Sometimes the legitimacy of these complaints can

Inspected By:veronica_nunez

00072846524

0007284

6524

C-2
8

be settled through the scrutiny of an objective assessment (e.g., EKG, pulse oximetry, and painful stimuli), but usually these are symptoms that are hard to disconfirm with examination (e.g., abdominal pain).

In short, crews and cops tend to look at arrested and jailed subjects with intense suspicion. Indeed, such subjects have an obvious material goal in presenting themselves as sick. And, from the standpoint of both crews and cops, the ability to "pull incarceritis" gives their subjects significant power. It affects how such people are "cleaned up" from a given area by momentarily redirecting their trajectory from the jail to the hospital.

THE STREET-SWEEPERS

When teaching me about the complexities of ambulance work, the paramedics and EMTs I shadowed and worked with often spoke of analogous jobs. I mentioned in previous chapters how these men and women described themselves as being like doctors, taxi drivers, and even social workers. Another common reference point was the sanitation worker.

Ambulance work often means cleaning public spaces of dirty bodies. In some ways, the ambulance is like a street-sweeper, barreling through the county and brushing up matter out of place. This can involve the removal of those limp and leaking bodies that are left after horrific car accidents, critical gunshots, and other "legitimate" emergencies. However, more often than not, this involves the removal of subjects with "bullshit" problems. Such cleanup work is frequently shared with law enforcement and is often directly shaped by police action (e.g., writing 5150 holds).

There are some important parallels between crew and cop labor with respect to coercion (e.g., limb restraint), but the shared task of street-sweeping is what most commonly links paramedicine and policing. The ambulance regularly touches—and is sometimes outright manipulated by—the punitive hand of the state through the cleanup work that draws crews and cops together.

6 Burden Shuffling

Paramedics and EMTs sometimes use a vocabulary of war when talking about their work. Most exchange "war stories." Many describe neighborhoods with lots of gunshot calls as "war zones." Some even see themselves as crucial but unrecognized soldiers in a "war on drugs." In addition to these phrasings, actual war is understood by many to be the cradle of civilian ambulance operations. Several treatment technologies for traumatic injury, like the "combat application tourniquet," are historically rooted in military medicine. Indeed, textbooks used in EMT and paramedic training programs frequently point to the treatment lessons learned through combat medicine during American-involved conflicts like those in Korea, Vietnam, and Afghanistan.[1] War, no matter how sanitized it might seem to be from the streets of Agonia, is a common reference point for ambulance crews.

There are, however, more immediate battles. In addition to their daily struggles with patients (as detailed in part 1) and management (to be detailed in part 3), crews often conflict with other frontline workers like nurses and cops. Ultimately, these horizontal battles are battles over *work* and they shape how shared subjects are processed. In my fieldwork, I identified three general forms of horizontal conflict: jurisdictional struggle, finger pointing, and burden shuffling.

Jurisdictional struggle happens when one party accuses the other of encroaching on their duties and it tends to only occur during more legitimate cases. For example, crews and cops sometimes elbow one another on gunshot scenes. Crews accuse cops of "getting in the way" by asking the wounded too many investigative questions in the ambulance while cops accuse crews of unnecessarily tampering with evidence. Likewise, nurses and paramedics sometimes struggle with one another over the appropriate medical intervention. Much of this seems to stem from the fact that nurses, while better trained, have less autonomy than paramedics. The latter can "push" a number of medications in the field per standing orders while the former often need physician approval first. If frustrated with a paramedic's decision to administer a certain intervention, a nurse will sometimes accuse the paramedic of too eagerly pushing medicine in the field instead of waiting for the hospital to do it. In my experience, these lateral struggles over jurisdictional claim are rare. More often than not, the cases these workers share are generally seen as undesirable by all parties. There is often little motivation to push another worker out of the way to access a given case.

Finger pointing is also pretty rare. This happens when workers blame someone else for causing a serious error or, more likely, for increasing the perceived risk of such an error. Crews sometimes accuse the police of failing to sufficiently "secure" a shared scene, therefore exposing them and their patients to significant risk of injury. Additionally, nurses sometimes blame crews for missing critical signs during their field assessments and then inappropriately fixing their patients up. Like jurisdictional struggle, finger pointing tends to happen on more legit calls.

Given my observations as a ride-along and my experiences as an EMT, I am confident that burden shuffling is by far the most common form of horizontal conflict. Such struggle primarily occurs over bullshit, over mostly undesirable cases. Indeed, for crews, police, and nurses, the bulk of potential or actual ambulance clientele comes with work to be avoided. While protocols may generally designate which party is responsible for specific cases at specific times, they never seem to perfectly determine who will actually work these cases. Discretion also plays an important role and workers across the board know this. Nurses know that crews have some control over which hospital they transport many of their patients to and crews know that cops have some agency in summoning ambulances,

writing 5150s, and making arrests. These discretionary acts often generate tension between different frontline workers. Sometimes this tension
plays out as a heated argument, but it usually platforms a colder war made
of playful bickering and covert shit-talking.

Regardless, the accusation is usually the same: someone is strategically
shuffling bullshit onto someone else. This is a "shuffle" in a double sense.
First, it's an evasive and sometimes sly attempt to *shuffle out* of one's duty
to manage an undesirable case. The point is to hand it to someone else by
sneakily bowing out of the situation. Second, in doing the first, this strategy entails a mixing up of clientele that's kind of like *shuffling up* a deck of
cards. People don't disappear as a result of burden shuffling. They're just
reordered and then dealt to a different worker.

SHUFFLING JOSE

While an EMT, I worked a number of day shifts with Kyle. Like me, Kyle is
a white man around thirty years of age. Unlike me, Kyle is really into fitness
and weightlifting in particular. I imagine I gave him the same blank stare
when he talked about his gym and diet routine as he gave me when I talked
about my academic interests. Still, Kyle was one of my favorite people to
work with. We seemed to spend most of our shifts together smiling and
laughing as we exchanged absurd stories of both paramedicine and
parenthood.

On this particular shift, Kyle and I felt a little lucky. Earlier, the ambulance gods gave us a legit call: a vehicle rollover where we found a woman
with collar bone, forearm, and ankle deformities. Later in the shift, they
blessed us with a thirty-minute lunch break. We didn't get it until we were
already eight hours into our shift, but we were happy nonetheless.

But then the gods punished us. Our break was cut about ten minutes
short. All of sudden our in-rig computer flickered and a dispatcher's voice
came through our radio's speakers: "Unit twenty-one eighteen, I need to
pull you from your code seven [lunch] for a delta [second highest priority]
unconscious male." "Copy," I said over radio while chewing my food.

I shoved the rest of my sandwich in my mouth, put the ambulance in
drive, and drove Kyle and myself through some busy weekday traffic. I

blared our sirens and occasionally pumped the air horn to pressure other drivers to the shoulder of the road. Kyle hoped this call would be another legit one. I too was hopeful. Unconscious? This dispatch category is so vague and so promising. Maybe this person got knocked out in a fight. Maybe he faded into darkness after a heroin overdose. Maybe the call was for a diabetic who slipped into a hypoglycemic coma.

However, the person we were summoned to was none of these things. Instead, he was "just drunk." After only a couple of minutes of driving, we arrived on scene to find cops standing around a bus stop bench on top of which lay a Latino man around thirty-five years of age.[2] Kyle noticed this man before he even got out of the ambulance. It's Jose. He's a regular and on this particular day he was sporting a hospital wristband from a local emergency department.

Jose was pretty out of it, rolling his head back and forth. Sunlight splashed his face and his eyes were squinted. His lips were curled into a smile, through which he mumbled some incomprehensible speech. The pitch of his voice shifted in a songlike fashion. I think he was humming, perhaps even singing, underneath those mumbles. Kyle quickly concurred with the cops that this was nothing more than intoxication. There was even a smoking gun of sorts: an empty liquor bottle was tipped over next to Jose's bench-turned-bed.

This was a bullshit call, but Kyle and I both knew there was no getting out of it. Jose was clearly too intoxicated for us to leave and he probably couldn't sign a release form even if we gave it to him. The police officers, who were the ones who initially responded to the call and then activated the ambulance for "unconsciousness," clearly had the upper hand. They decided this bench needed to be cleaned up, but instead of doing the cleanup work themselves (e.g., through arrest for public intoxication) they summoned me and Kyle to do it. Jail wasn't even mentioned on scene, but we knew what the cops' likely defense would have been because we had both heard it several times before: "too drunk for jail." Ultimately, the police shuffled the burden onto us and they had protocol on their side.

As we loaded Jose into the ambulance, one of the officers asked us in a serious tone, "Can't you guys take him to a different hospital?" This cop correctly assumed we were going to return Jose to the hospital listed on his wristband. He confessed that he didn't want Jose to get quickly discharged from the hospital and then return to his beat. This officer wanted Jose out of the area for as long as possible. "We don't know where we're going yet," said Kyle before citing protocol, "but we need to go to the 'closest, most appropriate facility.'" The officer, seemingly unsatisfied and unconvinced, simply walked away. Indeed, we *could* have taken Jose to a hospital in a neighboring city within Agonia County but there wasn't anything for us to gain by doing so. Kyle generally liked the area we were in. The next-closest hospital was embedded in a far busier territory. Plus, neither of us was in the mood to simply help the guy out who inadvertently pulled us from our lunch break to clean up this bus stop.

Inside the ambulance, Kyle asked what I thought about the cop's suggestion that we head to a more distant hospital. "Fuck him," I said before arguing that we should just go to the emergency department that recently discharged Jose. I noted that Jose clearly hangs out in this area if the cop knows him this well and wants him out of his beat. "I'm not trying to fuck up his [Jose's] day that bad," I added. Kyle agreed and noted that taking Jose to a different hospital would also be more difficult to justify to the nurses. They would probably ask us why we didn't take the patient to the facility he was just discharged from.

Even so, it's not like we brought Jose to nurses with open arms ready to help him out. The triage nurse at the hospital sighed when she saw me and Kyle wheel Jose in on a gurney. She asked why we brought him to this particular facility. Kyle noted it was the closest hospital. Maybe it was because I was tired, but this nurse's response pissed me off: a slight shrug of the shoulders, a head shake, and glance at one of her colleagues. It was as if she were asking her coworker with nonverbal cues, "Can you believe these guys?" I snapped back with some attempted wit in my voice, "He was ten blocks away. Had your band on from yesterday. Figured we'd return to sender." Kyle chuckled and I smiled as the nurse stared me down. Feeling a little guilty for picking an argument, I then noted how one of the officers on scene wanted us to go to another hospital. "It was probably Officer Jones," she said matter of factly, "He's always looking out for us." "Yeah," I responded. "I don't think this guy was looking out for you. He seemed more interested in getting [Jose] out of his beat." The nurse didn't reply but she did assign us a bed to drop the patient onto. We took the burden police shuffled onto us and shuffled it onto this particular team of nurses.

Jose's case is telling. Police initially responded to the scene and deter-mined that he needed to be removed from the bus stop bench. Somewhere between a fully discretionary actor and a cog in a machine, one of the officers then summoned me and Kyle to take their subject away. He then requested that we transport Jose out of the area, but we chose to go to the closest hospital instead. We could have granted the cop's wish but decided not to. With the burden shuffled onto us, we then shuffled it onto nurses at a particular emergency department. We reasoned this transport desti-nation would make our shift easier. We believed this would keep us out of the really busy areas of the county for a bit longer. As a bonus, our prefer-ence was consistent with protocol, easily justified under nurse scrutiny, and it matched Jose's assumed interest to remain in this part of Agonia.

JAIL OR HOSPITAL?

As noted in the previous chapter, ambulance crews and law enforcement converge on scenes that need to be cleaned up. But who is going to actu-ally do the work? Are ambulance crews going to transport someone to the hospital, or are the police going to arrest someone and take them to jail?

For crews, the answer is usually predetermined. Either the subject in question wills it (e.g., through so-called incarceritis) or the police do. With a powerful toolkit of protocols at their disposal, law enforcement in the county can strategically "cut paperwork" that forces someone to undergo mental health evaluation or simply claim that a person is so drunk or high that they need medical attention. Jail may register as an option for many of these cases, but by the time paramedics and EMTs arrive on scene the police have usually already decided that the ambulance will carry the body away. They don't diagnose, but cops have a curious ability to successfully medicalize human problems, and they frequently do so to shuffle out of undesirable cases.

However, an ambulance ride is not always so predetermined. Sometimes the alternative of arrest is mentioned on scenes that crews share with cops. From time to time, the police articulate the jail as an explicit substi-tute for the hospital. They usually do so to verbally strong-arm a relatively lucid person into the ambulance. Put simply, the police will occasionally use the threat of incarceration as a strategy to shuffle so-called bullshit into the ambulance.

The same situation seems to repeat itself. A cop arrives on scene first and determines that someone needs to be cleaned up from the area, usually because they're drunk or otherwise disordered. For whatever reason, the officer doesn't want to arrest his subject and so he does his best to *medicalize* the event. He opts not to write a 5150 or perhaps doesn't even consider it. Instead, he simply decides the person should just go to the emergency department for some other medical problem, usually intoxication. He summons an ambulance crew to do the transport. Maybe he thinks it's faster and easier than taking the subject himself.

The responding crew, however, doesn't typically want the call. It's bullshit. "Total bullshit." Not only is it not legit, it is arguably not even "medical." So, the paramedic *demedicalizes* the event, generally rejecting the cop's classification. She double confirms this with the subject's lack of a chief complaint and her own examination (e.g., collection of vital signs). Upon confirming that the would-be patient does not want to go to the hospital and that he or she is "alert and oriented" (and therefore capable of making their own medical decisions), the paramedic then tells the officer that she cannot transport. Sometimes she offers some version of this punch line: "We're not in the business of kidnapping people against their will."

One of my partners liked to call maneuvers like this "cop blocking." The idea is simple. If the paramedic can demedicalize the case, then the officer will be unable push his or her subject into the ambulance.

This is where it's necessary that I distinguish between what I saw and what I heard. Multiple workers at MRT told me that they successfully blocked the police from shuffling drunks and otherwise undesirable cases into the ambulance. They told me the police simply dismissed the crew and handled the case some other way. One paramedic told me he thought the officer he successfully blocked ended up taking the person in question to the hospital himself. But I heard of outcomes like these far more than I actually saw them. On a couple of occasions, I saw crews successfully block the police from shuffling in a drunk person when the subject convinced law enforcement that they could leave the area safely under their own accord. Such outcomes were rare though. It was more common for the police, upon learning that their subject did not consent to ambulance transport, to offer an ultimatum: jail or hospital?

Consider a few excerpts from the patient care reports (italics and parenthetic notes added):

ATF [arrived to find] 53 y.o. [year-old] male sitting upright on bus. Bus driver attempted to wake pt [patient] and had a hard time doing so. Pt is AOX4 [alert and oriented] with normal VS [vital signs] *denying any and all medical complaints,* reporting he has had a few beers today. *Police advised pt he could either go to jail or the hospital. Pt chose the hospital.*

On scene, find 25 y/o [year-old] male pt [patient] AOx4 [alert and oriented] sitting upright on the curb alongside [city police]. *Pt does not appear to be in any acute distress or show any signs of obvious trauma.* Pt was found by PD [police] sleeping in a bush, incontinent of urine, and under the influence of ETOH [alcohol]. *Pt denies any pain or medical complaint and was given the option of jail or the hospital by PD.* Pt moved to gurney and transported code 2 [without lights and sirens] to [hospital] without incident.

Patient is a 63 yo [year-old] homeless man that was sitting out front of 7-11 [convenience store] and staff called PD [police] to shoo him away and when the officer arrived on scene the *officer asked the pt* [patient] *if he wanted to go to Jail or the Hospital and he said Hospital. PD then requested EMS [ambulance crew] and stated pt had a seizure.* Upon arrival pt found sitting awake and in no obvious distress or discomfort being attended to by [fire medic] with officer standing by. Upon pt contact pt a&ox4 [alert and oriented] and *states he did not have a seizure.*

The threat of incarceration provides law enforcement with another way to shuffle undesirable cases into the ambulance, and the excerpts above help illustrate this point. There is, however, something important these narratives miss. Crews may want to avoid the bullshit cases the police try to bully into the ambulance, but this doesn't mean they're advocating for arrest. In my experience, most would prefer that the police simply dismiss the cleanup altogether, leaving matter out of place. This is at least partially why we see crews attempting to demedicalize cases rather than criminalize them.[3]

Ultimately, when they share undesirable tasks, cops usually have the tools to successfully pressure crews to do the cleanup work. In addition to the easily written green sheet (i.e., 5150 holds) and the loosely justified argument that someone is too inebriated for jail, police can verbally pressure people into the ambulance with a jail-or-hospital ultimatum. But, while crews might feel generally powerless in relation to the cops who shuffle bullshit onto them, they have some power to determine how they shuffle bullshit onto nurses. I consider this next.

STRATEGIC TRANSPORTS

Where do ambulance crews transport their patients? There are over a dozen emergency departments in Agonia County. Yet, on paper, ambulance crews don't have much of a choice on where they can go. County protocols mandate that crews take their patients to the closest, most appropriate facility. Appropriateness usually refers to the hospital's specializations relative to both the primary impression and the severity of the emergency. For example, critically injured patients should go to the closest trauma center and those suffering a heart attack should be taken to the closest hospital with a catheterization lab. Thus, appropriateness tends to only matter for more legit calls.

However, at the risk of sounding like a broken record, most calls are closer to the bullshit end of the continuum. The next consideration, per protocol, is "patient choice." If the patient is not so critical that he or she must be taken to a specialty facility or even just to the closest emergency department, then the patient can typically choose an emergency department "within reason." This usually means one out of the three or four closest hospitals.[4]

For sure, there are many ambulance patients who articulate particular preferences for where they go. Some hate or love a particular hospital, given their past experiences or stereotypes. Whiter and wealthier patients sometimes command crews not to take them to a "ghetto hospital." Many patients with chronic illness want to make sure they go to the same hospital every time to assure a continuity of care. Some patients seem to even deliberately exploit the patient choice protocol so they can be transported to a particular area of the county.[5] So long as these requests are within reason, they're usually fulfilled.

Many notable exceptions withstanding, patient demand is not usually so particular. This is where worker discretion creeps into the picture.

During a "stay and play," crews often negotiate a specific transport destination with their clientele. Paramedics, and to a lesser extent EMTs, discuss some transport options with their patients and they frequently pressure them to go to a particular hospital. They emphasize a sometimes true but sometimes false benefit to the patient: shorter wait times, superior care, better sandwiches, and the like.

However, there is often a hidden interest in these negotiations. Unbeknownst to patients, crews are often intentionally recommending hospitals they believe will improve their shift in some way or another. Sometimes this means recommending a hospital in an area the crew is more familiar with or a hospital they believe has faster triage times during that particular moment. However, these strategic transport recommendations are usually driven by one of three specific ends.

First, during the eleventh hour of their shifts, ambulance crews will typically try to convince their patients to go to hospitals that will bring them closer to their designated sign-out locations. Indeed, paramedics and EMTs are often very invested in transport negotiations during their final call, or what they hope is their final call, of the shift. These negotiations constitute workers' primary tactic for mitigating the risk of shift overtime, which is almost universally despised. The idea is simple. If my partner and I are required to return the ambulance and clock-out at central headquarters, or the "barn," then we want our final transport to be to a hospital that is as close as possible to that location. That way, if we're dismissed from duty at the conclusion of the transport, then we only have a short drive back to the barn. The further our final hospital is from our sign-out location, the longer our drive back to headquarters. As this distance increases so too do our odds of getting "pulled back" into 911 service should the availability of ambulances suddenly and substantially decrease. In other words, after being relieved from duty, an ambulance crew can be summoned back into service so long as they are still in their rig. Workers therefore have a clear interest in having the final transport of their shifts be to hospitals as close as reasonably possible to their sign-out locations.

Second, crews sometimes hope to transport their patients to a hospital that's located in a less busy and therefore a wealthier and a whiter area of Agonia. They reason that by taking someone to a hospital that's in a less demanding territory of the county the dispatchers will be more likely to post them near that hospital once they complete the call. They see this as a way to push the ambulance into an area that may slow their shift a bit. It should, in their estimation, reduce their chances of getting another call right after they complete the current one. Indeed, this was Mark and Danny's reasoning in chapter 4 when they agreed to transport Rob to a hospital in a neighboring city of Agonia County.

Third, crews occasionally wish to avoid the county's primary psychiatric hospital because it's often seen as inconvenient (e.g., away from their sign-out location, long triage times, and in a relatively busy area). They do this by more or less fabricating a "medical clearance" transport for 5150 cases. In green sheeting someone, the police mandate that their subjects undergo a mental health evaluation at "a designated facility," usually meaning the county's primary psychiatric emergency department. However, should a 5150 patient present with a *medical* problem (as somehow distinct from a mental problem), the crew should transport to the closest, most appropriate hospital. Medical clearance protocols provide crews with quite a bit of latitude to remedicalize a number of 5150 subjects. For example, just as cops can decide that someone is too drunk for jail, crews can often decide that a 5150 subject is too drunk for the psychiatric facility. This is what happened with Miles in chapter 5. Ambulance crews can also lean on some "borderline" vital signs to justify a medical clearance transport (e.g., a heart rate above 120 beats per minute). Sometimes they "fish" a medical chief complaint out of a 5150 subject even if it's unrelated to the 911 event. This usually happens through a battery of questions: "Any chest pain?" "Any nausea?" "Any dizziness?" Some crews get pretty direct: "Tell me you have abdominal pain so you don't have to go to [psychiatric facility]." While occasionally mixed into a seemingly authentic concern for the patient (many workers problematically assume that medical clearance can mean an early discharge if the green sheet is weakly justified), 5150 hospital transports are usually driven by a concern to benefit the crew. More often than not this means remedicalizing a case so that they can transport the patient to a hospital with faster triage times in a less busy territory.

Thus, while the methods are complicated and the intentions are subtle, ambulance workers find ways to shuffle bullshit cases onto particular hospitals. These strategies largely come with the assumption that the next call will be closer to the bullshit end of the continuum and that it should be avoided for as long as possible. They're usually part of a larger attempt to slow the shift down or end the shift on time, but these strategies shouldn't be equated with an attempt to avoid work altogether. Crews are generally eager to speed things up and even extend their shift past their off-duty time if the call is vocationally fulfilling. But, as gambling men and women, they usually bet the next call is not so legit and this is often a motivation and justification for shuffling bullshit cases onto particular hospitals.

Nurses are not ignorant of these strategies. Triage nurses are often skeptical of crews' transport decisions. Those who work in smaller emergency departments just outside the core of Agonia are especially suspicious. They frequently interrogate crews in the triage bay by asking two questions, "Where'd you pick her up?" and "Why'd you bring her here?" If a crew names a pickup location that's obviously closer to one or two different hospitals, their defense is usually the same: "patient request." This is why it's important that crews convince their patients that the recommended destinations are in their best interests. Nurses are not always buying it though and they frequently suspect strategic transports that serve the interests of crews above patients.[6]

But what can nurses do? The short answer is not much. Federal law, not to mention state and local policies, prevents nurses from turning away the patients whom crews fix up for them. However, many paramedics and EMTs are convinced that nurses find ways to slow or discourage this burden shuffling. Some believe that nurses underhandedly prolong triage for bullshit cases as a strategy to discourage future transport.[7] More directly, some nurses contact MRT field supervisors to complain. This, however, is rare as it requires a bit of proof (e.g., patient testimonial) to be successful. Ultimately, nurses don't have many tools to resist the burdensome cases that are strategically shuffled onto them by ambulance crews.

CHOOSE YOUR BATTLES

Let's summarize the chapter so far. In answering the question of who is going to do the work on undesirable cases, the police frequently summon ambulance crews and crews frequently nominate nurses at particular hospitals. Knowing the rules and regulations is a necessary but insufficient condition for understanding this process of burden shuffling. The protocols for things like involuntary psychiatric holds, patient consent, and medical clearance are useless without labor on the ground to interpret and implement them. Workers discretionarily navigate inter- and intraagency regulations to shuffle undesirable cases onto others. Most tensions between crews and their nurse and police counterparts can be linked to these discretionary decisions. The stratagem here is pretty simple if you're a frontline worker: navigate the protocols to shuffle the burden in a way that somehow makes *your* shift easier.

We should, however, be careful not to reduce the relations between crews and their police and nurse counterparts to pure calculated struggle. The horizontal relationships between crews and these other frontline workers are certainly better defined by concord than conflict. The relatively smooth handoffs we saw in the previous two chapters are more typical than the conflicts and tensions just revealed.

This makes sense when you consider the general solidarity shared between workers on the streets. As fix-up workers, crews and nurses see themselves more as partners than as enemies on the front lines of emergency medicine. Both parties are generally quick to back each other when a patient gives either of them any "trouble." Ambulance crews sometimes bring nurses coffee and many nurses give crews key codes to hospital staff break rooms so they can grab free snacks. Likewise, there is more harmony than hostility between crews and cops. By and large, cops are quick to physically defend crews during their occasional scuffles with patients. Many paramedics and EMTs also like to express their solidarity with law enforcement by covering their MRT badges with a black bar to mourn the not-so-rare death of a cop.

Such interagency solidarity was probably one of the reasons why burden shuffling was not strategized on all the so-called bullshit calls I saw in the field. This at least seemed to be the case for many ambulance workers. They frequently bit their tongues during interactions with cops and nurses, and then privately complained to me about how they got "stuck" with some bullshit. They'd tell me how a nurse seemed to prolong triage or a cop seemed to write a bogus green sheet. These frustrated ambulance workers often justified their lack of a defense as an overall concern for "keeping the peace." From their point of view, picking an argument with a nurse or cop may be a bad idea. They could awkwardly run into these workers later on and some even noted a perceived risk of revenge (e.g., longer triage in response to strategic transporting).

Still, lateral solidarity and a general motivation to keep the peace are not the only factors that shape burden shuffling. Workers' cold and warm interactions with clientele may also play a role. The more sympathetic the crew, the less likely they seem to strategically shuffle burden in a calculated effort to improve their shift. For calls more in a "gray area" than "total bullshit," crews seem less likely to coach transports to hospitals that might make their shifts easier at the possible expense of patients' convenience. The "kinds of people" to be shuffled can also matter. For example, because whiter, cleaner, and older clientele tend to yield more sympathy from crews, they seem less likely to be treated as passive pawns in a subtle game to improve workers' shifts.

Nonetheless, solidarity across the front lines and sympathy for clientele don't prevent burden shuffling. They simply reduce the likelihood of such a strategy and its related conflicts and tensions. As these factors reduce the motivations for burden shuffling, other factors are increasing these same motivations. For example, as I frequently recorded in my field notes, when crews entered the eleventh hour of their shifts, they were often explicitly interested in shuffling bullshit cases onto nurses closer to their sign-out location. Likewise, a few cops even admitted to my paramedic partners and me that they summoned ambulance services because they didn't want to get held past their off-duty time at the jail. These officers, however, only admitted this retrospectively, as they confessed to past sins.

Thus, as both fix-up workers (regulators of spaces in bodies) and cleanup workers (regulators of bodies in spaces), ambulance crews are caught in productive but often strained relations with nurses and cops. These frontline workers frequently clash over the shuffling of so-called bullshit cases.

This chapter concludes part 2. Where part 1 illustrated how ambulance crews recognize and churn through a plethora of human suffering near the bottom of the polarized city, part 2 has shown that they don't do so in isolation. Crews instead process a disproportionately poor and nonwhite clientele through their recurrent interactions with other frontline workers like nurses and cops. It is through these horizontal relations on the front lines that suffering bodies are not only bandaged but also sorted.

We can't stop here though. For as important as this horizontality is, verticality is perhaps even more critical. Bureaucratic and capitalistic forces rain on, and reign over, the tops of ambulances. We've already encountered some of this in my ongoing discussions of protocols and my occasional references to management, but in part 3 I will offer a deeper analysis of verticality and will do so by examining the hierarchical relations that ambulance crews enter into during the labor process. This will not only clarify how suffering populations are handled by way of the ambulance but also help explain some of the interactions observed between frontline workers.

PART III   Hustling Bodies

THE AMBULANCE UNDERNEATH
BUREAUCRACY AND CAPITAL

If we hope to understand how ambulance crews are handling their subjects, then we must make sense of forces imposed on these frontline workers from outside and above them. So, unlike part 2, which had us stepping into the streets and hospitals just outside the rig, part 3 has us locating the ambulance underneath a nexus of bureaucratic and capitalistic pressures. Returning to the map sketched in the introduction, we're going to start at the top and work our way down. We'll begin inside a manager meeting at MRT's headquarters before heading into the supervisor rig and then again into the ambulance.

Profit and policy will be key themes during our descent. MRT's tireless pursuit of profit is important not only because it motivates high ambulance transport invoices, which tend to land on disadvantaged populations, but also because it influences the manner and context in which crews handle their subjects. For somewhat obvious reasons, MRT managers constantly pressure crews to improve their performance and more specifically the number of transports they complete. Among other things, these pressures contribute to crew exhaustion and exacerbate their already tense relations with patients and other frontline workers like nurses and cops.

This vertical analysis, however, cannot be reduced to an account of profiteers over workers. We'll see how the naked self-interest of capital is tightly swaddled by the public policy interest of the local bureaucracy that surveils this firm. Agonia County EMS, often following federal, state, and county mandates, establishes many protocols that workers on the ground must execute and thus MRT management must generally assure. These include the clinical procedures listed in the thick protocol book that supervisor Eric tossed into my lap, which I discussed in the introduction. They also include policies that contradict the profit motives of MRT and shape management's relationship to labor as a consequence.

This intermingling of capitalistic and bureaucratic forces from above the ambulance affect but don't fully determine the internal and horizontal features detailed in parts 1 and 2. For example, there are probably many reasons why someone who calls 911 is met by a "dick" ambulance worker, but conditions largely generated by managers and protocols are especially suspect. Long hours, low pay, few breaks, heavy caseloads, and waves of vocationally unfulfilling tasks are but some of the exhausting and agitating forces that can wear crews down into generally cold people workers. Additionally, ambulance crews are often interacting with patients, nurses, and police in particular ways as part of a subtler struggle with capital and bureaucracy.

I realize that an analysis of company managers and formal procedures can seem like a strange detour for the book at hand. However, understanding the vertical relations that crews are embedded in is essential for understanding the ambulance as an institution that governs urban suffering. Such relations provide some necessary context for making sense of how crew labor amounts to a bandaging of bodies. Agonia County EMS protocols clarify workers' scopes of practice, specify the tools needed inside the ambulance, and detail step-by-step instructions for treatment and transport. These guidelines narrow crews' possible interventions. They also force workers to respond to essentially anyone who requests their services, regardless of their opinions of medical necessity. Yet, while the policy interests of the county explain why crews must offer particular responses and why they have to work so-called bullshit, the profit interests of the company better explain why any given crew has to work so hard.

County protocols tell crews that they have to wrap people in gauze, but company managers tell them to wrap as many people as possible.

Again, these vertical relations don't just matter for understanding what's happening inside the ambulance. They also matter for making sense of the horizontal relations between ambulance crews and other frontline workers. In other words, verticality also structures the sorting of bodies. Protocols, as we saw in part 2, specify the conditions for transferring subjects from the squad car to the ambulance and from the ambulance to the hospital. Indeed, it's impossible to discuss a sorting of clientele without considering how the official rules for things like involuntary psychiatric holds and patient choice condition the interactions between crews and their nurse and police counterparts. The forces of lean production, pushed more by capital than by bureaucracy, are also important for making sense of horizontal relations. These are forces that intensify paramedics and EMTs' interests in pacing their shifts. What I'm calling "burden shuffling" starts to make more sense when such verticality is considered. Strategically transporting nonurgent patients to hospitals that crews believe will make their shifts easier or attempting to block the undesirable cases that cops are trying to push into their rigs can often be read as efforts to combat the forces of lean production. How people are sorted can affect shift pacing, and, in turn, this pacing can affect how people are sorted.

The vertical relations of production also help clarify another mechanism for how urban suffering is handled on the front lines: *hustling bodies*. People are not just bandaged and sorted. They're also hustled. I'm not referring to how MRT's contract with Agonia County allows the firm to charge people and/or their insurance providers thousands of dollars for ambulance rides. The firm's navigation of a fee-for-service market constitutes a hustle of sorts, but not one best revealed on the front lines. Crews never collect payments from clientele, and billing is rarely discussed inside the ambulance. Paramedics and EMTs are instead engaged in a different hustle. Their hustle doesn't concern a swindling of money from patients, but instead a swift processing of them. Ambulance workers hustle people along through hurried interventions. Forces from above not only pressure workers to bandage a lot of people; those forces also encourage them to do so quickly.

Indeed, there's a rapidity to ambulance-based people work. Some variably "legitimate" crisis strikes. An ambulance crew responds. They treat, transport, and move on to the next case. Hustling people through points of intervention is normal and is directly promoted by both county protocols and company management. The forces of lean production in particular encourage a high transport-to-crew ratio and this usually translates into crews rushing through interventions.

7 The Barn

Previous chapters mention MRT's Agonia County headquarters, or the "barn." This chapter takes us inside this building and walks us upstairs. It's here, during daily management meetings, that we can best see the relationship between bureaucracy and capital and some of the consequences this relationship has for ambulance crews. As I'll also make clear, understanding what's happening in the barn is key to understanding how patients are handled by workers on the ground. Not unlike the many paramedics and EMTs who enter and exit this building every day, we'll stop here briefly.

UPSTAIRS

MRT's headquarters is located in a two-story building. As an EMT, I got to know the first floor pretty well. I'd enter through the garage where rigs were repaired and restocked, tuck my uniform shirt in, and clock in for work using a fingerprint scanner located toward the center of the building. I'd then approach a nearby counter, where a vehicle service technician would sign me out some keys, a computer, and a pair of radios.

From here, I'd head outside to my assigned ambulance and set it up. I'd log in to the computer and double-check that critical equipment was functioning correctly. Depending on the preferences of my paramedic partner, I'd sometimes hang strips of medical tape off a ceiling bar in the back of the ambulance for easy access, assemble some saline locks, and complete other preparations. Meanwhile, my partner would retrieve and lock the "narc box" in a safe in the back of the rig before I'd "go available" over the radio: "Good evening. Unit twenty-two twenty-three logging on." The dispatcher would then assign us a street intersection to "post" at and wait for a 911 call or she would assign us a call directly if one happened to be pending. Either way, we weren't staying at headquarters. I'd drive the ambulance off the premises and wouldn't return for twelve to fourteen hours.

While working, I spent more time in Agonia County's busiest hospitals waiting for beds than I did in the barn. Headquarters was just a place I encountered during the very beginnings and very ends of my shifts. And, even then, I only regularly accessed the first level, where rigs were parked and the equipment counter was located.

I'd rarely venture upstairs. The second floor of MRT's headquarters constituted a somewhat mysterious space for workers. For many, it seemed to be occupied by villainous managers and a supporting cast of office goons: number crunchers, paper pushers, and other pseudoworkers. From below, it's imagined as a kind of fake, boring, and cushy world, insulated from the real, exciting, and harsh one that paramedics and EMTs confront daily.

However, before I was an EMT, I went upstairs several times. I'd accompany supervisors like Eric as they were pulled from the streets to attend meetings with both middle and upper managers. These meetings, here called "Daily-Ops," were held in a large conference room. Usually in attendance were the chief of MRT's local operations, the contract manager, the personnel manager, the clinical director, daytime field supervisors, and other specialized managers. These were regular gatherings to "check the pulse" of the firm.

TIME AND PUNISHMENT

In the Daily-Ops meetings I observed firsthand and in the many more meeting notes I read, Karen, one of MRT's upper managers, always spoke the most. She would start any given meeting by telling her fellow managers how many late calls the firm had run in the past twenty-four hours and the types of calls that were late. These simple statistics tended to only concern others in the room to the extent that they did or didn't indicate contractual compliance.

The details are complicated. The contract, part of what I'm calling "official protocol," specifies strict requirements for ambulance response times (i.e., the time a crew arrives on an emergency scene minus the time that call was initially dispatched to the MRT fleet by the county dispatcher). The required response times vary according to two factors, and Karen tended to speak as if everyone in the room knew this. First, the contract specifies three area types for ranking each square kilometer of Agonia County by its call volume density. The corresponding expectation is intuitive: busier areas should receive faster ambulances. Second, the alpha-to-echo triage categories mentioned in the introduction establish another intuitive ranking: the higher the triage, the shorter the expected response time.

Whenever Karen mentioned that there had been a late echo call the night before, a sigh or two could usually be heard in the room. However, I never heard such sighs for late charlie or bravo responses. That's because the consequences are simply more severe for higher-priority late calls.

Through the authority granted to them by the County Board of Supervisors, Agonia County EMS negatively incentivizes response time compliance by fining MRT for tardy ambulances. Agonia County EMS doesn't, however, fine MRT for individual late calls unless they're greater than 150 percent of the expected response time. Instead, they calculate the firm's late call percentages across four major sectors within the county and issue fines if MRT's monthly rate of late calls is greater than 10 percent for a given triage category within any of these areas. For example, Agonia County EMS will fine MRT $50,000 should they have a monthly compliance rate below 90 percent for the highest-priority triage level within any of the sectors. If that late call happens to be greater than 150 percent of the allotted time, then the monthly fine will swell by $5,000. And that's just for the late echo responses. The late delta, charlie, bravo, and alpha calls can snowball into some much heftier fines. Without providing me with a month-by-month breakdown of fines paid, management told me these fines could reach nearly $400,000 a month even when more than nine-tenths of MRT's *overall* responses were "on time."

As I said, the details are complicated. But the major concern for management is simple. Late ambulances can lead to hefty fines.

The contract between the county and the company certainly specifies much more than response time requirements. Among other things, it details how much the firm can charge per transport and the amount of money MRT has to pay annually to help finance the county dispatch center and related infrastructure. However, for Karen and her peers in the Daily-Ops meetings, the central item of concern seems to always be the response time requirements. As I show next, these requirements are an important part of an unspoken dilemma for management and it's a dilemma that concerns the poor's heavy use of the ambulance.

POVERTY AS UNSPOKEN DILEMMA

Attending the Daily-Ops meetings, reviewing the contract, and talking to managers helped me unearth an unspoken but nevertheless central dilemma that MRT management faces. *If the firm aids the poor, they will continuously waste resources on a mostly unprofitable clientele. But, if the firm abandons the poor, the county bureaucracy will fine them for violating protocol.*

Let's break it down. In the introduction, I noted that over half of MRT's invoices are billed to either uninsured or means-tested Medicaid patients. This isn't all that surprising, given what we know about the insurance status of ambulance patients nationally.[1] Per management, uninsured people often don't pay their bills and Medicaid covers about 10 percent of a $2,000 to $3,000 transport. As such, thicker flows of revenue come down from the hills of Agonia County and from the wealthier pockets of its suburbs, where people are more likely to have private insurance. It is also assumed, at least by a few managers, that residents in these areas are more likely to call 911 for reasons that insurance providers will recognize as "medically necessary" and therefore cover in full or nearly in full. Yet, despite the relatively thinner revenue flows from the more destitute flatlands of the county, MRT cannot just abandon the poor. The response time fines negatively incentivize the firm to keep areas with the highest demand stocked with the most ambulances. And, as also demonstrated in the introduction, the areas with the highest demand are typically the areas with the highest rates of poverty.

Management at MRT, like management in any organization, faces a number of challenges. However, what I'm branding the poverty dilemma is a central one for leadership at the studied firm. To be clear, I never heard anyone say "poverty" or "poor" during the Daily-Ops meetings and the contract lacks this language as well. Daily-Ops participants occasionally mentioned the challenges of "frequent flyers" who didn't pay and the "busy areas" of the county, but I never heard anyone upstairs explicitly discuss Agonia County's poor residents and their heavy use of ambulance services. Nevertheless, by examining MRT's economic and legal circumstances, it becomes clear that the dilemma exists. Aiding poor patients hurts the firm, but abandoning the poor hurts more.

The pressing question is not whether the dilemma exists or how it's articulated, but how management responds to it. How do they alleviate financial loss amid the bureaucratic pressure to serve a largely unprofitable clientele?

MRT can't talk their way out of the poverty dilemma, but they can attempt to negotiate some provisions that make it less painful. In the span of just a few years, MRT was able to amend the service agreement with Agonia County EMS to incrementally jack up the baseline price of transport, from around $1,500 to $2,000 (plus additional charges for miles traveled and oxygen used). This didn't affect Medicaid reimbursements and it probably didn't do much to increase revenue from uninsured patients, but it almost certainly thickened the flows of revenue from privately insured patients. MRT also requested and received some relief from paying certain agreed-upon fees to the county, and they successfully advocated for some minor tweaks to the fine schedule. Additionally, Ralph, MRT's chief of local operations, was known to lobby the state legislature with some of his peers in the industry. They pressured the state to increase Medicaid reimbursements for ambulance transports.[2] This largely amounted to asking for modest increases of a couple hundred dollars per transport, crumbs in the grand scheme of things.

THE LEAN FLEET

While negotiations with county and state governments aren't insignificant, they don't constitute MRT's primary strategy in responding to the poverty dilemma or the pursuit of profit more generally. The firm's go-to tactic is more quintessentially capitalist: intensify the exploitation of wage labor, or, in other words, increase the amount of surplus that management can appropriate from workers. Put even more simply, management aims to increase a transport-to-crew ratio. The more hospital trips a given crew can handle, the better. It's a kind of plug-your-nose-and-do-it-quick philosophy. The obvious solution is to pressure crews to grind through a large number of transports. It doesn't guarantee profit, but it should help minimize loss. At least that seems to be the general sentiment upstairs.

Management tries to increase a transport-to-crew ratio by deploying what I call "the lean fleet." I'm inspired by sociologist Alan Sears's account of how contemporary welfare states at the turn of the millennium have absorbed principles of lean production—systematic efforts to decrease waste by increasing the efficiency and the flexibility of labor.[3] Of course, managers' concerted attempts to orient the front lines into lean bodies of production shouldn't be limited to a discussion of outsourced for-profit service providers like MRT. Strategies to increase frontline efficiency and flexibility can be seen in police departments, nonprofits, and welfare offices.[4] The articulated end might be profit, but it doesn't need to be. More opaque goals like "efficient performance" and "fiscal responsibility" may motivate organizational heads to pursue a lean workforce.[5]

In the case of MRT specifically, leanness can be understood as a kind of goldilocks status between thinness and fatness. Management wants to avoid a fleet that's too thin, because although it would reduce labor costs it would also increase the risk of late calls. If there are too few ambulances on the streets, especially in some of the busier and thus generally poorer areas of the county, then the firm risks late call penalties imposed by Agonia County EMS. At the same time, management wants to also avoid a fleet that's too fat, one that would reduce the risk of late calls but would in turn raise labor costs. If there are too many ambulances, more crews will be sitting around on post and completing relatively few transports. Understandably, management wants to hit that sweet spot between thin and fat.

This very concern was routinely taken up during the Daily-Ops meetings I observed. Following her summary of a late call from the past twenty-four hours, Karen would typically then give the floor to Bruce. Where Karen's specialty is the contract, Bruce's specialty is personnel. He's responsible for ensuring ambulances are stocked with workers, a somewhat difficult task, given MRT's high employee turnover and call-out rates.

The firm tends to maintain a kind of skeletal schedule of full-time regular employees, but it's almost never enough to cover anticipated demand. Bruce has an obligation to layer some meat onto the bones by publishing an auxiliary schedule, which he tends to do every couple of days. This is typically filled by a flexible army of part-time laborers or full-time workers looking to collect some overtime pay. If Bruce struggles to fill these additional shifts or if he's concerned that they won't fill easily, he will incentivize portions of the schedule.

Bruce has two carrots, one more expensive than the other. The cheaper carrot is a promise to erase a portion of an employee's absence or tardy records. These are simply referred to as "incentive shifts" and they aren't always filled. The more expensive carrot, however, is almost guaranteed to work: a promise to pay double the wage. For reasons that will be discussed in chapter 9, these are oxymoronically called "voluntary mandation shifts," but they're more colloquially known as just "mandation" or "mando" shifts.

When I attended Daily-Ops meetings, most of us would stare at a calendar displayed on a wall-mounted monitor as Bruce told us which shifts would be generated, which would be incentivized with absence/tardy forgiveness, and which would be upgraded to double pay. By expanding and sweetening the schedule, Bruce almost certainly reduced the company's chances of being fined by the county. He always needed to be careful though. While more crews on the street could decrease the likelihood of late call fines, too many crews could in turn mean "too much post time" (i.e., the amount of paid time a crew spends parked at or near a designated street intersection waiting for a 911 call). There was always the risk in these meetings that Bruce would add too much meat to the schedule. This would make the fleet more fat than lean.

While important, the day-to-day pliability of the fleet's size is but one aspect of labor's leanness. Crews in the field need to also handle tasks in an efficient manner. If possible, they should transport their patients to nearby emergency departments and take as little time as necessary at these hospitals before returning to the streets for another 911 call. Indeed, managers upstairs closely monitor crews' "drop times" (i.e., time spent at hospitals) and regularly remind the fleet of their surveillance. For example, when I was an employee, Bruce emailed the fleet essentially every morning with a spreadsheet that logged crews' hospital drop times from the previous day. He always highlighted in red those crews with the longest times and he sometimes noted in these emails that the overall fleet could "do better."

At the same time, managers at the barn use other tactics to ensure that the fleet doesn't act too hastily or carelessly. They randomly audit medical records to see if workers are administering appropriate care consistent with county protocols. In accordance with the company's insurance, automated road safety surveillance equipment is also installed into every MRT ambulance. While crews are obviously pressured to respond to 911 calls quickly, they're discouraged from driving too fast, braking too abruptly, and turning too sharply. Management does a lot to pressure the fleet to self-regulate their labor.

Still, deploying an efficient and flexible workforce from headquarters is easier said than done. There are two contradictory conditions that hinder leanness: official protocols and worker discretion. On the one hand, protocols curb workforce flexibility. The protocol book lays out many procedures that thwart discretion, such as a policy to transport all green-sheeted cases (i.e., those the police place on involuntary psychiatric holds). Protocols do not reduce workers to cogs in a machine, but they limit labor flexibility in a significant way. On the other hand, labor discretion, although a necessary condition of frontline labor flexibility, also threatens leanness. Miles away from the barn, workers can choose to extend their time at hospitals, pressure patients to go to emergency departments in less busy territories, and commit other sins against the interests of management.

Fortunately for those who sit at the Daily-Ops conference table, there's a mobile team of managers who regularly leave the barn to pressure a lean ambulance fleet: the field supervisors. There are four on duty at any given time. Two usually show up to these meetings. The other two usually call in because they're tasked with supervising operations further from the barn. Nighttime supervisors, who are probably sleeping during the 9:00 AM meetings, are asked to read the minutes. However, their absence doesn't really seem to matter since the supervisors who are in attendance don't usually speak anyway.

In my experience, supervisors were rarely asked by those at the table to participate in the conversation. These middle managers instead sat on the periphery and listened. Sometimes an ethnographer sat next to them. When the Daily-Ops meeting would adjourn around 9:30 AM, the two supervisors on the phone would hang up and the two at the barn would head out to their supervisor rigs. Indeed, they're meant for the streets. Upper management needs them on patrol.

8 Supervision

We've been in a supervisor rig before (figure 9). Eric drove me around some of MRT's busiest neighborhoods in one in the introduction. It was in this rig that I peered out into a "little nexus of evil" and listened to him talk about "zombies" and other caricatures.

Before summarizing that sightseeing tour, I noted that Eric had two general tasks that day. One was to show me the ropes, but the other was far more important: monitor the largest segment of MRT's 911 ambulance fleet, the portion servicing the urban core of Agonia County. Indeed, Eric's generous tour occurred amid his managerial tasks. It occurred between his visits to hospitals, his phone calls with crews, and his attendance at a Daily-Ops meeting.

I shadowed Eric and other supervisors several times in the year following that first day of fieldwork. It didn't take long for these middle managers to stop their courtesy tours and just do their jobs with me next to them. I sometimes helped them, although not in a very consequential way. From the passenger seat, I transcribed a couple of emails for supervisors and assisted their navigation of traffic. I sometimes helped them keep their eyes on the road by reading them the dispatcher call notes that popped up on the rig's computer. While on the 911 scenes that these supervisors were

Figure 9. A supervisor rig.
Note: Author's photo.

summoned to, I occasionally helped them carry equipment and collect information from bystanders. Ultimately, though, I was just along for the ride. Maybe they were just being nice, but most supervisors said they appreciated the company and they often encouraged me to ride along with them again. So, I did.

A DIFFERENT KIND OF BULLSHIT

Each of the eight supervisors I shadowed provided three simple justifications for their movement from paramedic to manager: money, ease, and vocation. First, the pay is higher inside the supervisor rig. No one shared their exact salary with me. In fact, the couple whom I directly asked about compensation skirted the question with vague answers. One thing's for sure though, the baseline supervisor salary is more "comfortable" than getting paid to work full-time on the ambulance. One supervisor told me that if he worked as hard as a veteran paramedic who pulled a lot overtime shifts (150 percent wage) and mandation shifts (200 percent wage), he'd be able to make more money. However, this would require several more hours of work. In terms of the forty-hour workweek, compensation is clearly and unsurprisingly better for supervisors.

Second, while supervision isn't easy, it's not as exhausting as working on the ambulance. Few supervisors seemed to ever admit this to their crews, but they often told me that their job was not as labor-intensive as being a full-time paramedic. As I did ride-alongs with both ambulance crews and supervisors, I quickly learned that the latter enjoy significantly more downtime. Supervisors and I regularly went out to eat and I sometimes watched entire movies with one of them on a portable DVD player. On a few occasions, supervisors parked in abandoned parking lots so that we could nap. Don't judge us though. When 3:00 AM hits and you've been patrolling the fleet since 5:00 PM the previous day, let's see how easy you can stay awake in a warm SUV. And, in the napping supervisor's defense, he doesn't fully check out but instead learns to "half sleep" with "one eye open." This means dozing off while still being conscious of radio traffic in case he gets summoned to a call. In short, while supervision is not gravy, Eric and his peers nevertheless admitted to me that it's easier than working on the ambulance.

Third, and most importantly according to the supervisors I shadowed, there's a vocational perk to their middle-management position. Supervisors get to not only observe but also assist crews on many of the most legit calls (figure 10). Per the contract with Agonia County, MRT supervisors are dispatched to *every* echo call (i.e., cardiac and respiratory arrest), every multi-casualty incident, and several other high-profile events (e.g., all shootings and some other severe trauma cases). While many of these calls are false alarms (e.g., a cardiac arrest dispatch for someone sleeping on the sidewalk), a good portion of them are legit. They're just not very frequent. It's not uncommon for supervisors to catch just a couple of calls in a shift. When they do respond to these high-severity emergencies, supervisors frequently help crews push drugs, intubate, and do other deep clinical interventions into the body. These calls really belong to the paramedics, who will continue care inside their ambulances, but supervisors nonetheless play a consequential role for many of these responses. They get to watch and work some of the "best calls" in the system while avoiding the mundane bullshit that most crews have to deal with. In some ways, supervisors get to live out a paramedical fantasy by exclusively responding to legit calls.

But, while the position of supervisor may come with some perks, it also comes with some downsides. As Grant once told me, the job comes with "a different kind of bullshit." Supervisors like him are frequently replacing broken equipment in the field and writing lengthy incident reports for

Figure 10. A supervisor on a high-priority scene. *Note:* Author's photo.

things like ambulance-involved wrecks and patient-on-crew assaults. They're sometimes called to neutralize the conflicts between crews and other workers in and out of the organization. A bit more exciting, but still far from doing legit clinical work in the field, supervisors are often talking to fire captains, police sergeants, and charge nurses about ways to manage the frontlines at their intersections. For example, supervisors and charge nurses somewhat frequently discuss whether or not to place a busy hospital on a temporary ambulance bypass status. To top it off, supervisors have to deal with some other mundane tasks at the barn, like attending Daily-Ops meetings. None of these activities, however, really captures the main grind of field supervision: the interlocking tasks of "watching levels" and "clearing hospitals."

WATCHING LEVELS

Several months after Eric's introductory tour, I found myself back in his SUV as we ate breakfast together. We were parked outside a grocery store near the epicenter of his supervision zone. We had just left yet another Daily-Ops briefing at headquarters, and, per usual, I had some questions about what was said in the meeting. This conversation quickly carried us into a discussion of management's tactics more generally. As he munched his food and sipped his coffee, Eric told me about the ways people at the barn calculate crews' hospital drop times, track their driving performance, and audit their paperwork.

The topic then shifted a bit. Perhaps in an effort to signal his similarity to labor, Eric said, "You need to understand that upper management is micro managing us too." He explained to me how people upstairs in the barn often look at the late calls, long drop times, and other poor perform- ance measures as indicators of weak supervision. Upper managers like Ralph, Karen, and Bruce count on supervisors to find ways to prevent, or at least reduce, these poor performances.

Of course, just as those at the barn know that crews can't fully control a number of circumstances, they also know that supervisors can't fully control fleet performance. For example, the posting locations for ambu- lance crews, while part of a "dynamic system," are preapproved by Agonia County EMS and are managed by the county dispatchers, who assign posts to crews directly. Supervisors also can't control the fact that emer- gency departments are perpetually overwhelmed with patients and that cops can loosely justify involuntary psychiatric holds.

However, within reason, upper management expects Eric and his peers to do what they can to maintain "levels." This is a general term used throughout the industry. The current level refers to the number of ambu- lances that are presently available to respond to new 911 calls. Because this number fluctuates so frequently, people often speak of plural levels. Depending on the day and hour, there can be nearly fifty ambulances out in Agonia County, but levels are often lower than a dozen. Every supervi- sor I shadowed carefully monitored the levels during my time with them. They regularly looked at their in-rig computers and counted the number of ambulances available (figure 11).

I learned early on in my fieldwork that supervisors become alarmed by low levels for two major reasons. First, low levels mean a thin fleet and thus an increased likelihood the firm will catch a late call. While upper management hates late calls because they can lead to fines from the county

Figure 11. View from inside a supervisor rig. *Notes:* Per usual,
the in-rig computer is opened to a screen for monitoring levels.
Author's photo.

government, supervisors dread late calls because they can bring heat from
the barn. According to Eric, upper managers often imply that supervisors
are at least partially to blame for the tardy responses that occur under
their watch.

Second, low levels can prevent crews from ending their shifts on time.
County dispatchers cannot dismiss ambulance crews from duty unless it's
level eight or higher. In other words, if you're working on an ambulance,
and you've completed all twelve hours of your shift, the dispatcher cannot
relieve you and your partner until there are more than seven ambulances
available to respond to new calls. You may be forced to work for up to
fourteen hours total. Upper management doesn't like this because those
additional two hours come with a 50-percent wage increase. Nevertheless,
shift extensions don't just come with some heat from above. They also
come with some heat from below. Even with the wage bonus, ambulance
workers almost universally hate being held past a dozen hours. In speaking to this latter issue, supervisor Steve once told me he generally feels bad
for paramedics and EMTs who get held over, but he also hates the "whining
and bitching" he gets from crews when they're forced to work past their

off-duty time. Supervisors are in the business of working an easy shift and aiding some legit calls. The less drama the better.

As such, supervisors prefer levels to be as high as possible. In this regard, their interests are more aligned with labor in the field than with management in the barn. Supervisors and crews overwhelming desire "fat" levels. Neither wants the goldilocks fleet that upper management hopes for, the one that's perfectly sized to avoid the fines that come with thinness and the wasted labor power that comes with fatness. When levels are relatively fat, crews go home on time and get longer "breaks" on post between calls. This reduces heat from below. It also somewhat strangely reduces heat from above. While upper management clearly despises fat levels because it threatens efficiency, supervisors are not expected, or at least not provided with the methods, to trim excess labor power. They can't, for example, just start sending workers home during a slow day. Thus, from the standpoint of both workers and supervisors, fat levels are operational bliss.

Unfortunately, levels are rarely fat. Bruce does what he can from the barn to keep them lean and this produces a challenge for supervisors. They can't just passively watch levels and shrug their shoulders. Instead, they're pressured by upper management to lift levels, especially when the number of available ambulances dips into "level shit." And when it strikes "level zero," as seems to happen several times a week, supervisors need to scramble to fatten the number of available ambulances.

CLEARING HOSPITALS

There are a few ways supervisors can try to increase levels. They can ask incoming crews to rush their rig setup at the barn and head out into the streets as soon as possible. They can encourage others to avoid long hospital transports and thus trim the time between the call and the return to 911 availability. If there's an incident involving multiple patients, they can recommend that more than one patient go to the hospital in a single ambulance. Supervisors can even speak to patients with "bullshit" complaints directly and encourage them to reconsider a hospital transport via ambulance. While these strategies can be somewhat effective, they're

Figure 12. A busy emergency department ambulance bay.
Note: Author's photo.

trivial in the grand scheme of things and they often depend on special circumstances. The go-to tactic is more practical: get crews who are at the hospital back into the streets as soon as possible. This is called "clearing hospitals."

The problem to be solved is captured in figure 12. Ambulances often accumulate in emergency department parking lots. This is a stressful but not an uncommon sight for supervisors. The ambulances in that photo can't be dispatched to new 911 calls at that very moment because the crews attached to them are technically in the process of completing the transports for their previously assigned responses.

But how can supervisors help get these ambulances back into the streets? Like many things, "full house" emergency departments are often out of their control. Supervisors can't affect the number of available beds at the hospital. Likewise, they can't change the protocols that force crews to transport anyone who wants to go. Supervisors also recognize the challenges that emergency department staff face, such as busy waiting rooms and strict regulations requiring that they assess anyone who comes looking for aid. They know such challenges help explain why ambulance crews often have to "hold the wall" and wait several minutes for a bed assignment. Related to this, supervisors know that crews cannot just drop a body off on a bed and return to service right away. Protocols command them to write and print patient care reports before they return to the streets. Crews also need to clean their ambulances and reprepare the equipment they used.

These are some strong impediments to fast drop times, but supervisors nevertheless find ways to help clear hospitals. One option is to talk with nursing staff, and charge nurses in particular. A phone call might do the trick, but most supervisors told me that face-to-face interactions work best.

Sometimes a simple question can do wonders. "Y'all short-staffed today or something?" supervisor Lisa once asked a charge nurse. The nurse apologized and found Lisa's wall-holding crews some beds "like magic." Just as supervisors will help charge nurses out by placing an exceptionally busy hospital on a two-hour ambulance bypass, nurses will sometimes help supervisors by bumping ambulance patients a few triage notches above their already privileged status in the queue.

There is, however, a more effective way to clear hospitals: pressure paramedics and EMTs to return to service sooner rather than later. The point is to discourage crews from "milking" their drop times. Again, a simple face-to-face question can do wonders.

Every shift I spent with supervisors involved them driving to hospitals when levels were low and asking crews questions like "Can you clear [i.e., return to service] soon?" and "Have you printed yet [i.e., completed your paperwork]?" Such questions were often prefaced with some brief yet ostensibly friendly conversations about legit, comical, or bizarre calls. Sometimes supervisors even contextualized these questions with details that were not always truthful. These included claims that it was level zero, that other crews were past the twelve-hour mark and were trying to go home, and that managers at the barn were more closely monitoring drop times on that particular day.

Regardless of the specific tactic, supervisors' intentions are pretty obvious to crews. They typically come to the hospital to light some fire under their asses and lift levels. And while supervisors frequently question ambulance crews, they don't always have to. Their mere presence at the hospital is often enough to motivate crews to return to service. When a supervisor drives into an ambulance bay, it's not uncommon to hear crews suddenly announce their availability for a new 911 call over the radio. "They scatter like cockroaches," supervisor Grant once told me as we heard a couple of crews clear over the radio shortly after he parked in a hospital ambulance bay.

Supervisors don't just randomly select hospitals to clear. They use the same in-rig computer program that tells them where their crews are and what level it is. This program shows them how many ambulances are at each hospital and how long each crew has been there. Supervisors' computers also tell them whether or not crews at hospitals have printed their patient care reports and are therefore (probably) technically ready to return to service. When they feel the urge to clear a hospital, supervisors will usually select ones that have four or more crews or ones where a single crew has been at the hospital for over fifty minutes. Less often, they will get a call from management at the barn requesting them to go clear a particular hospital.

Again, the point is to discourage crews from "milking" their drop times. The assumption here is that crews are deliberately extending the amount of time they're spending at the hospital in an effort to avoid work. There's a significant degree of truth to this assumption and it became very obvious to me once I started working as an EMT. For example, when it was my turn to write the patient care report at the hospital, my coworkers taught me to complete the paperwork but wait ten to fifteen minutes before actually printing the document. This would help prevent management from knowing that we were actually ready to return to service and it would give us a few minutes to take a break. Drop time milking certainly exists and it happens on far more transports than not. And, this is not a secret to anyone at MRT.

It's also not a secret that supervisors are generally tolerant of crews doing *some* milking throughout the shifts. As previously noted, crews do not return to ambulance stations between calls. They're instead "posted" at particular street intersections and these posting assignments can change on a minute-to-minute basis. This means crews are working twelve-hour shifts that basically repeat the following chain of events: post-call-hospital-post. But it's actually worse than that because posting assignments change so often. Crews are frequently driving between posts when they're not running calls. So, the chain actually tends to look more like this: post-post-call-hospital-post-call-hospital-post-post-post-call. The post-post links are "post moves" and they occur when dispatchers command crews to cover another area of the county. This produces incredible flexibility but also incredible exhaustion. The chain only breaks when the shift ends, the ambulance breaks down, or a worker falls ill.

Supervisors generally accept the fact that hospital ambulance bays sort of function as improvised break rooms for paramedics and EMTs working under a regime of dynamic posting.[1] With levels typically being lean or low, crews rarely get official meal breaks and so they often use their time at the hospital to eat. Additionally, emergency departments are in many ways the only places where workers can count on the presence of accessible restrooms. But accessibility isn't everything. Ambulance workers are not likely to be interrupted while they're in an emergency department bathroom. This is very significant. Try working on an ambulance and taking a shit at the Starbucks near your assigned post. The ambulance gods almost guarantee that you will catch a 911 call as soon as you sit on the toilet. Beyond meal and restroom breaks, the hospital also provides a place for crews to "catch their breath" before heading back into the streets.

Eric, Grant, Lisa, and other supervisors understand that crews want to take a few minutes to "recharge" before returning to service. However, they expect this to be limited to around ten minutes every couple or so transports. They also hope crews will be flexible and forgiving. More specifically, they hope crews will be willing to postpone or forgo such informal breaks for the benefit of "the system" when it's level shit. But expectations and hopes only go so far. Supervisors often feel compelled to harass crews over the amount of time they spend at the hospital. For good reason, they're suspicious that crews are doing what they can to push their drop times to the max. They're suspicious that many, if not most, are a bunch of slackers.

THE LAZY FLEET

It was one thing to watch supervisors try to clear hospitals and another thing to be one of the workers they tried to clear. During one of my first shifts as an EMT, I found myself with Lance, my field training officer, at a particularly busy hospital. It was around midnight. We had completed yet another transport. Vince, our paramedic partner, had finished the paper-work for this call and I had cleaned the ambulance. It was about six hours since we had left the barn for the night and we hadn't received any official meal breaks. Experience told me that we probably wouldn't get a break in the next six hours either. So, I used this time in the ambulance bay to drink coffee and eat food. Lance sat with me in the back of our open-door ambulance and Vince reentered the hospital to take a piss.

Suddenly, supervisor Jim drove into the bay, parked his rig, and walked directly toward Lance and me. While we had been at this hospital for about an hour, we had only been sitting for a couple minutes. In addition to the long triage, we had a messy cleanup. Nevertheless, we knew the drill. Jim had come to clear this hospital. Because we had been there the longest out of any of the other crews in the bay, Jim focused on us first.

He greeted us and claimed calls were dropping (i.e., it's busy). Lance then told the supervisor what he apparently wanted to hear, "We're about to clear, and not just cause you showed up." "I appreciate that," responded Jim. I continued to chew my food and swig my lukewarm coffee. Lance then asked with a smile if someone at the barn had called Jim and sent him to this particular ambulance bay. Jim admitted this was the case. Attempting to keep the conversation light, Lance continued, "They always got you guys out here doing that, huh?" Jim seemed irritated by this ques-tion. Speaking of the particular woman who called him from the barn, he said, "She's just doing her job. I'm just doing my job. And my job is to make sure you guys do your job. If we all do our jobs then everything will work out." Lance and I nodded but said nothing in return. Jim must have thought he had just dropped the mic or something. He abruptly walked away and approached another crew. They were his next prey.

Looking back on this exchange, Jim said something to Lance that I mostly heard supervisors say privately to me when I rode along with them. It's this idea that if crews do their jobs and do them well (i.e., efficiently), then life will be easier for management.

As supervisor Steve once told me beyond the earshot of labor, "I'm cool with crews as long as they don't make *me* work." He clarified that this didn't mean the legit clinical work that he was generally happy to assist crews with on scene, but rather what Grant called a "different kind of bullshit." Echoing the sentiments of his peers, Steve told me he doesn't want to be a "babysitter."

Indeed, supervisors generally don't like to watch levels and clear hospitals. The latter in particular can require a lot of tedious driving and awkward conversations. For people still committed to the craft of paramedicine, these foreman-like tasks are simply not very rewarding. And, when supervisors aren't responding to high-priority calls, they would rather be eating out, watching movies, taking naps, or killing time in other leisurely ways. Some seem to think that they deserve this as a reward for working the streets for so long. Whether or not this is a reasonable opinion, people don't always get what they deserve. Such supervisor ease depends on a number of factors like the volume of 911 calls, the availability of hospital beds, and the number of shifts that Bruce has added to the schedule.

Yet, the most frustrating threat to a cushy supervisor shift exists right beneath them: a fleet of allegedly lazy employees.[2] While supervisors verbalize sympathy for the hardships of a busy workforce, they also see crews as generally shiftless and opportunistic in their efforts to avoid work. Because crews like to extend their hospital drop times, supervisors have to drive between hospitals and "get on them."

The comedy here is obvious to an ethnographer who drifts between the worlds of management and labor: supervisors suspect and despise a "lazy fleet" because it hinders their own leisure. An apparent laziness from below forces the middle to work more of that bullshit of a different kind. No one's laughing with me though, especially not the supervisors.

9 Payback

We now step out of the supervisor rig and continue our descent downward. In order to understand how the vertical forces detailed in the previous two chapters shape the frontline regulation of urban suffering, we must consider how said forces are filtered through the practices of crews. In other words, we must account for workers' responses to those forces imposed onto them from outside and above the ambulance.

BLOODLUST

For labor, obedience is the most typical response to bureaucratic and capitalistic pressures. In continually selling their capacity to work for a wage, crews remain largely subservient to capital and bureaucracy. They generally adhere to the explicit commands of protocol and management.

The evidence in support of this obedience is somewhat obvious. They respond to every call the county dispatchers give them and most note the "tight leash" the dispatchers have over their movements throughout the county. Moreover, because protocol commands it, and because punishment for disobedience is too high to ignore, crews frequently transport a mass of bodies they'd prefer to leave behind. Inside the ambulance, para-medics and EMTs frequently execute the protocol-determined interventions for each medical problem they identify. And, despite a caseload packed with vocationally unfulfilling duties, crews work hard in response to their close surveillance by upper managers and field supervisors.[1]

Still, as I've argued throughout this book, ambulance workers are not cogs in a machine. In fact, neither protocols nor managers expect them to be. The protocol book published by Agonia County EMS is written for critical thinkers and emphasizes things like "provider judgment." Likewise, management at the firm encourages a flexible workforce that's adaptable to an array of clinical and operational uncertainties. Forces from above encourage, and in many ways produce, discretionary workers inside the ambulance.

Worker discretion is, however, a double-edged sword. It can help trim labor into a lean body by making it more flexible, but it can also slice into management's bottom line. Crews can use moments of discretion to pursue their own interests against the interests of management. We saw a bit of this in the last chapter as crews attempted to extend their hospital drop times at the expense of lean levels and frustrated supervisors. Thus, while labor's obedience may be likely, it's never fully guaranteed.

Workers frequently counter the interests of management through both individual and collective action. The crews' labor union, as an upward force that confronts (even if it often concedes to) capital, is itself an important actor. A few months into my employment at MRT, my "brothers and sisters" negotiated a nearly two-dollar wage increase for myself and other rookie EMTs. And, when I accidently backed my ambulance into a pole at the hospital and significantly damaged the rear bumper, my partner told me not to sweat it because the union would have my back.

But, for as consequential as the union is, labor's daily struggle with management occurs in a less formalized or collective fashion. More so as an EMT than as a ride-along, I learned how crews attenuate their own suffering as frontline workers charged with executing the will of MRT managers and Agonia County bureaucrats. My coworkers taught me some "little tricks" on how to *pace the shift* (i.e., slow production) and *swell the check* (i.e., increase earnings).

The material benefits of a paced and pricy shift are significant, but there's another reward for pulling some of the tricks covered in this chapter: feelings of vengeance. Like many of my colleagues, I found something simply thrilling about "working the system" for my own benefit. The little tricks for what I'm calling shift pacing and check swelling constitute a kind of upward violence, or at least many workers like to think that they do. These are ways to scratch and slash the underbelly of that beastly mixture of capitalistic and bureaucratic forces. As one senior paramedic once put it to me as he summarized some of the tactics I detail next, "I'm here to bleed these motherfuckers dry."

SHIFT PACING

My partners and I often began work hoping that we'd limit how much our asses got kicked with calls. It's not that we didn't want to work or work hard. As noted in chapter 2, crews overwhelmingly desire "legit" calls, which are usually more physically, mentally, and emotionally exhausting than the usual "bullshit." However, we couldn't choose which calls we responded to and what we were assigned was usually much closer to the bullshit end of the continuum than the legit end. So, while we hoped for some hard work that was vocationally fulfilling, we also wanted to pace our handling of the more mundane cases.

Yet, besides praying to the ambulance gods, what could we do? Many of the factors that determine shift pacing, like the call volume and our posting assignments, were simply out of our control. Luckily, we had a few tricks up our sleeves, some of which I've already touched on a bit in previous chapters.

As discussed in chapter 6, paramedics and EMTs can do strategic transporting. By guiding "patient choice" during so-called bullshit cases, crews can help steer the direction of the ambulance. They frequently do so by recommending that their patients go to hospitals they believe will somehow improve their shifts. I previously noted three basic ends of strategic transports: (1) go to a hospital that's relatively close to the barn during the eleventh hour, (2) go to a hospital in a typically less busy area of the county, or (3) avoid the county's primary psychiatric facility. These are important ways that crews horizontally shuffle undesirable cases onto nurses at particular hospitals, but they're arguably better understood as part and parcel of a vertical struggle.

Strategic transports are often used in a larger effort to pace the shift. The first end reduces the likelihood that a crew will catch a "holdover call." This trick reduces the time spent traveling between the final transport and the crew's designated sign-out location, and it's a simple attempt to avoid forced overtime.[2] The second end directs the ambulance toward relatively less busy areas, and it orients an even more explicit effort to pace the shift. Crews hope that after such transports they'll be assigned a less busy post nearby, thus extending their time between calls. Spending lots of time on a post is generally rare, but when it happens it's doubly satisfying: you get a much-needed break and MRT has to pay you to sit in a parked ambulance. The third end, which involves avoiding the county's primary psychiatric facility in favor of a closer emergency department, is often similarly motivated. As also noted in chapter 6, crews occasionally "fish" for a medical complaint when handling cases where the police force a seventy-two-hour psychiatric hold. Paramedics and EMTs often do this because they want to remain in a relatively less busy area of the county.

Another shift-pacing trick involves what I call "post delaying." Of the dozen or so posts regularly assigned to crews, paramedics and EMTs generally despise three or four that are in the county's poorest and densest areas. These are sometimes described as "ghetto posts." While crews know that legit calls concentrate near these particular intersections, they also know that there's a high likelihood of catching a bullshit call in these areas. And, because these parts of the county are generally busier than the rest of Agonia, workers accurately predict that their time on these posts will typically be brief. Crews generally assume that any informal downtime at these particular intersections will be short because they'll most likely be interrupted with a bullshit call. As such, crews are incentivized to avoid these ghetto posts. Still, they can't outright disobey a posting assignment. The best they can do is stall their arrival.

For example, my partners and I would sometimes take slower routes to these posts (e.g., city streets rather than highways) in hopes of being reassigned to a more desirable post en route. More commonly, though, we did something we called "the five-minute rule." When a county dispatcher assigned us an undesirable post, we would acknowledge the assignment over the radio but wait five minutes until we actually started driving toward that intersection. This was usually just enough time to dodge any scrutiny from dispatchers or supervisors. If we were lucky, the five-minute rule would lead to a closer post assignment as other crews became available for service following the completion of their hospital transports (thus changing the geography of available ambulances and possibly the post assignments).

While strategic transporting and post delaying are significant, perhaps the most effective method for pacing the shift was discussed in the previous chapter: extending drop times. Indeed, the supervisors are right. Crews *are* taking more time than needed at the hospital. After handing patient care off to nurses, completing paperwork, cleaning the ambulance, and reprepping equipment, crews often take a few minutes to eat, use the restroom, and otherwise relax. They do this in a busy 911 system that has them running a ton of bullshit and does not have them returning to an ambulance station between calls. Because it's well known that most supervisors will start to question crews once they've been at the hospital for over fifty minutes, many push their drop time to just around this duration (unless it's the eleventh hour and they want to rush back to the barn to end the shift on time).[3]

Drop time extending frustrates upper management far more than strategic transporting and post delaying. Largely oblivious to the day-to-day specifics of triage and other factors that affect time spent at the hospital (e.g., messy cleanups and complicated paperwork), upper management seems to only see numbers.[4] Still, they don't like what they see: a daily average drop time of about fifty minutes for the entire fleet. Combined with crews' time spent driving to the call, responding on scene, and then driving to the hospital, this means that each case will likely account for over ninety minutes of a crew's shift. More time per case means a lower transport-to-crew ratio, the very thing that managers at the barn want to avoid.

In addition to pressuring the supervisors to watch levels and clear hospitals, upper management encourages crews to trim their drop times directly. Their most aggressive attempt to do so during my fieldwork came early in my employment at MRT. Management struck a deal with the union that incentivized shorter drop times. They added two carrots. First, the firm agreed to pay us a 3-percent quarterly earnings bonus if the fleet's average drop time for that quarter was less than forty minutes.[5] The plan was to have crews hold one another accountable in the ambulance bays. If one crew was taking too long it would obviously lower the fleet average and hurt everyone's chances at getting the bonus. To facilitate peer-policing, management allowed crews to access a limited "supervisor view" on their computers so that they could monitor their coworkers' drop times. Second, management agreed to reward individual workers with exceptionally low drop times by permitting them to wear a company-approved "T-shirt" during the following month. This reward was relatively small, but it wasn't insignificant to many workers. It meant temporarily ditching a thick and itchy uniform button-up.

These efforts to tempt labor out of the ambulance bays with cash and comfort largely failed. "Fuck those greedy motherfuckers, I'm not changing shit," said one of my partners a few days after the new incentives were put in place. His comments seemed to capture the general opinion of labor, at least as I encountered it inside rigs and ambulance bays. Many doubted the possibility of lowering a collective drop time average below forty minutes. Several workers figured we'd just work hard to return to the streets quickly but not actually get rewarded (e.g., lower the average drop time to forty-one minutes). Workers also reasoned that a 3-percent quarterly bonus, which many suspected would be taxed higher than our regular earnings, might not be worth "killing ourselves" over. You could just pace the shift as usual and then pick up a few additional shifts to make some more money. Workers also generally hated the idea of policing one another and figured any serious attempts to reach the forty-minute goal would raise tensions with nurses over triage times.[6] Nevertheless, a minority of workers were apparently motivated by the T-shirt incentive and about one to two dozen employees were allowed to leave their button-ups at home every month. These eager crews were exceptional though. For the most part, the workers I talked to saw the T-shirts as something not worth sacrificing a paced shift over. They'd rather preserve their energy against the explicit wishes of management.

CHECK SWELLING

Pacing the shift against the interests of management is one way crews can get some payback. Indeed, a slower-paced shift means fewer transports and thus less revenue. We can think of this as hurting management by making the fleet a bit costlier. But, while shift pacing may increase the relative price of labor, workers don't see a monetary benefit in doing things like strategic transporting, post delaying, and drop time extending. Shift pacing simply helps protect them from exhaustion.

Luckily, workers have another bag of tricks at their disposal. I brand these tricks "check-swelling" strategies. They don't necessarily protect workers from exhaustion, but, like shift pacing, they help make the fleet more expensive. The benefit to workers is obvious: more pay per shift.

For example, thanks in large part to the union and California labor law, workers can often pick up shifts that pay higher than their base wage. One obvious way to do this is by picking up overtime shifts, which pay 150 percent of the hourly wage. Holiday shifts also come with this benefit. Another option is to pick up night shifts over day shifts because the former come with a few more dollars per hour. Sometimes there's even the option of combining these increases (e.g., an overtime-holiday-night cocktail).

There are some more subtle ways to swell the check too. One trick is to "run the clock." Some workers intentionally punch the clock a few minutes earlier or later than necessary. To the annoyance of management, several employees come into the barn and clock in before they're appropriately dressed (e.g., without the uniform shirt on). Moreover, should they return to headquarters a few minutes before their shift is scheduled to end, some will hang around the barn a bit before clocking out. Because crews cannot punch the clock more than eighteen minutes early or late without offering a written explanation, this strategy can at best only yield about an extra half-hour of pay per shift (i.e., eighteen minutes early plus eighteen minutes late). While this is a somewhat petty effort, if done enough in a biweekly pay period it can noticeably increase a person's paycheck.

An even sneakier trick involves what I call "lunch dodging." While workers frequently complain that they don't get the two thirty-minute meal breaks they're promised, they have a material interest in not receiving these breaks. The firm pays workers an extra hour of pay for each break missed.[7] The actual strategies of lunch dodging are mixed into the strategies of drop time extending. Longer drop times not only provide some time and space for meal consumption; they also reduce the likelihood of getting a meal break since these cannot be issued to a crew when they're technically in the process of completing a transport. Indeed, when management incentivized shorter drop times, a number of workers expressed concern that this could actually hurt worker pay. Shorter drop times could lift levels and potentially increase the likelihood of receiving meal breaks. This would obviously reduce the likelihood of receiving the special compensation for missing such official meal periods. Not all crews want to dodge lunches, but a good number of them certainly do.

The most obvious way to swell the check concerns the so-called mando shifts that I briefly mentioned in chapter 7. Remember that Bruce from the barn will frequently post these in an effort to thicken up a thin schedule.

The particular features of mando shifts were forged through struggles between labor and management well before my entry into the field.[8] According to some of the more senior workers I shadowed and worked with, management has long reserved the "right" to *force mandate* employees into work under the argument that ambulances, like squad cars and fire engines, are essential public infrastructure. Meanwhile, organized labor has long argued that forced mandation is a management-produced problem; it marks the company's failure to hire enough people and schedule enough shifts ahead of time. At some point, management offered a concession that softened mando: double pay. Added to this, labor convinced management to make mandation "voluntary" before forcing it. Now, Bruce must publish mando shifts for voluntary pick up before he can force mandate anyone. Perhaps as an effect of more experienced workers running the union, labor caught another crumb: senior employees (and thus the highest-paid workers) get first dibs on these double-pay shifts.

Because I was a rookie EMT at the bottom of the seniority list, I could only occasionally participate in the "voluntary mandation" program. In order for me to snag these shifts, mando needed to be "deep." This meant that the number of voluntary mandation shifts needed to be greater than the number of relatively senior employees interested in these shifts. Lucky for me, mando was frequently deep right after I was hired. I was able to catch these shifts from time to time and my coworkers taught me how to do so effectively. When I heard rumors that mando was deep, I would pick up few or no straight pay shifts and would instead wait for management to publish the double pay shifts for me to request or "bid on." This strategy came with some risks though. Sometimes mando wasn't deep enough for me to win a bid, leaving me with an empty or near empty schedule.

MRT continued an EMT hiring wave a couple months into my employment and this provided management with more workers to populate ambulances. Mando didn't disappear, but it suddenly dried up for rookies like me.[9] Still, while it lasted, mandation felt great. Like many of my peers on mando, I'd show up to work with a little pep in my step, bragging to my coworkers about the mando shift I got. The shift came not only with extra pay but also with a sense of vengeance. As one of my paramedic partners on mando said one shift, "That's what they [management] get." Our mandation shifts were like sanctions we imposed from below. They were fines not for late calls, but for the firm's failure to retain staff. We relished in the opportunity to collect on these penalties.

THE DEFIANT FLEET

Ambulance crews are not entirely passive to the downward pressures of management and bureaucracy. They may be exploited and generally obedient, but they find some innovative, albeit modest, ways to undermine those who control and coordinate their labor. From this point of view, workers don't constitute much of a lean or a lazy fleet. Instead, they're a *defiant fleet,* or at least that's how many paramedics and EMTs like to see themselves. Several workers described the fleet to me as something "rebellious," "punk," and "anticorporate." A "fuck management" maxim frequently accompanied their justifications for shift pacing and check swelling.

These efforts certainly frustrate people above labor, but they never seriously threaten capital or bureaucracy. In fact, the argument could be made that the strategies detailed in this chapter actually help facilitate worker exploitation by making it more tolerable overall. These little tricks may indicate labor's attempts to direct some harm upward without fundamentally challenging those above them. Even so, these efforts signal mild and momentary breaks from obedience, and understanding them is important for three interconnected reasons.

First, the little tricks summarized in this chapter help clarify the *suffering of crews* by showcasing their efforts to mitigate it. For some readers, it might seem outright ridiculous that I discuss such a thing amid the hardships we've already encountered beneath these workers' boots. I sympathize with this critique. But, while crews are generally whiter, richer, and healthier than the people they work on, they're not immune to some of the same basic forces that social scientists insist are hurting people toward the bottom of the American social hierarchy. The encroachment of the market into essentially all arenas of society, the intensification of social insecurity, and the polarization of life chances may leave a few groups unharmed, but ambulance workers are not such a group. In many ways, shift pacing and check swelling mark crews' daily efforts to ameliorate their particular experiences in an advanced capitalist society.

More to the point, these are tricks for alleviating the pains of low wages and long hours.[10] Many paramedics and EMTs see the strategies I've detailed in this chapter as essential to their survival. Several depend on things like overtime and mandation pay to cover their living expenses. For some, catching too many meal breaks (and thus missing out on the corresponding compensation) can seriously threaten their ability to pay their bills. Many with dependents to support feel a strong pressure to work sixty hours a week. Others are driven to "pull doubles," which usually means they work a twelve-hour shift, sleep in their car in the barn parking lot for a couple hours, and then return for another dozen hours of work. A few even have second jobs at other ambulance firms and at organizations unrelated to paramedicine.

Given such circumstances, the defiant strategies I've outlined can mean a lot to workers and not just because they can come with some refreshing feelings of vengeance. Swelling the check, even if by a little, can mean paying one's bills on time or having a bit more spending cash in one of the nation's most expensive states to live in. The motivations for shift pacing also start to seem more reasonable. For labor, pacing the shift is not just a way for them to lift their middle fingers at management; it's also a way for them to catch their breath in a system that has them running from call to call for multiple hours a day, several days a week. Extending their hospital drop times and doing related tricks can help keep them from running into the ground.

Second, the tactics detailed in this chapter show us that crews are neither total tools nor total victims of the downward forces of capital and bureaucracy. Paramedics and EMTs don't just struggle with pain-in-the-ass clientele. They also struggle with those who kick their asses with difficult shifts.

My job seemed to have me wresting drunk and disorderly patients every couple of shifts, but my partners and I were more consistently grappling with forces above us. We tied wrists to gurneys and forced masks over spitting heads, but we more frequently struggled to pace our shift and swell our checks. Getting some revenge on MRT, and to a lesser extent on Agonia County EMS, held much of our focus while at work. In some respects, it was easy to lose sight of the patients beneath us as we focused on ways to survive and screw those above us.

Thus, there's a third reason why it's important to understand the defiant strategies of paramedics and EMTs. Ambulance patients may experience some collateral effects of labor's daily struggles with management and protocol. In workers' efforts to swell their checks, they are quick to become exhausted and this seems to increase their dickish interactions with patients. Worker frustration, and the cold and apathetic hands that tend to come with it, cannot be totally explained by the mismatch in vocation and labor I detailed in chapter 3. Yes, most of the paramedics and EMTs I met are generally vexed by so-called bullshit, but such distress is magnified when they're tired. It's really easy to lose sympathy for clientele when you're on the sixtieth hour of work for the week and you've managed to dodge a lot of meal breaks. Even mando, which has you working for double the pay, probably has you working more hours than you initially anticipated.

But it's not just check swelling and the exhaustion that tends to accompany it that matter for ambulance patients. Shift pacing seems to come with its own collateral effects. In doing things like drop time extension, crews are affecting ambulance coverage.

Indeed, my partners and I often found ourselves resting in hospital ambulance bays as calls dropped nearby. If a call seemed legit, like for a cardiac arrest or a gunshot wound, we'd sometimes quickly return to service and try to snag it. But this was rare. We mostly remained idle until we felt compelled to return to the streets after an informal break or until a supervisor came to clear the hospital.

Post delaying can also come at the cost of thinning ambulance coverage in the busier and thus the more vulnerable areas of Agonia County. While such geographic holes in coverage may be temporary and not frequent enough to adjust the overall pattern of timeliness observed in disadvantaged neighborhoods, the risk for tardy ambulances may be at least partially pinned on the defiant strategies of ambulance crews.

Additionally, strategic transporting can bring patients to hospitals that may not be ideal for them. Many of the low-priority patients who more or less get duped into selecting a hospital in a less busy territory of Agonia County get transported to hospitals farther away from the areas they dwell in. This can mean a longer and more challenging return back to these areas following hospital discharge. And, because strategic transporting typically means avoiding the busiest emergency departments, crews are often keeping patients away from the hospitals with the more robust social service programming (e.g., on-site social workers, psychiatric care, and taxi vouchers). Collateral effects like these can seem inconsequential in an institution that is officially oriented toward "saving lives," but there's reason to believe they can chip away at the already low life chances of some of the county's most vulnerable residents.

To sum up, if managers in the barn hope the fleet is something lean and those in the supervisor rig suspect the fleet is something lazy, then the fleet knows itself as something defiant. Even I, someone with probably more sympathy for management than the average worker because of my history as a ride-along, got caught up in the little tricks for payback. I too wanted to pace the shift and swell the check and I too found such minor acts of vengeance to be emotionally and materially rewarding. As such, I too must take some responsibility for the collateral effects that might be linked to this conduct.

This chapter concludes part 3. The vertical relations detailed in these three chapters not only contextualize a bandaging and a sorting of bodies; they also help detail a hustling of bodies. Due to a particular constellation of bureaucratic and capitalistic forces, ambulance crews hastily process their clientele.

To be clear, this doesn't mean that people aren't waiting or that they aren't waiting long.[11] Suggesting that people are generally rushed *through* an intervention is not the same as saying that people are generally rushed *toward* an intervention. Ambulance patients in fact experience a lot of waiting (e.g., for the crew to arrive on scene, for the nurse to assign them a bed, and for a physician to eventually see them). But these periods of limbo are separated by flashpoints of intervention (e.g., rapid exams, quick triage decisions, and fast treatments).

Understanding this hustling of clientele necessitates an understanding of the vertical relations of production. Protocols designate quick treatments to stabilize crises, and management encourages an acceleration of people processing to increase the fleet's productivity. Additionally, workers are generally self-motivated to push through cases quickly so that they can free up some time for informal breaks.

If bandaging bodies helps account for the depth of interventions and sorting bodies helps account for the breadth of interventions, then hustling bodies helps account for the speed of interventions. An examination of an ambulance labor process illustrates how state responses to urban suffering are not just shallow and diffused but also hurried. Outside the ambulance, we can see this in temporary housing, one-time cash assistance, and other short-lived interventions that frontline workers hustle people through. Yet the ambulance might be the best example. The flashing lights and loud sirens that allow its crews to rush superficial treatments to people are emblematic of a state that's made not just of reactionary but also of rapid interventions.

Conclusion

Quitting my EMT job was a bittersweet feeling. The bitterness came from saying goodbye to friends, sliding back into the seemingly less consequential world of the academy, and departing from a profession that I learned to love. The sweetness came from ditching an unpleasant mixture of long hours and low pay, freeing up more time to write, and abandoning a career that hardened my sentiment.

As mentioned in chapter 3, I finally had enough of the ambulance after running a call for a woman who was raped and left for dead on the outskirts of Agonia County. I was going to quit anyway, but this particular case was so nauseating that I decided to walk away sooner than expected. In many ways, this was the moment that most separated me from many of my colleagues at MRT. When things got difficult, I had the privilege of running away from the misery of ambulance work. I tolerated many horrors for sure, but that was always easier to do when I was more energized, curious, and dependent on an ambulance paycheck. Things were different by the time my partner and I were sent to treat and transport the last person I saw writhing in pain in the back of an ambulance. I was more exhausted than ever, the intellectual wonder that lead me into the ambulance as a ride-along had mostly been tamed, and the economic troubles that ushered me into this vehicle as an employee had been fixed. The time to leave was inching closer and witnessing the aftermath of this woman's assault was the last straw for me.

A few days after this call, I posted a farewell note on the union's private message board. I reflected on my sociological interests in ambulance operations and expressed my gratitude to a workforce that welcomed me as both an intrusive ride-along and a fledgling EMT. The responses I received from a number of my coworkers made my departure even more difficult. However, more than anything, these messages assured me that my pivot from ride-along to EMT was worthwhile. "It's admirable that you had the humility to hop out of your ivory tower and join us plebes in the trenches," wrote one paramedic. "It was genuinely uplifting to see someone who was willing to work in the field to get a better understanding," said someone else. "You caught on quick bro and it was good working with you!"

Others said they just generally appreciated how I got my "hands dirty" in an effort to better understand paramedicine. Many seemed to imply that simply working in the ambulance tapped into some special, superior, or sacred knowledge. I was honored but also somewhat horrified by these kinds of responses to my departure. I imagine all ethnographers leave their field sites feeling a little daunted by the responsibility of accurately depicting the people and places they study, but the confidence many of my coworkers placed in me as a fellow insider only amplified this pressure. In the end, I'm not sure this book could ever meet the high expectations of my former colleagues, but I hope it comes close.

AMBULANCE CREWS ON THE FRONT LINES OF URBAN SUFFERING

Sociologists don't tend to write about the ambulance, but when they do they rarely ponder its frequent interactions with structurally vulnerable populations in the American city. I was motivated before, during, and after my fieldwork to understand the ambulance as an institution for governing urban suffering. This inevitably honed my focus on how ambulance crews are disproportionately handling bodies toward the bottom of the economically and racially polarized city.

Such an endeavor meant I had to break from some competing framings of the ambulance. The primary framing is essentially the public relations image propagated by emergency medical service bureaucracies, ambulance provider agencies, and paramedic and EMT labor unions. It's this vision of the ambulance as an institution that aids anyone and everyone in medical crisis, regardless of their physical or social location. Yet there's an alternative framing of the ambulance that rubs against this one and it's propagated by a significant number of academics and journalists. It's this idea that the ambulance is frequently missing in poor neighborhoods because of people's reluctance to dial 911 or some systemic biases in ambulance dispatch.

These framings aren't totally wrong, but they're misleading. Paramedics and EMTs respond up and down the polarized city and there's evidence suggesting that poor people and people of color choose to avoid them due to concerns over billing, timing, and surveillance. Yet both of these framings ignore one of the most important features of the ambulance: it's an institution that's heavily utilized by vulnerable populations. For example, regardless of severity or type of emergency, neighborhood-level poverty is positively and strongly associated with ambulance responses.[1] There's also evidence suggesting that the majority of the individuals who encounter ambulance crews are either uninsured or covered by Medicaid. The ambulance is perhaps best framed as a prevalent and busy institution in the lives of those who suffer most in the American city.

I don't think the ambulance should only be understood as an institution for handling economically and racially oppressed populations. As noted in the introduction, suffering is not exclusive to poor people or people of color. Misery just tends to accumulate toward the bottom of a complex urban hierarchy. I nevertheless see the ambulance as both a suitable and a strategic case for studying the management of down-and-out populations. For one thing, it's parked at some critical intersections identified in this literature (e.g., between welfare and penality and between policy and profit).

But, in order to make sense of the ambulance as such, I've argued that we need to adjust our ways of thinking about the frontline governance of urban suffering. Early into this case study I found myself inspired by, but also frustrated with, extant frameworks like those sketching the ambidextrous state and those examining street-level bureaucracies. I never expected these frameworks to explain everything, but they came with some significant blind spots that made it difficult for me to comprehend what I was seeing in the field. If they weren't forgetting workers, then they were ignoring the horizontal relations between institutions or neglecting the vertical intricacies within them.

To help remedy this problem, I've pushed for a labor-centric vision for understanding how suffering bodies are handled by institutions on the ground. This didn't mean a total abandonment of existing theory (i.e., the trap of empiricism), nor did it mean a pure synthesis of previous models and concepts (i.e., the trap of theoreticism).[2] Instead, it meant piecing together useful bits of theory into something new that could help me navigate the case at hand. And it meant linking existing themes in the scholarship by embracing the special and surprising lessons learned from my case.

This book has treated the regulation of urban suffering as a labor process. I've argued that doing so forces us to account for frontline workers, their lateral intersections, and the vertical associations they're locked in. This refocusing is simple. Start by considering what frontline workers are changing or maintaining. All labor processes involve a transformation or regulation of the world by the hands and minds of workers utilizing the instruments of production. This is true whether we're talking about physical manufacturing, knowledge production, service labor, or so-called people work. With respect to how institutions on the streets handle urban suffering, labor-produced transformations and regulations can be seen, as I stated before, in the sheltering of unhoused people, in the feeding of hungry mouths, and even in the beating of supposedly dangerous subjects. Sometimes frontline labor can simply mean the processing of people into "clients" (e.g., patients and inmates) so that other workers can monitor and adjust them. The results may be micro and momentary, but they are transformations and regulations nonetheless. And, of course, these efforts are only made possible through the social relations of production. Productive activity is enabled and constrained by the relations workers enter into with fellow laborers at their sides and with those who attempt to control and coordinate their labor from above.

I first entered a world of people work where crews are *bandaging bodies* by providing a number of stabilizing and superficial responses to complex problems. I then stepped out of the ambulance and into the streets to find crews, nurses, and police collectively *sorting bodies* across medical and penal sites. Finally, I made my way into ambulance headquarters, down to the supervisor rig, and back into the ambulance to make sense of why crews are *hustling bodies* through rapid points of intervention.

My analysis does not come without weakness. In concentrating on workers and their work, I too generated some blind spots in how we understand the frontline governance of urban suffering. Indeed, the lived experiences of clientele can easily be neglected by such an approach. I'm certainly guilty of this. It's an easy sin to commit when your analytical frame directs your attention to the labor process. There are also some important aspects to how suffering populations are governed that seem to unfold outside of, or at least significantly far from, the activities underlined by a labor-centric approach. For example, contract negotiations between MRT and Agonia County and the development of 911 transport policies at multiple levels of government are not very visible in an ambulance, a supervisor rig, or even a daily management meeting. These blind spots are significant. Nevertheless, if the goal is to understand *how* urban suffering is handled at ground level, then a labor-centric approach proves useful. The next section details this general framework in greater detail and considers its applicability to other cases.

BEYOND THE AMBULANCE

The labor-centric framework I've used throughout this book can be distilled into three propositions. First, suffering bodies are often handled by frontline workers who are embedded in both vertical and horizontal relations of production. In other words, the practical and relational components of a labor process are essential to understanding how state, state-delegated, and related institutions govern suffering. The people who aid, punish, and otherwise react to variably recognized problems are necessarily caught in productive relations with management from above and with fellow workers at their sides. These multidirectional associations shape workers' interactions with their clientele.

Second, these relations are intersectional and interdependent. This suggests that we should examine the front lines of governance, the horizontality of governance, and the verticality of governance in relation to one another. For example, this is why we can't make sense of burden shuffling, a horizontal process, without accounting for a crew's practical engagements with, and varied preferences for, the subjects of their labor. We must understand their frustration with "bullshit." But this isn't enough either. We must also account for the vertical forces that exhaust paramedics and EMTs and compel them to work so many vocationally unfulfilling cases. Crews' strategies of burden shuffling are often intermixed with their more subtle tactics to mitigate their exploitation as wage laborers.

Third, the life chances of those processed on the front lines are altered through a vertically and horizontally structured labor process. For the case study at hand, I've attempted to demonstrate this through the three mechanics of bandaging bodies, sorting bodies, and hustling bodies. However, it's perhaps most obvious through the second. Workers, doubly caught in vertical and horizontal relations of production, funnel people into hospitals or jails. Relative to one another, the first destination protects and extends life chances while the latter severs them. The specific hospitals that ambulance crews transport to may also come with some collateral effects for patients. For example, some emergency departments have weaker social services and some are obviously farther from the places individual patients tend to dwell. Understanding how bodies are sorted across these spaces requires a simultaneous examination of policy execution *and* the work conditions that influence this execution. Frontline laborers, as both calculating and emotional actors, often sort their subjects in a way that benefits themselves against the interests of management and other workers.

In the end, I hope this case study inspires others not only to see the ambulance as an institution for governing urban suffering but also to see such governance more generally as a labor process. The specific concepts used throughout the previous chapters (e.g., people work, burden shuffling, and the lean fleet) may be applicable to other cases. However, in my opinion, the simple claim that suffering populations are governed by frontline workers embedded in horizontal and vertical relations of production is far more useful. Consider, for example, the relevance this

framework might have for two massive institutions that disproportionately handle poor people and people of color in the United States: the
welfare office and the prison.

More folk term than official title, the welfare office usually exists as a
branch of a local social services bureaucracy. Caseworkers transform the
world by admitting clientele into benefits programs (e.g., food stamps and
temporary cash assistance) and referring them to other street-level agencies (e.g., job-training programs and community health centers). They
also work to inspirit responsible, entrepreneurial, and self-governing sub-
jectivities among their clientele.[3] The framework established in this book
predicts that the lateral relations between overwhelmed frontline workers
constitute an important dimension to how the welfare office operates.
Caseworkers, for example, may engage in something like burden shuffling
with the Left-handed agencies they refer clientele to and the Right-
handed agencies that share their jurisdiction (e.g., for subjects who receive
public assistance but who are also under correctional supervision).
Regardless of the specifics, a labor process examination of the welfare
office would necessitate an examination of the horizontal relations of production, and this would almost certainly mean observing how frontline
workers interact across organizations or departments. This approach
would also call for an examination of bureaucratic authority (e.g., the use
of strict performance standards for caseworker labor) and capitalistic
influence (e.g., delegating specific operations like Medicaid administration to private firms and the absorption of market principles through
strategies akin to lean production).

The labor-centric framework I use throughout this book may also help
demystify the prison. Despite claims that the American penitentiary is like
a "warehouse," the laborers of the prison do more than keep an exorbitant
number of poor people and people of color locked up. For sure, prison
guards work to keep inmates in cells, rotating them daily through the
spaces of the cafeteria and the yard and discretionarily punishing them for
incompliance.[4] However, the prison is also a place for regulating subjects
from the inside out. Nurses, counselors, and life skills instructors focused
on transforming prisoner mind-sets compose a consequential, albeit an
understudied, part of the correctional labor force under mass incarceration.[5] The framework I advance suggests that we cannot understand the

practical component of carceral labor without also analyzing the relations these workers are caught in. In addition to importing subjects from courts and jails and later exporting the bulk of these people into parole offices, the penitentiary is internally structured by the intramural relations between guards, counselors, educators, nurses, and other laborers who make and maintain prison operations. Of course, in thinking about prison operations as a labor process, such an inquiry would also need to examine the vertical relations of production. And while the hierarchical relations between inmates and staff that sociologists have long focused on are certainly important, the framework proposed here is equally concerned with relations between staff and those who control and coordinate their labor.[6]

Whatever its capacity to inform other cases, it's important to distinguish this labor-centric framework from some of the scholarship that inspires it. I'm indebted to a theory of street-level bureaucracy, but I'm not convinced that such an approach calls for a deep-enough analysis of production.[7] We should move beyond the once innovative but increasingly banal claim that policy is "made" by frontline workers. It's not enough to say that policy is made. We must consider what exactly is transformed and regulated by labor (e.g., spaces in bodies and bodies in spaces). This has implications for the social relations established between workers, clientele, and management. Among other things, a deeper examination of production motivates a horizontal framing that helps us see how frontline workers labor with and against each other *across* locations and professions. Since the beginning, street-level bureaucracy scholars have claimed that multiple front lines are managing poor and otherwise vulnerable populations, but few have studied the sideways interactions between workers of distinct vocations. In examining the everyday productions of a splintered and seemingly hollow state, the labor-centric prospective I advance assumes such a state includes people-processing sites that are variably porous. From this point of view, the lateral associations between workers affect the life chances of their clientele in a manner inexplicable to theories that narrowly focuses on vertical conditions.

This labor-centric framework also adds to some of the other ways that social scientists think about the regulation of urban suffering. It builds upon some of the theories that largely ignore frontline labor, like those that tend to emphasize an ambidextrous state.[8] The distinction between the protective Left hand and the repressive Right hand certainly helps us situate the ambulance between the hospital emergency department and the police squad car. However, in generally neglecting the actual execution of aid and punishment, such a framework tells us little about how destitute and stigmatized people are managed at ground level. Studies of the frontline labor process can help fill this gap and show us how workers embedded in complex relations of production influence the governance of suffering populations.[9]

Then there are the scholars who examine the interactions between workers, especially between those in professions that are more protective or Left-handed and those in professions that are more repressive or Right-handed.[10] My analysis differs from many of these studies in that I couple a horizontal examination with a vertical one. Thus, in considering the interactions between workers (e.g., crews, nurses, and police), I also examine the interactions between workers and those who attempt to control and coordinate their labor from above. I also consider how these horizontal and vertical relations influence each other.

I like to think I stand on the shoulders of giants. My analysis is influenced by previous theories and research. However, the labor-centric framework I advance offers something new and it's more than just a synthesis of existing scholarship. I should also note that I don't want readers to desert the perspectives I'm clearly inspired by. I just want those who are puzzled by the governance of urban suffering to consider the usefulness of a labor process analysis. Much can be gained by doing so.

DOWN THE RIG

I'm going to end this book in a way similar to how I ended a few shifts at MRT: by "downing the rig." At work, this meant pulling my ambulance out of service for mechanical reasons. Assuming I didn't need a tow, I'd drive back to the barn for repairs or for a different ambulance if one was available (it often wasn't). I'd sometimes wait out the remainder of my shift at headquarters. Other times, the fleet mechanics would resolve the problem before I returned to the streets to finish out my twelve hours. For example, I once downed a rig because it kept overheating. My partner and

I returned to the barn and waited a couple hours for the mechanics to repair the ambulance before we returned to service. I'm not exactly sure how the mechanics repaired our rig.

I'm also not exactly sure how the ambulance can be fixed to better serve the populations that depend on it most, be it for people who turn to the ambulance for assistance or for people who count on it for a paycheck. The analysis offered in the previous chapters can nevertheless point us to some general repairs and reforms.

As such, I'm less interested in ending this book with specific policy recommendations. I'm no more a policy writer than a fleet mechanic. I'm merely motivated to down the rig and point to a few possibilities for change. The "check engine" light is on and I'm bringing the ambulance into the garage. I can only hope that a coalition of civil society groups, labor unions, elected officials, and other stakeholders will actually put in the work to fix what's broken and modify what needs improvement. I'm just dropping this vehicle off with three general recommendations: decommodify the ambulance, transform the vocation, and strengthen a safety net beyond the rig.

Let's start with decommodification. Those tasked with repairing and reforming the ambulance should consider pulling it away from the market and making it less capitalistic. Others suggest that deprivatization could lead to some better working conditions for crews and less expensive services for clientele.[11] This may be true, but it's not enough. So-called public ambulance operations, like those run by fire departments, usually depend on fee-for-service models similar to MRT. The leaders of such operations are also pressured to run an efficient and flexible workforce as they navigate a "transport market." The pursuit of profit may not be the name of the game for public ambulance providers, but the pursuit of "fiscal responsibility" may have similar effects anyway if money is primarily earned through clientele fees and primarily spent on labor power. I encourage more serious inquiries into the promises of entitlement-based ambulance provision, where fee revenue is eclipsed by tax revenue and private insurance is replaced by public insurance. This should be coupled with an effort to reduce caseloads for crews by fattening the fleet. Public investments can be made to add more ambulances (and ambulance stations) to the streets, irrespective of their profitability. This decommodification project should also include efforts to increase compensation, benefits, and protections for crews. They'd remain dependent on selling their labor power for a wage, but perhaps not so dependent that many would have to work overtime shifts or second jobs to make ends meet. The analysis fleshed out in this book suggests that such a change could reduce worker frustration and increase their sympathy for clientele. Ultimately, what I'm calling ambulance decommodification has the potential to doubly improve working conditions and quality of care.

My analysis also encourages a transformation of vocation. Throughout the United States, local EMS bureaucracies are experimenting with "community paramedicine" programs that deliberately integrate nonemergency medical services into the ambulance (e.g., having crews run postdischarge follow-up appointments).[12] While much of this seems to be motivated by efforts to increase operational efficiency by reducing "unnecessary" transports in the long run, my fieldwork suggests that such programming could benefit many patients. However, I encourage an even broader scope, one that integrates a vision not only of "primary care" but also of "social work." Future research should consider how crews could be given tools for linking patients to housing, food, and other "nonmedical" resources. I suspect that this would require a reconfiguration not only of tools but also of training. Integrating the "structural competency" pedagogies that are increasingly used in other medical professions into paramedic and EMT training programs is one option.[13] This would have aspiring ambulance workers learning about the more "upstream" conditions that they would ideally be better equipped to address in the field. An even more dramatic change would have us replacing the lesser-trained position of the EMT with that of a social worker who is also trained in basic life support skills.[14] Ultimately, the point would be to expand the scope of the ambulance to better match demand on the ground. Among other things, this might help reduce the frustrations of both crews and patients.

We can't, however, expect the ambulance to do everything. I lastly encourage advocates of paramedical reform to join broader efforts to strengthen the welfare state. This could include a call for programming that's been demonstrated to mitigate medical crises (e.g., widespread naloxone distribution and citizen CPR training).[15] However, this could also include more general strategies for improving the life chances of vulnerable populations. The goals here don't need to be too complicated: universal health care, secure housing, and a more generous welfare state overall.[16] The point is not to eliminate a bandaging of suffering bodies, but to promote efforts that reduce the risks of wounding. Likewise, we can't expect to stop the sorting of human problems across a division of frontline labor, but we can make some important adjustments to the possibilities of sorting. For example, we can change policies that allow for the coercive hospitalization of down-and-out populations (e.g., loosely justified involuntary psychiatric holds and strong-armed ambulance trips) and encourage better-fit programming (e.g., mobile mental health crisis response teams and sobering centers).[17] And, while conscious of the long waits people encounter on the front lines, we can work to develop interventions that are not so hustled and fractured (e.g., long-term and integrated health care).

In the end, we can't expect the regulation of urban suffering to disappear. By all reasonable accounts, suffering seems forever weighed toward the bottom of the economically and racially polarized metropolis. The relative wealth of a few depends on the relative poverty of many in advanced capitalist societies and the racial order continues to color inequalities in life chances. Among other things, we can expect bodies toward the bottom of the urban hierarchy to disproportionately leak, gasp, scream, quiver, ache, and starve. Barring the emergence of a truly classless and antiracist society, the state will continue to govern the downward distribution of suffering, be it by aiding, punishing, or neglecting those who carry the brunt of hardship. The question is not *will* suffering populations be governed, but *how* they will be governed. I simply hope this book demonstrates that an examination of the ambulance, and the ambulance labor process in particular, can help answer this question.

Notes on Data and Methods

I remember lying on the floor in a stuffy office building. My eyes were closed. A young woman tore off my shirt and pants. She was an EMT student and I was her pretend gunshot patient.

"I'm checking for B-P-DOC," she announced as she pressed her gloved hands against my bare sternum and began to slide her palms across my abdomen. "No acronyms," commanded the clipboard-wielding proctor who sat in a chair and watched this aspiring EMT examine my body. "Sorry, um, I mean bleeding, pain, deformities, open wounds, and crepitus."

The proctor was speaking in the same monotone voice he had been using with the dozen or so other EMT students who had examined my pretend injury: "OK, you notice blood on the right anterior chest, it's a sucking chest wound." The student responded swiftly and confidently, "I'm going to treat using occlusive dressing, using tape on three sides to prevent a tension pneumo (pneumothorax)."

That's where desperation brought me. To the floor, half-naked, and pretending to be injured. At the time, I knew I wanted to study the ambulance. I just wasn't yet sure how to do it. Spending time at this EMT school seemed like a good way to address the problem. The instructors and fellow volunteers were some of the few people I knew who worked in ambulances.

I met most of them a few months earlier when I was a student in the program. Indeed, I was once in the same position as the woman who examined me on the floor. I too was peeling back the eyelids of strangers to check their pupils and flashing a small light in their ears to act as if I were looking for blood. Almost certainly unlike hers, though, my primary goal in completing the program was to inspire a research project.

I enrolled in the EMT program roughly two years after the conversation I had with James outside of his transitional housing facility in Portland. I reasoned an entry-level training like this would help demystify paramedical operations and introduce me to people in the industry. Entering the six-week program only cost me about $3,000 and a perquisite CPR certificate. Once I was in, I spent eight hours a day for four days a week listening to introductory lectures on anatomy and physiology and learning how to treat simulated emergencies. When I graduated the program, I continued to show up to the school as a volunteer.

That's how I eventually made my way on the carpet, pretending I was unconscious and shot. I figured volunteering at the school would give me a chance to talk to some experienced paramedics and EMTs about how to design an ambulance ethnography. However, this was only partially the case. The people I met at the school offered great insight into the profession, but they couldn't imagine a way for me to access the ambulance as a researcher. They encouraged me to speak with more "powerful" people in the world of emergency medicine.

So, that's what I did, and luck eventually came my way. After meeting with a few emergency room physicians and briefly interning for a public health bureaucracy, I networked my way into a meeting with leading administrators at Agonia County EMS. They, in turn, referred me to upper management MRT.

FIELD OBSERVATIONS

About a year after I completed my EMT training, I entered the firm's headquarters. There, I met Jared, the company's medical director, and Laura, the clinical director whose responsibilities included managing the firm's "ride-along" activities. During this meeting, I pitched an exploratory study that would involve me shadowing ambulance crews as a ride-along. I admitted a somewhat intentional lack of focus but noted my interest in the role that ambulances play in poor neighborhoods. Projecting my own Hollywood-based fantasies of ambulance work, I mentioned this could mean a focus on gunshot wounds and other high-severity trauma calls.

Both Laura and Jared were encouraging. Laura, who claimed sociology was one of her favorite courses from college, volunteered to help with the logistics of scheduling my ride-along shifts. She even solicited some free framing advice. Presumably relying more on stereotypes than research, she insisted my research would be "really interesting" if I could somehow answer why Latinos were prone to stabbing one another while blacks were partial to shooting their foe. I politely nodded and agreed that could be interesting. Jared, a bit closer to my wavelength, encouraged me to think about the ways ambulance crews could "better communicate" with marginalized populations. Again, I nodded and expressed appreciation.

Ultimately, the three of us didn't know exactly where my analysis would take me, but Jared and Laura were surprisingly open to letting a nosy researcher poke his head around the organization. Following their behind-closed-doors confirmation with other upper managers, they even recommended that I shadow MRT field supervisors. They said this would give me more of a "bird's-eye" view of how the organization functioned. And, because the supervisors are dispatched to monitor and assist a number of high-priority responses like those for gunshot wounds, they told me this would increase my chances of seeing calls like these.

I had struck gold and the next year was dedicated to conducting these ride-along observations. Laura allowed me to request any ambulance or supervisor shift so long as it wasn't on a rig with an assigned intern or trainee. I selected days and nights, weekdays and weekends, and crews and supervisors. None of the eight supervisors, twenty-five paramedics, or fourteen EMTs I asked to shadow denied my request and several encouraged me to request their shifts again (which I often did). Through shadowing these people, I conversed with many more crews and managers as well as other parties like patients, cops, and nurses.

Crews and supervisors generally, although incompletely, welcomed me into the world of paramedicine. My EMT training provided me with a superficial knowledge of ambulance work and helped me examine clinical decision-making in the field. I did not work as an EMT during this first year, but I attempted to lightly assist crews and supervisors throughout their shifts. I often carried, cleaned, and prepped equipment for crews and I sometimes helped supervisors with simple paperwork duties. On a few occasions I directly assisted with emergency care when events became unusually hectic (e.g., manually stabilized a broken femur, maintained pressure on a stab wound, and helped hold down a fist-swinging person). However, the rapport I built with the men and women I shadowed might have more to do with our similar social profiles. Like many of the crews and supervisors at MRT, I am a white male and I come from a working-class family far away from the neighborhoods the ambulance frequents most. On the other hand, my status as a ride-along separated me from those I shadowed: some teased me for being a naïve "college boy," some were irritated by my "politically correct" stances on 911 "system abusers," and some were frustrated when, as a *doctoral* candidate, I was unable to offer smart clinical advice.

I took detailed field notes as a ride-along. When with crews, I focused my notes on their interactions with patients, supervisors, nurses, and police. While with supervisors, I focused my notes on their interactions with crews and upper management. I jotted many events and some conversations as they occurred, but I typically put pen to paper during "downtime" as I sat in hospital ambulance bays, in ambulance-posting locations, and at headquarters. I also used downtime to informally interview crews and supervisors. Management forbid me from using an audio recorder, so all conversations were paraphrased in my notes. Following each shift or set of consecutive shifts, I expanded my jottings into more detailed narratives. As with many ethnographers, my techniques for note taking were directly inspired by a book by Robert Emerson, Rachel Fretz, and Linda Shaw.[1]

At the beginning of my fieldwork I articulated general interests in the everyday operations of urban paramedicine, but I also stressed an early fascination in "trauma work" (i.e., the management of physically injured patients). I assumed I would extend Eddie Palmer's ethnographic description of ambulance workers as "trauma junkies" who are vocationally driven to aid wounded citizens.[2] Early into my fieldwork, crews labeled me the "trauma guy" and a few joked that I had "come for blood."

I couldn't help but think that people were laughing at me and my focus on trauma. They had good reason to. It became readily apparent in the field that the high-profile trauma responses that define the ambulance in mainstream fiction, local news media, and my EMT training program were not very common. I certainly saw crews rushing punctured, crushed, and broken bodies to the trauma center, and they were mostly collecting these patients from disadvantaged neighborhoods as expected. Such events, however, only accounted for a sliver of the calls I saw crews responding to. Not only were most calls not so "severe," even the severe ones weren't typically "traumatic." They were instead more "medical," meaning they involved crises of illness more than crises of injury.

I needed to abandon the cliché of ambulance work as trauma work. As one supervisor I shadowed early on noted, "You don't want your (doctoral) thesis to be like that show *Trauma,*" referencing a canceled NBC drama he liked to mock for its technical inaccuracies and its overall sensationalization of ambulance work. To favor intense trauma responses over less severe events, let alone other high-severity contacts that were not injury-based (e.g., asthma attacks, strokes, and diabetic comas), meant that I would probably reproduce Hollywood fantasies of the ambulance.

It wasn't long before I knew that this project would be less about "trauma work" and more about how ambulance work involves a laboring of suffering bodies more generally. I began to comb through my field notes seeking patterns that complemented and challenged existing scholarship on how suffering populations are governed in the American city. This meant thinking about the ambulance as more than just a medical institution. It meant situating my case among studies of prisons, welfare offices, and other institutions that tend to handle people who agonize near the bottom of a complex urban hierarchy.

I utilized the "extended case method" to advance this endeavor.[3] Beyond my extension into the everyday lives of ambulance crews and supervisors, I aimed to link the microprocesses of ambulance operations to extralocal forces and this necessitated an extension of theory. In other words, I needed a theoretical framework to help make the connections between activities on the ground and the social forces outside and above my field site. Ultimately, the mission of this ethnography was neither a misguided attempt to restate "commonsense" folk categories nor a pointless surrender to scholastic traditions.[4] Instead, I aimed to use theory to see and organize data and use data to stress and evolve theory.

After twelve months of shadowing crews and paramedics, I observed 279 calls. However, I wasn't done yet. For reasons detailed in the preface, I pivoted from a ride-along to a novice EMT.

When adding in these additional calls, I encountered 566 ambulance cases and shadowed or worked with forty-eight paramedics, nineteen EMTs, and eight supervisors across twenty-one consecutive months. Combined with the time I spent training as an EMT, I logged over sixteen hundred hours in the field and compiled nearly five hundred single-spaced pages of typed field notes.

I used a qualitative data analysis software program (ATLAS.ti, version 8.1.3) to code my field notes and help develop the key analytical themes deployed throughout this book (e.g., legit calls). However, besides assembling some simple "code cooccurrence tables" (e.g., tabulating the simultaneous occurrence of legit codes and police codes on the same calls), I did not use the analytical tools in this program. Instead, I basically used this software to index my notes for easy reference while writing.

Table 2 summarizes some of the observed demographics of crews, patients, and supervisors during this time. These data are not drawn from a probability sample, and most rely on *my* imperfect determination of people's race, gender, and age. Next, I detail my transition into, and experiences as, a novice EMT.

BECOMING AN EMT

My shift from ride-along to EMT involved a series of rituals. I only briefly covered these in the preface: a fitness and agility trial, a mannequin-based skills exam, and a fifty-question multiple-choice test covering anatomy and physiology, pre-hospital emergency procedures, and other topics. As you might expect, the details are a bit more complicated.

The EMT training I completed was not enough to become employable at the studied firm. I had to also pass a three-day refresher course, a physical exam, and a written ambulance driver's certificate test at the DMV. Once I completed these relatively easy tasks, I applied to MRT and listed three people at the firm as references: an EMT, a supervisor, and someone in upper management.

The employee-run hiring committee then invited me to a panel interview and a mannequin-based skills test, both of which included evaluators who knew me from my fieldwork. In the interview, I clarified my long-term goals of becoming a sociology professor and doing research in medical institutions. I talked about my research and my desire to learn more about ambulance work. I also confessed to

Table 2   Field Observation Demographics (%)

	Supervisor (n = 8)	Paramedic (n = 48)	EMT (n = 19)	Patient (n = 566)
		Gender		
Male	74.63	75.00	73.68	52.12
Female	25.37	25.00	26.32	45.94
Other/Unknown	.00	.00	.00	1.94
		Race		
White	100.00	72.92	42.11	26.33
Black	.00	8.33	10.53	42.58
Latino	.00	12.50	36.84	14.49
Asian	.00	6.25	10.53	7.95
Other/Unknown	.00	.00	.00	8.66
		Age		
Child/Teen	.00	.00	.00	6.54
20–59	100.00	97.92	100.00	60.95
60+	.00	2.08	.00	30.21
Unknown	.00	.00	.00	2.3

SOURCE: Author's field notes, 2015–2016.

NOTE: Nonprobability sample. Demographics largely dependent on author's interpretation. For events involving more than one patient, demographics are collected for the primary (i.e., most severe) patient. Some percentages do not total 100 due to rounding.

feeling inconsequential in academia and wanting to do something "that mattered." I ultimately stand by my presentation of self in this meeting, even though I couldn't help but put on my "interview face."

The interviewers then asked me to change into some exercise-appropriate clothes for a skills test. I showed a couple paramedics how I could shove an airway adjunct into a mannequin's mouth and ventilate using a bag-valve mask. I then showed them how I would control active bleeding with a tourniquet and told them why I would hypothetically apply a cervical collar to an unconscious person at the bottom of an imaginary stairway.

A few days later, someone from the hiring committee called to invite me to participate in MRT's final prehire challenge: the physical agility test. Among other things, I was tasked with briskly carrying forty or so pounds of equipment up multiple flights of stairs, colifting a 210-pound mannequin off the ground, and performing ten consecutive minutes of compression-only CPR. I was left sore for days, but I was hired.

The company's "New EMT Hire Academy" constituted my first two weeks of employment. With over a dozen other new hires (also mostly male, white, and without 911 work experience), I learned county protocols and company rules. As one of my peers put it, much of this academy was "death by PowerPoint." However, we also spent a significant amount of hands-on time with the firm's equipment (e.g., gurney, monitor, and radio). The academy concluded with another written test and a final skills assessment (e.g., on splinting, spinal immobilization, and delivering a baby) before the instructors brought us to an empty parking lot to teach us how to drive an ambulance.

Once out of the classroom, I was trained for six weeks in the field. For the first week, I was assigned to Danny, who I mentioned a few times in the main text. While Danny obviously knew me from my previous fieldwork, he promised to make my life hell. True to his word, he spent much of three twelve-hour night shifts (from 6:00 PM to 6:00 AM) scolding me for my sloppy driving.

Following a stressful but effective set of shifts with Danny and his partner Mark, I was transferred to Lance, who we also met a few times in the main text. He was my field training officer, and he taught me some important on-the-job skills beyond driving. As he put it, much of this involved *unteaching* me a lot of what he considered to be stale and impractical lessons from the company academy. On our first shift, Lance said something along the lines of, "The academy teaches you all the stuff that keeps them [MRT] from getting sued, I'm going to teach you how to actually do the job." He taught me how to best use equipment, how to efficiently fill out paperwork, and many other technical aspects of the job. But more importantly, along with his regularly assigned partner Vince, Lance taught me a number of taken-for-granted tricks of the trade, like how to handle difficult patients with a firm and dickish voice.

Similar to Danny, Lance knew me well from my previous fieldwork, but he struggled to teach me. Frustrated after our first week together, he said, "It's weird, you're probably the most educated person I've trained, but I keep having to remind you to do the dumbest shit." Early into my training, Lance and Vince both criticized my shaky hands when I spiked IV bags and prepared other equipment. They were also especially irritated with my inability to remember where specific medications and devices were stored in the back of the ambulance. My mediocre knowledge of the county's major streets and highways didn't help either. As noted in the introduction, this led to me drawing and redrawing maps of Agonia County.

Luckily, after three or four weeks on the job and many hours of unpaid studying at home, I improved dramatically. I struck an imperfect rhythm with the technical and interactional aspects of the job. Repetition was my savior. In the end, Lance complimented my fast learning and assured me I would be a "good-enough" EMT.

As an intentionally funny conclusion to my field training, Lance bought me a can of chew. The tobacco chewing ambulance worker is a cliché that we had joked about earlier in my training. Lance said, "You're not leaving my ambulance until you chew. . . . Then you'll be a *real* EMT." I chewed and hated it. Vince was sure to video record my grimaces and awkward spits on his cellphone and share it with a number of our mutual friends at the company. Whether or not this made me a real EMT, I completed my field training that night and was finally free to work without a trainer.

As a part-time employee, I was able to pick up empty shifts on the schedule and cover shifts for full-time EMTs. This gave me the flexibility to spread my work across days and nights and weekdays and weekends. As with my time in training, most of my paramedic partners knew me from the previous year of field-work but those who did not know me always learned of my status as a sociology researcher interested in ambulance operations.

My job as an EMT meant driving a lot while my paramedic partners did most of the clinical work. When I wasn't behind the wheel, I was often on emergency scenes or in the back of the ambulance assisting paramedics by collecting patient vitals, securing limbs to the gurney, and starting my partners' paperwork. As supervisor Grant predicted, I was basically an assistant or "caddie" to paramedics. While many of the EMTs I met found these descriptions demeaning and rightfully noted that they oversimplified the complexity of EMT work, I found them to be pretty accurate. Even county protocols and company rules frame the EMT as a subordinate and supplemental agent to the paramedic. Still, as I noted in the preface, EMT work forced me to confront human suffering in a new and challenging way.

Throughout my nine-month tenure as an MRT employee, I maintained something that might be better described as a "field diary" than as "field notes." Because I was first and foremost an EMT, I did not jot notes in the field as frequently as I did when I was shadowing workers and supervisors. I nevertheless wrote brief notes during downtime, either when my partners and I were "on post" waiting for 911 calls or when we took informal breaks at hospitals between calls. And, not unlike during my time as a ride-along, I always expanded these short-hand notes into longer narratives from home following each shift or a set of consecutive shifts. However, in moving from field notes to a field diary, the content of my writing changed. More so than before, I turned the sociological gaze inward and noted my subjective reactions and acclimations to a world I had already spent a year watching from the sidelines. Among other things, this meant accounting for my own apathetic and sympathetic feelings toward clientele. It also meant contextualizing these personal experiences relative to the themes already detected through earlier fieldwork and through my ongoing conversations with fellow workers.

My critics would be right to note that this method relies heavily on the experiences of one person—myself conflated as both an agent and an object of analysis—and is therefore restricted in its generalizability. I don't deny this limitation. However, I also don't deny that my repositioning from ride-along to EMT was revelatory and significant for the overall analysis offered in this book. Any effort to scrub this experience from the text at hand would have been misleading at best and dishonest at worst. That is why I felt compelled to address this issue in the preface.

And, while an introspective account certainly focuses on a single person, I never analyzed my experiences in a vacuum. I instead made sense of my EMT work through the social relations I was embedded in. I frequently talked about what it was like to "become an EMT" with my colleagues, many of whom knew me first as a ride-along, and they in turn shared personal tips, stories, and opinions to help me make sense of my new location in social space. In other words, I (like anybody anywhere) made sense of myself in reference to others. Any suggestion that my reflections as a novice EMT come from "just a sample size of one" is therefore a bit inaccurate.

MEDICAL RECORDS

In addition to the ethnographic data, I collected 107,208 deidentified medical records. I secured every patient care report completed by an MRT crew in the year 2015. These records include data compiled through a computer-aided dispatch system (which automatically captures variables like the latitude and longitude coordinates of ambulance responses) and information produced by crews in the field (who manually log variables like primary impression). While these records provide weak demographic information (e.g., patient race is an optional field and billing status is often incomplete), they offer somewhat rich data with respect to location of events, medical interventions performed, and workers' narratives.[5] I used Stata/MP (version 13.1) to clean and analyze these data. Table 3 summarizes some relevant descriptive statistics.

To measure the severity of calls, I relied not on dispatch triage data but on the intervention data logged directly by paramedics and EMTs. Previous scholarship on critical and noncritical prehospital interventions—along with consultations with paramedics and EMTs in the field—inspired my decision to calculate frequencies for high-, medium-, and low-severity ambulance contacts.[6] I defined high-severity calls as patient care reports that included one or more of the following interventions: Adenosine, Albuterol, Amiodarone, Atropine, Atrovent, bag-valve mask, bronchodilators, calcium chloride, cardioversion, chest seal, continuous positive airway pressure, cardiopulmonary resuscitation, defibrillation, dextrose, dopamine, endotracheal intubation, epinephrine, glucagon, intraosseous infusion, King supraglottic airway, naloxone, nasopharyngeal airway,

Table 3 Descriptive Statistics on Patient Care Reports

	Mean	Standard Deviation	Min.	Max.
Female	.50	.50	.00	1.00
Age[a]	52.41	22.90	.00	109.00
Child/Teen	.08	.26	.00	1.00
20–59	.53	.50	.00	1.00
60+	.39	.49	.00	1.00
Dispatch Priority				
Alpha (lowest)	.25	.44	.00	1.00
Bravo	.20	.40	.00	1.00
Charlie	.23	.42	.00	1.00
Delta	.28	.45	.00	1.00
Echo (highest)	.03	.17	.00	1.00
Select Primary Impression				
Abdominal[a]	.10	.30	.00	1.00
Alt. Consciousness	.06	.24	.00	1.00
Cardiac	.04	.20	.00	1.00
Overdose/Intoxication	.04	.19	.00	1.00
Body Pain[b]	.12	.32	.00	1.00
Psychiatric/Behavioral	.11	.32	.00	1.00
Respiratory	.08	.27	.00	1.00
Seizure	.03	.18	.00	1.00
Stroke[c]	.01	.11	.00	1.00
Syncope/Near Syncope	.04	.19	.00	1.00
Trauma	.17	.38	.00	1.00
Weakness	.06	.23	.00	1.00
Select Scene Location				
Home	.52	.50	.00	1.00
Street	.16	.36	.00	1.00
Business	.11	.31	.00	1.00
Government Building	.05	.21	.00	1.00
Clinic/Assisted Living[d]	.10	.30	.00	1.00
Intervention Severity				
Low	.62	.48	.00	1.00
Medium	.23	.42	.00	1.00
High	.15	.35	.00	1.00
Crew-Cop Interactions	.21	.41	.00	1.00

SOURCE: MRT deidentified patient care reports, 2015.

NOTE: Observations = 107,208.

a. Includes gastrointestinal bleeding and nausea/vomiting.

b. Nontraumatic, noncardiac.

c. Includes transient ischemic attacks.

d. Includes hospitals, rehabilitation centers, and other medical facilities.

needle decompression, oropharyngeal airway, Pralidoxime (2-PAM), sodium bicarbonate, sodium thiosulfate, ST-elevation myocardial infarction alert, stroke alert, suction, tourniquet, transcutaneous pacing, trauma activation, or Versed. Consistent with previous research, I also coded patient care reports that indicated the "return of spontaneous circulation" as high-severity calls. I defined medium-severity calls as patient care reports that listed no high-severity treatments, but included at least one of the following interventions: aspirin, Benadryl, bleeding control, fentanyl, fluid bolus, glucose paste, nitroglycerin, high-flow oxygen, sepsis alert, spinal motion restriction (collar-only or full), splinting (traction and non-traction), vagal maneuver, or Zofran. I defined low-severity calls as patient care reports that listed no high or medium treatments. They could include the use of electrocardiograms, intravenous locks, icepacks, or low-flow oxygen. I dropped 119 cases (0.1 percent) where paramedics determined death in the field but neither high- nor medium-level interventions were performed. I assume these were calls where crews discovered obviously deceased bodies and didn't "work them."

In the introduction, I noted that I led a team that included a couple of emergency room physicians and a paramedic to run some neighborhood-level analyses on the patient care reports.[7] After eliminating records that fell outside of MRT's primary jurisdiction (e.g., mutual aid calls), we used an open-source geocoding software program (QGIS 2.14.6) to link over 90 percent of the remaining records with a US Census tract shape file for the county. While imperfect, census tracts have moderate to high face validity for approximating neighborhood.[8] Because we were interested in the relationship between neighborhood conditions and ambulance contacts, we identified and dropped cases where the open-ended narratives included keywords suggesting the response occurred on a major highway or bridge. We assumed such calls were more obviously detached from neighborhood conditions. We also layered the tract shape file with Google Maps to review each tract and confirm they were covered by MRT. Following these procedures, we were left with 88,027 records geocoded across three hundred census tracts.[9] We then merged the resulting tract-level file with demographic data from the American Community Survey five-year estimates for 2011 to 2015.[10] After the research team dissolved, I manually coded tracts with metropolitan train stations and tracts with jails or municipal police headquarters (which often include detention facilities).

Table 4 summarizes some of the descriptive statistics for these neighborhood-level data. I used a tract-level dataset to calculate age-adjusted MRT response rates and to run other analyses mentioned in the main text (e.g., regressing the frequency of patient care reports within a tract on poverty and other factors).

As noted in chapter 5, I identified medical records that indicated crew-cop interactions.[11] Table 5 lists the words and phrases I used to capture these interactions in the open-ended narratives that paramedics and EMTs write into their patient care reports. In these narratives, crews are supposed to document pertinent scene details. Such details should indicate whether or not a subject was

Table 4   Descriptive Statistics on Neighborhood-Level Data

	Mean	Standard Deviation	Min.	Max.
Ambulance Contacts	293.42	222.70	29.00	1317.00
Crew-Cop Interactions (%)	19.23	6.80	5.71	54.96
Poverty (%)	12.63	10.45	.00	49.64
Black or Latino (%)	36.78	23.43	.65	95.57
Metro Train Station	.05	.23	.00	1.00
Jail or Police Headquarters	.03	.18	.00	1.00
Density per 1,000 pop	10.18	7.19	.03	41.87
1,000 Population	4.52	1.60	.07	9.63

SOURCE: MRT deidentified patient care reports, 2015; American Community Survey Five-Year Estimates, 2011–2015.

NOTE: Observations = 300. Neighborhoods defined as census tracts.

Table 5   Terms and Phrases Used in the Automated Coding of Crew-Cop Interactions

POLICE	COP	COPS
PD	P.D.	LEO
L.E.O.	LAW ENF	OFFICER
SHERIF (sic)	DEPUTY	ARRESTED
UNDER ARREST	IN CUSTODY	HANDCUFF
HAND CUFF	SQUAD CAR	PATROL CAR
14 "XPD" ABBREVIATIONS		

NOTES: Partial strings (e.g., "LAW ENF") used to capture long and abbreviated texts. Common spelling errors accounted for (e.g., "HAND CUFF" and "SHERIF"). "ARREST" not used to avoid miscoding "cardiac arrest" and "respiratory arrest." Spaces and periods added after "COP" to avoid miscoding of "copy."

found under the supervision or care of a third party, like the police. The keyword, though, is *should*. I've written a number of patient care reports myself and I also watched many paramedics and EMTs do so. Whether due to laziness, forgetfulness, or habit, ambulance workers sometimes fail to document an interaction with law enforcement. Luckily, the ethnographic data suggest crews are usually documenting interactions with the police in their open-ended narratives and the

Table 6 Ordinary Least Squares Regression of Neighborhood-Level Percentages of Ambulance Calls Involving the Police

	Model 1	Model 2	Model 3
Poverty (10%)	1.19**	0.82	-0.11
95% CI	0.34,2.05	-0.28,1.91	-1.04,0.82
Black or Latino (10%)		0.25	0.49*
95% CI		-0.21,0.72	0.10,0.87
Metro Train Station			12.10***
95% CI			9.20,15.00
Jail or Police Headquarters			14.54***
95% CI			11.00,18.07
Density Per 1,000 pop	-0.06	-0.06	-0.02
95% CI	-0.18,0.07	-0.19,0.06	-0.12,0.09
Population Size (1,000)	0.42	0.39	0.16
95% CI	-0.07,0.90	-0.10,0.88	-0.25,0.56
Constant	16.41***	16.15***	15.92***
95% CI	13.65,19.17	13.35,18.95	13.60,18.23

SOURCE: MRT deidentified patient care reports, 2015; American Community Survey Five-Year Estimates, 2011–2015.

NOTES: Observations = 300. Neighborhoods defined as census tracts. CI, confidence interval.

* $p < .05$, ** $p < .01$, *** $p < .001$ (two-tailed tests).

finding that 20 percent of the records involve law enforcement is generally consistent with what I observed in the field.

I also examined crew-cop interactions at the neighborhood level. I used the same 88,027 patient care reports I geocoded across the three hundred census tracts covered by MRT's operations. For each tract, I then divided the frequency of reports that indicated an interaction with the police by the overall frequency of patient care reports and then multiplied the results by one hundred (mean = 19.2, standard deviation = 6.8). As discussed in chapter 5, I regressed the percentage of patient care reports that mentioned law enforcement within each tract on poverty and other factors. Table 6 summarizes the results. The first model suggests a small poverty effect. Controlling for population size and density, this model predicts that a ten-percentage-point increase in tract-level poverty is associated with a 1.2-percent increase in the overall share of crew-cop interactions. Not only is this association weak, the second model suggests that it's not statistically significant when adding in a variable for race (i.e., percentage black or Latino within a tract). It's also noteworthy that the race variable doesn't yield a statistically significant coefficient in this model. However, as evident in the third model, there are some other neighborhood-level factors that are associated with the percentage of crew-cop interactions. Accounting for the other factors just mentioned, tracts with metropolitan train stations and tracts with jails or municipal police headquarters are positively associated with the percentage of crew-cop interactions.

For the purposes of this book, the medical records augment the ethnographic data. They allowed me to triangulate some key patterns revealed in the field.

Notes

PREFACE

1. Seim 2016.
2. Anderson 2000, 138; Duneier 1999, 18; Sánchez-Jankowski 2008, 218.
3. Desmond 2016, 199–201; Stuart 2016, 218.
4. Douglas 1969; Mannon 1992; Metz 1981; Palmer 1983; Tangherlini 1998; see also Corman 2017.
5. Larkin et al. 2006; Meisel et al. 2011; Ruger, Richter, and Lewis 2008; Squire, Tamayo, and Tamayo-Sarver 2010; McConnel and Wilson 1998.
6. Piven and Cloward 1971; Soss, Fording, and Schram 2011; Wacquant 2009.
7. Lara-Millán 2014; Lipsky 1980; Moskos 2008; Watkins-Hayes 2009; see also Brodkin 2011; Ellis, Davis, and Rummery 1999; Evans 2011; Hupe and Hill 2007; Prottas 1979.
8. For reflections on a similar experience, see Sufrin's (2015, 2017) examination of jail-based medicine as both an anthropologist and a physician.

AUTHOR'S NOTE

1. Jerolmack and Murphy (2017) offer a strong critique of "masking" in ethnography. See also Contreras 2019 and Reyes 2018.

INTRODUCTION

1. The victim on this particular call, whom Eric assumed must be a "dealer" if he got shot on this block, had friends drive him to the closest hospital. Unfortunately, the hospital they took him to was not a trauma center and so an ambulance crew had to aid him anyway. They rushed him to a facility better equipped to handle the hemorrhaging in his belly.

2. This area seems to capture what Irwin (1985, 2) calls "rabble," the "lowest class of people," who are not just destitute but also detached and disrepute. Consistent with Irwin's prediction, police heavily patrol this area. However, so do ambulance crews, and instead of sweeping them into the jail these workers connect them to the hospital.

3. Engels ([1885] 1993). See also Chernomas and Hudson 2009; Farmer 2004; Holmes 2013.

4. Benach et al. 2014; Muntaner et al. 2010; Yuill 2005.

5. Bonilla-Silva 1997, 2001; Feagin 2006; Massey and Denton 1993.

6. Gee and Ford 2011; Jones 2002; Williams and Mohammed 2013.

7. Chakravarthy et al. 2010; Chong, Lee, and Victorino 2015; Cubbin and Smith 2002; Wintemute 2015; Yuma-Guerrero 2018; Zebib, Stoler, and Zakrison 2017.

8. Addo et al. 2012; Akinbami et al. 2012; Beckman et al. 2017; Begley et al. 2011; Cox et al. 2006; Davidson et al. 2003; Diez-Roux et al. 1995; Eisner et al. 2011; Elliott et al. 2009; Gottlieb, Beiser, and O'Connor 1995; Hawkins et al. 2012; Kelly 2005; Kerr et al. 2011; Marzuk et al. 1997; McNiel and Binder 2005; O'Driscoll et al. 2001; Phillips and Klein 2010; Visconti et al. 2015.

9. Link and Phelan 1995; Marmot 2004; see also Bourgois et al. 2017.

10. Dohan 2002; Gordon 1999, 2005; Gordon, Chudnofsky, and Hayward 2001; Hock et al. 2005; Malone 1998; Rodriguez 2009.

11. Soss, Fording, and Schram 2011; Wacquant 2009.

12. Gordon 1999; Hansen, Bourgois, and Drucker 2014.

13. Institute of Medicine 2007; Mears et al. 2012.

14. Jacobs et al. 2017. The fragmentation of ambulance operations makes it difficult to provide an exact number for the national distribution of private providers. A report published by the Federal Interagency Committee on Emergency Medical Services suggests 25 percent of agencies are privately run, but they include nontransporting agencies (e.g., first responder fire departments that are intended to stabilize patients on scene before an ambulance arrives) and non-911 ambulances (e.g., agencies that simply perform hospital transfers), and they're missing data for four states (California, Illinois, Virginia, and Washington) (Mears et al. 2012). *The Journal of Emergency Medical Services,* a popular publication in the industry, suggests that 40 percent of the largest two hundred cities in America have a private ambulance company doing "primary transports"

(Ragone 2012). However, their survey of 455 "leaders of the first responder and transport agencies" across the two hundred most populous cities in the United States only yielded a 21-percent response rate and they warn that their study is not peer-reviewed. A similar survey with an 86-percent response rate and conducted by researchers at Johns Hopkins University, but limited to seven Mid-Atlantic states (Delaware, Maryland, New Jersey, North Carolina, Pennsylvania, Virginia, and West Virginia), suggests that 31 percent of the population covered in their studied geography are serviced by a private "primary transport" agency (MacKenzie and Carlini 2008).

15. MRT holds over 80 percent of the 911 ambulance market in Agonia County in terms of population coverage and over 90 percent in terms of square-mile coverage. The remainder of the market is claimed by a handful of municipal fire departments. Before MRT's arrival a few years ago, Agonia County's 911 ambulances were provided by another large for-profit corporation. MRT undercut the competition with promises of cheaper and faster services—promises they said they could keep by deploying a more flexible labor force that would be "dynamically posted" to street intersections between 911 calls. This contrasted the more traditional "ambulance station" model of the previously contracted firm.

16. Institute of Medicine 2007; see also Avsec 2016; Haslam 2015; Maruca 2015; Washko 2015.

17. Biersdorfer 2017; Robinson 2004.

18. Cain 2018; Crum 2017; Rasmussen and Smith 2017; Zekman 2017.

19. Gratton et al. 2010; Honberg 2015; Lopez 2017; Lucas 2016; Myers 2017.

20. Bailey 2017; Hall et al. 2016; Rosenthal 2013; Zamosky 2013.

21. Desmond, Papachristos, and Kirk 2016; Latimore and Bergstein 2017; Mclean 2016; Sasson et al. 2015; Tobin, Davey, and Latkin 2005; see also Bohnert et al. 2011.

22. Bell (2009, 67), author of the most comprehensive history of the ambulance, quotes an unnamed observer in New York from the late nineteenth century as stating, "the ambulance subject is usually a person in poor circumstances. One rarely sees a well-dressed occupant being carried to the hospital by ambulance." In his own words, Bell (2009, 63) notes that around this time, "there was enough disease in the poisonous slums to keep the ambulance horses in Derby-winning trim." This link between paramedicine and poverty continues through his historical description leading up to the early twenty-first century. See also Abel 2011.

23. Bell 2009, 305; EMS1 2014.

24. Bell 2009, 326–27, 334–36; see also Institute of Medicine 2007. Previous ethnographic studies of the ambulance from the 1960s onward also offer clues suggesting the ambulance has long been present in poor neighborhoods, but the details are generally thin (Douglas 1969; Mannon 1992; Metz 1983; Tangherlini 1998).

25. Meisel et al. 2011; see also Ruger et al. 2006; Squire, Tamayo, and Tamayo-Sarver 2010.

26. Seim, English, and Sporer 2017.

27. We found that neighborhood poverty was positively associated with twelve major field diagnostic categories: abdominal, altered level of consciousness, cardiac, overdose/intoxication, nontraumatic pain, psychiatric/behavioral, respiratory, seizure, stroke, syncope/near syncope, trauma, and general weakness (Seim, English, and Sporer 2017). The patient care reports we examined obviously didn't include explicit indicators for what Eric and others call "legit" and "bullshit," but they do include details on the clinical interventions made by ambulance crews. Building upon previous scholarship on critical and noncritical prehospital interventions (Sporer et al. 2010), we calculated neighborhood-level ambulance frequencies by "high"-severity, "medium"-severity, and "low"-severity contacts. Regardless of severity level, we found evidence that poverty was positively and significantly associated with the frequency of ambulance contacts at the neighborhood level. See the appendix for additional details.

28. Our ambulance response time findings (Seim et al. 2018) flew in the face of both journalistic and scholarly claims that ambulances are especially late to aid the poor (Dillon 2013; Govindarajan and Schull 2003; Hsia et al. 2018; Kleindorfer et al. 2006; Love 2014). Unlike much of the previous examinations on neighborhood ambulance response times, we didn't limit our analysis to particular emergencies (e.g., heart attack and stroke). We also didn't operationalize neighborhood using zip code or zip code tabulation area (for a critique of using zip codes in health and health care studies, see Krieger et al. [2002] and Thomas et al. [2006]). That said, our study was imperfect. As Hsia et al. (2018) appropriately note, my team's findings were limited to one county. In the place I call Agonia and during the general period of time this book covers, we confidently concluded that MRT ambulances were not relatively tardy to poorer census tracts.

29. Bergin 2015; Dillon 2013; Gross 2018.

30. Bledsoe 2011; Brown and Sindelar 1993; Donovan 2009; Johnson 2011.

31. Corman 2017; Douglas 1969; Mannon 1992; Metz 1981; Palmer 1983; Tangherlini 1998.

32. Kleinman, Das, and Lock 1997.

33. Holmes 2013, 95. See also Farmer 1996; Kleinman, Das, and Lock 1997.

34. Benach et al. 2014; Desmond 2016; Kalleberg 2013; Shaw 2004.

35. Baradaran 2015; Chapman et al. 2011; Sampson, Wilson, and Katz 2018.

36. Collins and Mayer 2010; Hays 2003; Piven and Cloward 1971; Soss, Fording, and Schram 2011; Watkins-Hayes 2009.

37. Beckett and Herbert 2011; Irwin 2004; Moskos 2008; Stuart 2016; Wacquant 2009; Western 2006.

38. Evans, Richmond, and Shields 2005; Milward and Provan 2003; Marwell 2007; Morgan and Campbell 2011; Smith and Lipsky 1993.

39. Hansen, Bourgois, and Drucker 2014; see also Dohan 2002; Gordon 1999, 2005; Gordon, Chudnofsky, and Hayward 2001; Hock et al. 2005; Malone 1998; Rodriguez et al. 2009.

40. Even those institutions that are purportedly concerned with addressing the general problems of poor and otherwise vulnerable populations, like the county welfare office, are arguably "used mainly to temper the hardships of poverty and ensure that they do not become disruptive for the broader society" (Soss, Fording, and Schram 2011, 1). However, disinterests in eradicating material deprivation and interests in managing its corresponding symptoms are perhaps most obvious in those many institutions that do *not* articulate missions to eradicate poverty and other etiologies of suffering but are nevertheless present and busy in the lives of the poor (e.g., police and emergency departments).

41. Seim 2017.

42. Wacquant 2009.

43. Wacquant (2009) frames the regulation of poor populations as a process occurring through a *bureaucratic field*, extending Bourdieu's (1998, 1–10; 1999, 181–88) conception of the state. Indeed, it's in Bourdieu's work that we find these essential distinctions in verticality (e.g., "higher state nobility" and "lower state nobility") and horizontality (e.g., "Left hand" and "Right hand" of the state). Wacquant's model is more explicitly concerned with poverty. He marries Bourdieu's concepts with Piven and Cloward's (1971) *Regulating the Poor* and other examinations of how the state governs vulnerable populations. The result is a rich argument that is not thoroughly summarized here, but it essentially rests on a vertical and horizontal conception of state power. Wacquant briefly admits a somewhat obvious hierarchal division between "policymakers" from above and the "executants" of policy from below. However, this discussion is brief and in many ways it simply mimics Bourdieu's general division between higher and lower state nobility. Wacquant is far more concerned with explaining relations of horizontality. As part of this, he edits the concept of the Right hand to account for penality, where Bourdieu more or less limits it to the fiscal and pro-market interests of the state.

44. See also Peck 2010. For a critique of the Left-hand and Right-hand distinction, see Morgan and Orloff (2017). They're ultimately concerned that Bourdieu's ambidextrous but still two-handed state oversimplifies the "profusion and multiplicity" of states. This may be true, but Morgan and Orloff don't offer a replacement model that helps us better distinguish, or rather better *position*, state entities on the ground. For my purposes, the Left-Right separation proves useful since the ambulance exists between two quintessential cases of each in the American city: the Left-handed emergency department and the Right-handed squad car.

45. Lipsky 1980.

46. A strict reading of Lipsky's (1980, xi) definition of "street-level bureaucracy" might suggest that it is not really a theory concerning how relatively poor

and powerless populations are managed by the state since it accounts for those worksites where frontline laborers "interact with and have wide discretion over the dispensation of benefits or the allocation of public sanctions." But Lipsky (1980, 54–56) is clear: street-level bureaucracy clientele can be generally described as "nonvoluntary" because they need the resources provided by these agencies (e.g., welfare) or these agencies descend upon them without or with relatively little consent (e.g., policing). In his words, "The poorer the person, the more he or she is likely to be the nonvoluntary client of not one but several street-level bureaucracies" (Lipsky 1980, 54).

47. Brodkin 2011; Ellis, Davis, and Rummery 1999; Evans 2011; Prottas 1979; Watkins-Hayes 2009.

48. Irwin 1970; Seiter 2002.

49. Meléndez, Falcón, and Bivens 2003.

50. Hupe and Hill 2007, 295.

51. Comfort et al. 2015, 115.

52. Lara-Millán 2014.

53. Nolan 2011.

54. In a more recent piece, Lara-Millán (2017) even theorizes the vertical relation between "frontline workers" and "political leaders" as one where the latter consults the former on how to best classify subjects in or out of a given agency or department. This is done to advance a vision of "states as a series of people exchanges." Said exchanges essentially constitute sidewise processes (e.g., moving clientele from a correctional agency to a mental health agency through adjustments in screening and diagnosis). Thus, he considers verticality, but only to explain a more horizontal process (e.g., how political leaders rely on "frontline actors' expertise" to engage in a more lateral struggle with other agencies over who will relinquish or obtain "responsibility for people") (Lara-Millán 2017, 83, 96). Just as Wacquant mentions the executants of policy but favors the vertical and horizontal axes of governance and Lipsky assumes horizontality but focuses on verticality and labor, Lara-Millán points to vertical processes but he does so secondary to his analysis of frontline workers and the more horizontal exchange of governed subjects.

55. For more on similar cross-professional interactions, particularly between law enforcement and executants of the state's Left hand, see Parkinson 1980, Sufrin 2017, and Weiskoph 2005.

56. Burawoy 1979; Ikeler 2016; Leidner 1993; Lopez 2006; Sallaz 2009; Sherman 2007; Viscelli 2016. While they do not deploy the same language, Metz (1981), Mannon (1992), and Corman (2017) can be easily read as studies of an ambulance labor process. Indeed, the book at hand is inspired by the earlier inquiries into paramedic and EMT work. The key difference is that I consider how ambulance labor helps govern suffering as something that's disproportionately carried by down-and-out populations in the American city.

57. Marx (1867) 1978.

58. In more orthodox Marxian terminology, the capacity to work refers to "labour-power," which a person (e.g., a capitalist) buys to use (Marx [1867] 1978, 344). As later articulated by Braverman ([1974] 1998, 37), the worker sells *"not an agreed amount of labor, but the power to labor over an agreed period of time."* When labor power is then in use (i.e., activated) it is "labour itself" and this involves a transformation of the world into useful things or fragments of useful things that may (or may not) be sold for a profit (Marx [1867] 1978, 344). This process of activation and transformation is essentially what we understand to be the "labor process."

59. Burawoy 1979, 15.

60. Burawoy 1979, 15.

61. The vertical asymmetry between medical workers and their patients is an enduring theme in medical sociology and can be traced to Parsons's (1951) theorization of "therapist" and "patient." In no way do most medical encounters constitute moments of total domination, but whatever powers patients have (e.g., "patient rights") are usually overshadowed by the social and cultural authority of care providers (see also Starr 1982; Waitzkin 1991).

PART I. BANDAGING BODIES

1. Here lies another tension between my analysis and Wacquant's. In a plenary address to the Australian Sociological Association, he tells his audience that in order to comprehend the "building of the neoliberal Leviathan," we must abandon the "'ambulance' conception" of the state, which portrays government "as a reactive outfit that tackles 'social problems' such as poverty after they have taken root" (Wacquant 2013, 8). The state, he reasons, is not constituted as much by its reactions as by its capacity to stratify and classify. In his own words, the state "sets the basic coordinates of social space and produces inequality and marginality upstream, before it manages them downstream" (8). The state may generate marginality by legitimating and imposing social categories, but it still takes a reactionary form. I contend that the ambulance is an excellent reference point for understanding how the state, from far downstream, manages the social problems associated with destitution and stigmatization. We shouldn't abandon the ambulance conception of the state, but rather embrace it. Doing so does *not* necessitate an ignorance of the stratifying and classifying capacities of the state, as I'll demonstrate throughout this first set of chapters (e.g., triage, diagnosis, and the imposition of informal categories like "legit" and "bullshit").

2. For a more specific example of ambulance as analogy, see McKee (2015) who likens social housing provision to the ambulance. According to her, such housing in England is "now akin to an 'ambulance service,' which provides

assistance during an emergency or time of crisis, as opposed to being a fundamental right of citizenship and key component of the welfare state" (3).

CHAPTER ONE. PEOPLE WORK

1. Goffman 1961, 74–83.
2. Goffman 1961, 75, 84.
3. Eng 2017; Hseich 2014; Keisling 2015.
4. Foucault 1973, 190.
5. Waitzkin 1991.
6. Link and Phelan (1995) are often credited with the distinction between distal and proximal causes of morbidity and mortality.
7. Foucault 1973, 164.
8. Prottas 1979, 3–4.
9. I also found that crews tended to more quickly doubt the suffering of teenag-
ers. Workers often generalize these kinds of people as "whiny" and "hormonal."
10. Determining the race demographics inside the ambulance proves difficult. The patient care reports do not provide demographic data for workers or
valid race information for patients. Moreover, the 566 calls I encountered in the
fieldwork provide limited insight for a couple of reasons. First, they do not constitute a probability sample. Generalizability is seriously threatened. Second,
race demographics drawn from the fieldwork rely heavily on my vision of race. I
noted my interpretation of patient race in my field notes and it's unclear how well
this corresponds with people's self-identification. I generally did this for workers
too, except I did occasionally ask them what race they identified as. These flaws
in data collection are serious, but such data likely still capture some general patterns in the racial distribution of ambulance encounters. My fieldwork suggests
that nearly two-thirds (64 percent) of paramedics and EMTs are white while
about a quarter of patients (26 percent) are. It suggests that nearly half (43 percent) of patients are black, compared to about a tenth (9 percent) of workers. The
proportion of Latinos (19 percent among workers and 14 percent among clientele) and Asians (7 percent among workers and 8 percent among patients) suggests a relative match in distributions of these groups across the positions of
crew and clientele. I also coded 9 percent of patients as "other" or "unknown" in
my field notes. See the appendix (especially table 2) for additional details.
11. Of the patient care reports I examined, 50 percent of the cases were classified as female. I found roughly the same distribution in my fieldwork. I don't
have representative demographic data on MRT crews. However, of those I shadowed and worked with, 75 percent were male. This distribution seems to also
hold across paramedics (75 percent male) and EMTs (74 percent male). See the
appendix (especially table 2) for additional details.

12. I tested whether there were gendered differences in twelve-lead electro-cardiogram (EKG) screenings for the patient care reports classified as "chest pain" (5,688 encounters, or 5.3 percent of the MRT encounters in 2015). More accurately, I examined cases that fell into one of three primary impression categories determined by providers: chest pain that was not suspected to be cardiac, chest pain that was suspected to be cardiac, and chest pain that was associated with ST-elevation myocardial infarction (STEMI). Of these cases, just over half (50.6 percent) were women. I then performed a logistic regression analysis to estimate the odds of receiving a twelve-lead EKG for chest pain, which both training and protocol recommend irrespective of patient gender. The results suggest that, when controlling for age, female patients with chest pain have 40-percent lower odds of receiving this screening in a paramedical setting (odd ratio = 0.60, standard error = 0.09, p < .001). This finding is generally consistent with similar research in emergency departments (Arnold, Milner, and Vaccarino 2001). Admittedly, without details on medical history and some other potentially relevant data, my analysis may be especially vulnerable to omitted variable bias. Moreover, the patient care reports generally limit me to measuring chest pain as the provider's "primary impression." It's possible that patients articulate chest pain, but that paramedics and EMTs fail to document this. Nevertheless, I'm unaware of any clear theoretical or intuitive reason that would suggest that somehow correcting for this weakness in measurement would explain away the observed gender discrepancy. I should also note that I discovered some optimistic findings unrelated to chest pain. I ran the same analysis on cases where the primary impression was classified as "altered level of consciousness" and found no significant gendered differences in twelve-lead EKG screening when controlling for age. County protocols request this screening for these kinds of cases as well. Still, the gendered discrepancy in twelve-lead EKGs for chest pain patients is concerning.

13. Goffman 1961.

CHAPTER TWO. DITCH DOCTORS AND TAXI DRIVERS

1. I tested three folk hypotheses: (1) legit contacts are positively associated with full moons, (2) legit contacts are positively associated with warmer weather, and (3) legit contacts are positively associated with the first and fifteenth days of the month. Using the patient care reports, I assembled a dataset that captured daily MRT responses for every day in 2015 (n = 365). I then calculated two outcomes: the daily frequency of all MRT responses (mean = 294, standard deviation = 20.8) and the daily frequency of all MRT responses involving high-severity interventions (mean = 43, standard deviation = 7.3). As in other analyses in this book, I assume the latter outcome is a better but certainly an imperfect measure

of so-called legit ambulance calls. To this, I added day-level data on the occurrences of full moons and the maximum recorded temperatures for the county's core municipality. There were thirteen full-moon dates in 2015 and, unsurprisingly, they were not significantly associated with daily frequencies in either all MRT responses or high-severity MRT responses. When I operationalized "hot days" as dates where the maximum temperature was greater than 79 degrees Fahrenheit (less than 10 percent of the observed days), I did find a significant and positive relation between warmer weather and the frequency of *any* MRT response. This simple bivariate regression analysis estimated about nine more calls on hot days (ordinary least squares, coefficient = 8.54, standard error = 4.00, p < .05). However, when I specified the outcome to high-severity responses, and thus presumably closer to what crews consider to be "legit," no statistically significant relation was observed. I also tested whether the first and fifteenth days of the month were positively associated with daily frequencies in either all MRT contacts or high-severity contacts. I generated three dummy variables: one to flag the first day of the months, one to flag the fifteenth day of the months, and one to flag both the first and the fifteenth days of the months. None of these measures was significantly associated with the two outcomes. However, as noted in the main text, welfare benefits are not actually distributed on those dates, and the only reasoning I heard for the supposed increases in ambulance utilization on the first and fifteenth days of the months mentioned "welfare checks" as the key mechanism. So, I also tested whether or not the days in which benefits are actually distributed were associated with a higher frequency of legit runs. Per literature written for welfare recipients in the area, cash benefits are usually distributed between the first and third days of the month while food benefits are usually distributed between the first and tenth days. However, no significant relation was identified when using either of these alternative measures (i.e., between first and third days of the month or between first and tenth days of the month) to predict the daily frequency of high-severity responses. Likewise, I did not find such a relation between these particular dates and the daily frequency of all MRT responses.

2. Palmer 1983.

3. Through his ethnography of medical students, Becker (1993, 33) learned the difference between "crocks" and otherwise legitimate medical cases. The difference here is that paramedics and EMTs are concerned not only with real physical pathologies but also with emergencies that require timely interventions in the field. They often see patients with verified chronic problems but with stable symptoms as "bullshit" cases that are better placed in primary care settings than in emergency medicine (let alone the ambulance). That said, their preferences cannot be reduced to "emergency" alone. They are particularly interested in biomedical emergencies, and are therefore not as concerned with more emotional, social, or even "mental" crises.

4. Palmer 1983.

5. Douglas 1969, 10.

6. Metz 1981, 116–24.

7. Mannon 1992; Palmer 1983; Corman 2017. Mannon (1992, 101–45) might offer the most complexity by specifying certain forms of "good runs" (e.g., cases highlighted in the media, actual "saves," and cases that involve highly technical interventions) and "bad runs" (e.g., "dirty work" and "illegitimate runs"). His concept of "dirty work" often captures what I will call "nightmare calls" and his concept of "illegitimate runs" is generally synonymous with what I call "bullshit calls." There is, however, an essential difference in the observed frequency of "bullshit" and "illegitimate" calls when comparing my analysis with Mannon's. Perhaps because Mannon was researching a less impoverished county at a different period with a stronger overall safety net or because he imposed a stricter operationalization of his concept, he concludes that illegitimate calls "constitutes the smallest number of runs" (Mannon 1992, 125). I insist the opposite. In addition to drawing on over one hundred thousand patient care reports to suggest that most calls are "low-severity," my ethnographic data overwhelming suggest that crews assume most calls are closer to the bullshit end of the continuum.

8. Dohan 2002; Gordon 1999, 2005; Gordon, Chudnofsky, and Hayward 2001; Hock et al. 2005; Malone 1998; Rodriguez et al. 2009.

9. When Douglas (1969, 68–69), arguably the first ethnographer of the ambulance, studied crews, she noticed that the "driver" was like the "captain of the ship" and the "attendant" in the back was tasked with doing the less desirable people work. No longer. The paramedic (today's "attendant") now holds the more honorable position of regulating spaces in bodies while the EMT (today's "driver") handles the less respectable transformation of bodies in spaces. This inversion is likely due in large part to the professionalization of paramedicine, the increased technical scope of the trade, and the contemporary licensing guidelines that more clearly separate the roles of paramedics and EMTs. Regardless of the reason, one thing is for sure: crews today would be generally offended by Douglas's description of ambulance work as "essentially a truck-driving operation" (Douglas 1969, 8).

10. Sporer et al. 2010; see also Seim, English, and Sporer 2017 and Seim et al. 2018.

11. I confirmed the internal validity of this measurement though informal conversations with MRT paramedics and with a physician before imposing it on the medical records.

12. Seim 2017.

13. Many workers insist that the percentage of bullshit responses is higher in the so-called ghettos and hoods and lower in the wealthier and whiter territories. The reality seems to be a bit more complicated. Only a few neighborhoods (i.e., eleven of three hundred census tracts) have less than 50 percent bullshit

responses when we use the intervention data in the patient care reports to estimate severity. Consistent with workers' expectations, these areas are more suburban, have lower levels of poverty, and contain fewer residents of color. For example, the neighborhood with the lowest percentage of bullshit responses (39.7 percent) has a low poverty rate (6.5 percent) and few black or Latino residents (7.7 percent). There are, however, also plenty of wealthier and whiter residential areas that have high percentages of so-called bullshit responses. In fact, the neighborhood with the highest rate of low-severity interventions (77.4 percent) also has a low poverty rate (4 percent) and few black or Latino residents (6.5 percent). But, unlike the suburban neighborhood with the lowest rate of bullshit, this particular area is embedded in the gentrified core of the county and includes plenty of public and commercial spaces (e.g., train station, supermarket, and cafes). Fieldwork taught me that crews were often running into this neighborhood and one's like it to pick up people who do not dwell within formal housing in the area and who are frequently deemed as "out of place" (see chapter 5 for additional details). In contrast, there is simply less variation among areas with the highest proportion of poor residents and residents of color. For example, the ten poorest tracts have low-intervention severity rates between 56 and 71 percent. While insightful, these kinds of comparisons shouldn't distract us from the everyday experience of ambulance work. There are simply more calls near the bullshit end of the continuum than the legit end and all call severities seem to gravitate toward the bottom of the urban hierarchy.

14. Prottas 1979.

15. Mannon (1992, 132–37) discusses something similar: "futile runs." These are "occasions when an all-out effort is expended on a patient whose medical condition is so hopeless that the paramedics have little or no chance for success" (Mannon 1992, 131–32). See also Metz's (1981, 126–28) discussion of "the dead and the dying."

16. Weber (1948) 1991.

17. Goffman 1961.

CHAPTER THREE. FEELING THE AMBULANCE

1. Marmar et al. 2006; Newland et al. 2015; Stanley, Hom, and Joiner 2016.

2. Grevin 1996; Regehr, Goldberg, and Hughes 2002; Collopy et al. 2012.

3. Lipsky's (1980, 82–23) discussion of "coping mechanisms" among street-level bureaucrats (who all seem to face some version of the endless clientele problem) helped me make sense of my new job and the affect it had on my perception and conduct. As he would expect, I learned the taken-for-granted tips for limiting demand and maximizing available resources, and I quickly figured out how to modify my conception of both the job and the clientele to level my expectations.

But this was only part of the story. I had to also figure out a way to "stomach" the pain of my subjects.

4. I hold that my feelings of sympathy for clientele was authentic and not a foolish or automatic embrace of "emotional labor" (Hochschild 1983). Having heart does not mean having a so-called managed heart—a disposition attuned by and to the interests of those who controlled and coordinated my labor. Indeed, there were few "feeling rules" designated, let alone surveilled or enforced, by management at MRT.

5. Hochschild 1983.

6. Goffman 1961, 76.

PART TWO. SORTING BODIES

1. Wacquant 2009; Bourdieu 1998.

CHAPTER FOUR. THE FIX-UP WORKERS

1. Rui and Kang 2014.

2. Centers for Medicare and Medicaid 2012. See also Fields et al. 2001 and Taylor 2001.

3. Dohan 2002; Hock et al. 2005; Malone 1998.

4. Hansen, Bourgois, and Drucker 2014. See also Wamhoff and Wiseman 2005/2006.

CHAPTER FIVE. THE CLEANUP WORKERS

1. Estimates of crew-cop interactions are drawn from my examination of the patient care reports. I identified records where paramedics and EMTs mentioned the presence of law enforcement in their open-ended narratives. This technique almost certainly underestimates the number of times crews and cops interacted on the same scenes during the observed period. See the appendix (especially table 5) for additional details.

2. I regressed the percentage of patient care reports that mentioned law enforcement within each tract on poverty and other factors. See the appendix (especially table 6) for additional details.

3. Streets include highways and sidewalks. In my experience, crews usually classify calls at or near train stations as on a street.

4. The sample size for intervention severity is lower than the overall sample size. Less than 1 percent of cases ($n = 119$) are excluded from the severity scoring. I cut incidents where crews determined death on scene but did not perform a

"high"- or "medium"-level treatment. Sometimes these are called "discovery calls," referring to the discovery of death but the lack of deep intervention. Multiple informal conversations with crews suggested I should not count these cases as low/bullshit or high/legit, because the interventions are absent but the crisis (death) is real. There are more of these events than the patient care reports capture, but firefighters usually make the discovery first and agree to handle the paperwork.

5. My fieldwork suggests that crews and cops interact with many more drunk and high people than what is indicated in figure 8. Crews often understand their clientele to be intoxicated but they don't always list intoxication as the "primary impression" (i.e., the most significant medical problem).

6. Douglas (1966) 2002, 2.

7. Eazy-E 1992; Van Halen 1986.

8. Bittner 1967.

9. Hiday and Burns 2010.

10. Lamb, Weinberger, and DeCuir 2002.

11. Roth 2018; Slate and Johnson 2008.

12. James and Glaze 2006.

13. Roth 2018, 2; Slate and Johnson 2008, 3.

14. Engel and Silver 2001, 245; see also Novak and Engel 2005; Morabito 2007.

15. Berry 2014.

CHAPTER SIX. BURDEN SHUFFLING

1. In the opening pages of the textbook I was assigned during my EMT training, the authors write, "What happens to an injured person before he reaches a hospital is of critical importance. Wars helped to teach us this lesson. During the Korean and Vietnam conflicts, for example, it became obvious that injured soldiers benefit from emergency care in the field prior to transport. . . . We continue to learn about trauma care from the wars in Iraq and Afghanistan and to implement changes in EMS practice based upon the outcomes of those patients" (Mistovich and Karren 2010, 7). A popular trauma care textbook assigned to many paramedic students digs even further back to link paramedicine to Dominique Jean Larrey, Napoleon's chief military physician, who articulated some early principles for fast hospital transport by way of ambulance and care en route (Salomone and Pons 2011, 7).

2. Firefighters were also on scene, but Kyle dismissed them once they helped us load Jose onto the gurney.

3. On a couple of occasions, I saw crews parrot the threat of incarceration to convince clientele to go to the hospital. In both occasions, this was part of a

"CYA" (cover your ass) strategy. The crews worried about being held liable for some potential injury that could occur if they just left the patient, so they used the threat of incarceration to pressure hospital transport. These were, however, exceptional occurrences.

4. Protocols don't explicitly limit choice to the closest three or four hospitals. This is more an informal rule and one imposed by MRT management. Some patients request hospitals across the county or even in one of the neighboring counties, but these requests are rare and not usually guaranteed. The crew may very well want to do some of these longer transports because it can mean avoiding more bullshit, but management actively discourages these long-distance trips and actively monitors for them in real time.

5. For example, Benny, a middle-aged black man who bounced between transitional housing facilities, homeless shelters, and the streets, was known to call 911 from the central part of the county and mandate a transport to a hospital in the western part. After a given crew would take Benny to the parking lot of that hospital he'd abscond before entering the emergency department. He'd simply step off the gurney and walk out of the parking lot and down the street. When Benny wanted to return to the core of the county he'd frequently do the same thing: call 911 and demand a more central hospital. Crews would sometimes try to resist Benny's demands by telling him they'd only be willing to take him to the closest hospital and some even paid him off with cash or food to cancel the transport. These maneuvers were, however, risky violations of protocol and were far less common than just transporting Benny to where he wanted to go.

6. Strategic transports are not the only source of tension between crews and nurses over so-called bullshit cases. For example, nurses sometimes accuse crews of doing some lazy fix-up work (e.g., offering an incomplete assessment or not starting a courtesy IV). However, in my experience as both a ride-along and a worker, the crew-nurse tensions over bullshit cases usually concern transport decisions.

7. On a couple of occasions, supervisors questioned nurses about vindictively, or at least unreasonably, prolonging triage for low-severity cases. Nurses denied intentional delaying in both cases, but crews noticed lower triage times in the minutes and hours following supervisor intervention.

CHAPTER SEVEN. THE BARN

1. Meisel et al. 2011.

2. See also Elliott 2016.

3. Sears 1999.

4. Alexander 2000; Hohl 1996; Police Executive Research Forum 2011; Soss, Fording, and Schram 2011.

5. For similar a discussion, see the scholarship on "new public management" (e.g., Brodkin 2011; Hasenfeld and Garrow 2012; Suleiman 2003).

CHAPTER EIGHT. SUPERVISION

1. In a way, crews have limited access to something that resembles a break room. The barn includes a room with seats, vending machines, and a television. Sometimes, fresh donuts can be found in this room. However, workers rarely enter this space and when they do it's usually at the beginning and ends of their shifts.

2. I heard supervisors call crews a lot of names behind their backs: dumbasses, retards, losers, and the like. I also heard crews, in the relatively private space of the ambulance, tag supervisors with many of the same insults. However, the go-to insult from both directions was "lazy."

CHAPTER NINE. PAYBACK

1. Labor's obedience can also be seen in the way they respond to certain stimuli from above. When protocols change (e.g., certain drug dosage requirements) or when management makes specific requests (e.g., to clear the hospital), crews generally obey. Whether done deliberately or habitually, crews are largely executing the will of those above them.

2. Levels permitting, dispatchers dismiss crews from duty over the radio. However, crews can still be "pulled back" into service so long as the paramedic still has a "narc box" checked out under his or her name. Thus, when dismissed from duty, crews want to reach the barn and return the narc box to the counter as soon as possible. The faster they do this, the lower their odds of being pulled back into service, should levels suddenly dip or a high-priority call happen to drop nearby. Strategic transports during the eleventh hour almost always aim to reduce the distance between hospital and barn.

3. Because fifty minutes is a loose but well-known tolerance threshold for most supervisors, crews are especially interested in hospitals with shorter triage times. If for some reason a crew happens to "hold the wall" (i.e., wait in triage with their patient) for twenty minutes rather than thirty minutes, then they'll usually enjoy ten additional minutes of downtime in the ambulance bay before returning to service. Unless they're at the hospital too, supervisors don't know how long crews wait in triage (i.e., the time an ambulance patient lies down in a hospital bed minus the time of hospital arrival). Their in-rig computers simply tell them current drop times (i.e., present time in the ambulance bay minus the time of hospital arrival).

4. As noted in chapter 7, Bruce emailed the fleet every weekday morning that I was in the field to announce the average drop time from the previous day (or previous weekend if the email came on a Monday). In each of these emails, he attached a spreadsheet that named every crew and all of their drop times. Bruce highlighted everyone's longest drop time in these spreadsheets, which most people seemed to delete or ignore without ever opening. While these emails sometimes included a brief note on how fleet performance was subpar, they often included nothing but these data points and their averages. I'm not sure why Bruce sent these emails, but most of the workers I talked to about this insisted it was a form of intimidation. It seemed to be Bruce's way of saying, "I see you."

5. The monetary drop time bonus would increase to 4 percent if the fleet's average drop time lowered to thirty minutes. It would even rise to 5 percent if drop times fell to twenty-five minutes. For essentially every worker I talked to about this, the thirty- and twenty-minute drop times were laughable, given the typical conditions of hospital triage. The forty-minute goal, however, was not so ridiculous. Following the introduction of the policy, labor actively discussed this option in hospital ambulance bays and on a message board invisible to management.

6. Several paramedics also voiced concern over the legal risks involved in rushed drop times: the pressure to hurry back to service could encourage faster, and thus sloppier, paperwork. Should a paramedic get called into court as a witness or a defendant, their paperwork would be closely scrutinized.

7. Levels permitting and workers willing, management will sometimes request the dispatchers to dismiss a crew a half-hour early if that crew missed a meal break. When this happens, the crew clocks out early but they're paid for the entire shift as scheduled.

8. Most of the struggles over mandation shifts occurred before I started my fieldwork. In fact, per a few employees, some of these struggles predate MRT's arrival to Agonia County. When the previous ambulance provider left the county and MRT took over, the contract required MRT to honor the collective bargaining agreement the previous firm struck with labor.

9. During negotiations with the union, management won something that helped them squash the mando strategy I played. Another hierarchy in mandation availability was applied: full-time workers get dibs before part-time workers. Management admitted to labor in an email that they requested this change to prevent part-timers from picking up few or no straight pay shifts. They assumed, correctly in my estimation, that a handful of part-timers were avoiding straight pay shifts in hopes that they could fill up their calendars with mando.

10. See Jacobs et al. (2017) for a more detailed report on ambulance workers' low wages and long hours.

11. The sociologies of poverty and state sometimes meet at the sociology of time (Auyero 2012; Comfort 2003). I don't deny that poor and otherwise

disadvantaged populations are often waiting for resources and services. My goal is to showcase another temporal experience, that of frontline workers. While clientele are often waiting, workers are often pressured by forces from above to rush through multiple cases and complete interventions in a timely fashion. Thus, while queues may be long, once a person hits the top of the queue they're often rushed through the next stage by the quick hands of tired workers. This often means bodies are hustled from one waiting period to the next.

CONCLUSION

1. Seim, English, and Sporer 2017.

2. Bourdieu, Chamboredon, and Passeron (1968) 1991.

3. Korteweg 2003; see also Pulkingham, Fuller, and Kershaw 2010.

4. Lombardo 1989; see also Liebling, Price, and Shefer 2010; Crawley 2013.

5. Fry 1990; Seim 2016; Sufrin 2017; Weiskopf 2005.

6. Clemmer 1940; Sykes 1958.

7. Lipsky 1980. See also Brodkin 2011; Ellis, Davis, and Rummery 1999; Evans 2011; Prottas 1979; Watkins-Hayes 2009.

8. Wacquant 2009. See also Bourdieu 1998, 1999; Peck 2010; Morgan and Orloff 2017.

9. As noted elsewhere (Seim 2017), my analysis departs from a vision of "bureaucratic fields" and from field theory more generally in sociology. Like a field theorist, I highlight multidimensional relations and assume that state power is embedded in, and exercised through, vertical and horizontal struggle. However, I emphasize an analysis of production over an analysis of "position." Or, rather, I examine social positioning through an analysis of production. In doing so, I break with field theory á la Bourdieu and its various iterations across organizational, economic, and political sociology (Kluttz and Fligstein 2016). The definitive social relation according to my analysis is *not* an endless struggle over the different "species of capital" (e.g., economic, social, and cultural) that supposedly structure a field from top to bottom and side to side. Instead, the definitive struggle is over labor—its pace, its division, and its connections to capital more traditionally understood. This motivates the construction of analytical maps that can seem both familiar and foreign to field theory (e.g., figure 3 in the introduction).

10. Lara-Millán 2014; Nolan 2011. See also Parkinson 1980; Sufrin 2017; Weiskopf 2005.

11. Calams 2017; Jacobs et al. 2017; Ludwig 2010.

12. Kizer, Shore, and Moulin 2013; Krumperman 2010; Iezzoni, Dorner, and Ajayi 2016.

13. Hansen and Metzl 2016; Metzl and Hansen 2014; Neff et al. 2017.

14. See Campbell and Rasmussen (2012) for a similar discussion.

15. Giglio, Li, and DiMaggio 2015; Keane, Egan, and Hawk 2018; Stiell et al. 2003; Swor et al. 2008.

16. Lasser, Himmelstein, and Woolhandler 2006; Lundberg et al. 2008; Navarro et al. 2006; Padgett et al. 2011; Shaw 2004; Srebnik, Connor, and Sylla 2012; Wilper et al. 2009.

17. Kisely et al. 2010; Ross, Schullek, and Homan 2013; Scott 2000; Smith-Bernardin and Schneidermann 2012; Steadman and Naples 2005.

APPENDIX. NOTES ON DATA AND METHODS

1. Emerson, Fretz, and Shaw 2011.

2. Palmer 1983.

3. Burawoy 2009.

4. Bourdieu, Chamboredon, and Passeron (1968) 1971.

5. Over 51 percent of the patient care reports have missing race data. Of those records that include race responses, 50 percent of patients are categorized as "unknown" and 5 percent are listed as "other."

6. Sporer et al. 2010. See also Seim, English, and Sporer 2017; Seim et al. 2018.

7. Seim, English, and Sporer 2017; Seim et al. 2018.

8. Usually designed to capture between twelve hundred and eight thousand residents and partially determined through advice from "local participants" in the US Census Bureau's Participant Statistical Area Program, tract boundaries generally adhere to "visible and identifiable features" (e.g., highways, major streets, bodies of water) and also to "nonvisible legal boundaries" (e.g., municipal borders) (United States Census Bureau 2012).

9. We dropped 473 (less than 1 percent) of the geocoded patient care reports for the response time analysis due to missing or illogical time data.

10. The American Community Survey is an ongoing survey managed by the US Census Bureau and it supplements data from the decennial census with more detailed and up-to-date sociodemographic information (United States Census Bureau 2018).

11. Crews aren't provided with a "police on scene" box to check when completing their patient care reports, and the computer-aided dispatch system doesn't automatically populate these records with data indicating whether or not crews and police were sent to the same scene.

Reference List

Abel, Emily. 2011. "Patient Dumping in New York City, 1877–1917." *American Journal of Public Health* 101 (5): 789–95.

Addo, Juliet, Luis Ayerbe, Keerthi M. Mohan, Siobhan Crichton, Anita Sheldenkar, Ruoling Chen, Charles D. A. Wolfe, and Christopher McKevitt. 2012. "Socioeconomic Status and Stroke: An Updated Review." *Stroke* 43 (4): 1186–91.

Akinbami, Lara J., Jeanne E. Moorman, Cathy Bailey, Hatice S. Zahran, Michael King, Carol A. Johnson, and Xiang Liu. 2012. "Trends in Asthma Prevalence, Health Care Use, and Mortality in the United States, 2001–2010." *NCHS Data Brief* 94:1–8.

Alexander, Jennifer. 2000. "Adaptive Strategies of Nonprofit Human Service Organizations in an Era of Devolution and New Public Management." *Nonprofit Management and Leadership* 10 (3): 287–303.

Anderson, Elijah. 2000. *Code of the Street: Decency, Violence, and the Moral Life of the Inner City.* New York: W.W. Norton.

Arnold, Amy L., Kerry A. Milner, and Viola Vaccarino. 2001. "Sex and Race Differences in Electrocardiogram Use (the National Hospital Ambulatory Medical Care Survey)." *American Journal of Cardiology* 88 (9): 1037–40.

Auyero, Javier. 2012. *Patients of the State: The Politics of Waiting in Argentina.* Durham, NC: Duke University Press.

Avsec, Robert. 2016. "EMS Funding: 6 Alternative Sources." *EMS1*, June 7. www.ems1.com/ems-products/ambulances/articles/97701048-EMS-funding-6-alternative-sources.

Bailey, Melissa. 2017. "Ambulance Trips Can Leave You with Surprising—and Very Expensive—Bills." *Washington Post*, November 20. www.washingtonpost .com/national/health-science/ambulance-trips-can-leave-you-with-surprising—and-very-expensive—bills/2017/11/17/6be9280e-c313-11e7-84bc-5e285c7f4512_story.html?utm_term=.88cc35a08b5a.

Baradaran, Mehrsa. 2015. *How the Other Half Banks: Exclusion, Exploitation, and the Threat to Democracy*. Cambridge, MA: Harvard University Press.

Becker, Howard. 1993. "How I Learned What a Crock Was." *Journal of Contemporary Ethnography* 22 (1): 28–35.

Beckett, Katherine, and Steve Herbert. 2011. *Banished: The New Social Control in Urban America*. New York: Oxford University Press.

Beckman, Adam L., Jeph Herrin, Khurram Nasir, Nihar R. Desai, and Erica S. Spatz. 2017. "Trends in Cardiovascular Health of US Adults by Income, 2005–2014." *JAMA Cardiology* 2 (7): 814–16.

Begley, Charles, Rituparna Basu, David Lairson, Thomas Reynolds, Stephanie Dubinsky, Michael Newmark, Forbes Barnwell, Allen Hauser, and Dale Hesdorffer. 2011. "Socioeconomic Status, Health Care Use, and Outcomes: Persistence of Disparities over Time." *Epilepsia* 52 (5): 957–64.

Bell, Ryan Corbett. 2009. *The Ambulance: A History*. Jefferson, NC: McFarland.

Benach, J., A. Vives, M. Amable, C. Vanroelen, G. Tarafa, and C. Muntaner. 2014. "Precarious Employment: Understanding an Emerging Social Determinant of Health." *Annual Review of Public Health* 35 (1): 229–53.

Bergin, Brigid. 2015. "How Long Is Too Long to Wait for an Ambulance?" *WNYC*, December 9. www.wnyc.org/story/how-long-too-long-ambulance.

Berry, Steve. 2014. "Deciphering When Patients Feign Symptoms to Avoid Incarceration." *Journal of Emergency Medical Services*, August 7. www.jems .com/articles/print/volume-39/issue-8/departments-columns/berry-musing /deciphering-when-patients-feign-symptoms.html.

Biersdorfer, J.D. 2017. "An Alternate Plan in Case of a 911 Failure." *New York Times*, April 7. www.nytimes.com/2017/04/07/technology/personaltech /mobile-phones-911-alternate-plan.html.

Bittner, Egon. 1967. "Police Discretion in Emergency Apprehension of Mentally Ill Persons." *Social Problems* 14 (3): 278–92.

Bledsoe, Bryan. 2011. "EMS System Abuse: The Mystery of the Frequent Flyer." *Journal of Emergency Medical Services*, January 26. www.jems.com /articles/2011/01/ems-system-abuse.html.

Bohnert, Amy S.B., Arijit Nandi, Melissa Tracy, Magdalena Cerdá, Kenneth J. Tardiff, David Vlahov, and Sandro Galea. 2011. "Policing and Risk of

Overdose Mortality in Urban Neighborhoods." *Drug and Alcohol Dependence* 113 (1): 62–68.

Bonilla-Silva, Eduardo. 1997. "Rethinking Racism: Toward a Structural Interpretation." *American Sociological Review* 62 (3): 465–80.

———. 2001. *White Supremacy and Racism in the Post-Civil Rights Era.* Boulder, CO: Lynne Rienner.

Bourdieu, Pierre. 1998. *Acts of Resistance: Against the Tyranny of the Market.* New York: New Press.

———. 1999. *The Weight of the World: Social Suffering in Contemporary Society.* Stanford, CA: Stanford University Press.

Bourdieu, Pierre, Jean-Claude Chamboredon, and Jean-Claude Passeron. (1968) 1991. *Craft of Sociology: Epistemological Preliminaries.* New York: Walter de Gruyter.

Bourgois, Philippe, Seth M. Holmes, Kim Sue, and James Quesada. 2017. "Structural Vulnerability: Operationalizing the Concept to Address Health Disparities in Clinical Care." *Academic Medicine* 92 (3): 299–307.

Braverman, Harry. (1974) 1998. *Labor and Monopoly Capital: The Degradation of Work in the Twentieth Century.* New York: Monthly Review Press.

Brodkin, Evelyn Z. 2011. "Policy Work: Street-Level Organizations under New Managerialism." *Journal of Public Administration Research and Theory* 21 (suppl 2): i253–77.

Brown, Eric, and Jody Sindelar. 1993. "The Emergent Problem of Ambulance Misuse." *Annals of Emergency Medicine* 22 (4): 646–50.

Burawoy, Michael. 1979. *Manufacturing Consent: Changes in the Labor Process under Monopoly Capitalism.* Chicago: University of Chicago Press.

———. 2009. *The Extended Case Method: Four Countries, Four Decades, Four Great Transformations, and One Theoretical Tradition.* Berkeley: University of California Press.

Cain, Sara. 2018. "Hamilton's 'Code Zero' Ambulance Shortages Hit Five-Year-High in January." *Global News,* January 30. https://globalnews.ca/news/3995973/hamilton-code-zero-ambulance-shortages.

Calams, Sarah. 2017. "Private vs. Public Ambulance Services: What's the Difference?" *EMS1,* October 23. www.ems1.com/private-public-dispute/articles/344259048-Private-vs-public-ambulance-services-Whats-the-difference.

Campbell, Hilary, and Brian Rasmussen. 2012. "Riding Third: Social Work in Ambulance Work." *Health & Social Work* 37 (2): 90–97.

Centers for Medicare and Medicaid. 2012. "Emergency Medical Treatment & Labor Act (EMTALA)." www.cms.gov/Regulations-and-Guidance/Legislation/EMTALA.

Chakravarthy, Bharath, Craig L. Anderson, John Ludlow, Shahram Lotfipour, and Federico E. Vaca. 2010. "The Relationship of Pedestrian Injuries to

Socioeconomic Characteristics in a Large Southern California County." *Traffic Injury Prevention* 11 (5): 508–13.

Chapman, Chris, Jennifer Laird, Nicole Ifill, and Angelina KewalRamani. 2011. *Trends in High School Dropout and Completion Rates in the United States: 1972–2009.* Washington, DC: National Center for Education Statistics, US Department of Education.

Chernomas, Robert, and Ian Hudson. 2009. "Social Murder: The Long-Term Effects of Conservative Economic Policy." *International Journal of Health Services* 39 (1): 107–21.

Chong, Vincent E., Wayne S. Lee, and Gregory P. Victorino. 2015. "Neighborhood Socioeconomic Status Is Associated with Violent Reinjury." *Journal of Surgical Research* 199 (1): 177–82.

Clemmer, Donald. 1940. *The Prison Community.* New York: Holt, Rinehart and Winston.

Collins, Jane L., and Victoria Mayer. 2010. *Both Hands Tied: Welfare Reform and the Race to the Bottom in the Low-Wage Labor Market.* Chicago: University of Chicago Press.

Collopy, Kevin T. 2012. "Are You under Stress in EMS?" *EMS World,* September 10. www.emsworld.com/article/10776875/are-you-under-stress-ems.

Comfort, Megan L. 2003. "In The Tube At San Quentin: The 'Secondary Prisonization' of Women Visiting Inmates." *Journal of Contemporary Ethnography* 32 (1): 77–107.

Comfort, Megan, Andrea M. Lopez, Christina Powers, Alex H. Kral, and Jennifer Lorvick. 2015. "How Institutions Deprive: Ethnography, Social Work, and Interventionist Ethics among the Hypermarginalized." *RSF* 1 (1): 100–119.

Contreras, Randol. 2019. "Transparency and Unmasking Issues in Ethnographic Crime Research: Methodological Considerations." *Sociological Forum* 34 (2): 293–312.

Corman, Michael K. 2017. *Paramedics on and off the Streets: Emergency Medical Services in the Age of Technological Governance.* Toronto, ON: University of Toronto Press.

Cox, Anna M., Christopher McKevitt, Anthony G. Rudd, and Charles DA Wolfe. 2006. "Socioeconomic Status and Stroke." *Lancet Neurology* 5 (2): 181–88.

Crawley, Elaine. 2013. *Doing Prison Work: The Public and Private Lives of Prison Officers.* New York: Routledge.

Crum, William. 2017. "Ambulance Availability Troubles Persist in Oklahoma City, but Have Eased since 2015." *NewsOK,* October 17. http://newsok.com /ambulance-availability-troubles-persist-in-oklahoma-city-but-have-eased-since-2015/article/5568413.

Cubbin, Catherine, and Gordon S. Smith. 2002. "Socioeconomic Inequalities in Injury: Critical Issues in Design and Analysis." *Annual Review of Public Health* 23 (1): 349–75.

Davidson, Peter J., Rachel L. McLean, Alex H. Kral, Alice A. Gleghorn, Brian R. Edlin, and Andrew R. Moss. 2003. "Fatal Heroin-Related Overdose in San Francisco, 1997–2000: A Case for Targeted Intervention." *Journal of Urban Health: Bulletin of the New York Academy of Medicine* 80 (2): 261–73.

Desmond, Matthew. 2016. *Evicted: Poverty and Profit in the American City.* New York: Crown.

Desmond, Matthew, Andrew V. Papachristos, and David S. Kirk. 2016. "Police Violence and Citizen Crime Reporting in the Black Community." *American Sociological Review* 81 (5): 857–76.

Diez-Roux, Ana V., F. Javier Nieto, Herman A. Tyroler, Larry D. Crum, and Moyses Szklo. 1995. "Social Inequalities and Atherosclerosis: The Atherosclerosis Risk in Communities Study." *American Journal of Epidemiology* 141 (10): 960–72.

Dillon, Liam. 2013. "Close Calls: When Emergency Help Comes Late." *Voice of San Diego,* July 22. www.voiceofsandiego.org/neighborhoods/close-calls-when-emergency-help-comes-late/).

Dohan, Daniel. 2002. "Managing Indigent Care: A Case Study of a Safety-Net Emergency Department." *Health Services Research* 37 (2): 361–76.

Donovan, Robert. 2009. "Why Ambulance Abuse Happens and How to Fix It." *EMS1,* December 16. www.ems1.com/ems-management/articles/682274-Why-ambulance-abuse-happens-and-how-to-fix-it.

Douglas, Dorothy J. 1969. *Occupational and Therapeutic Contingencies of Ambulance Services in Metropolitan Areas.* Unpublished PhD thesis, University of California, Davis.

Douglas, Mary. (1966) 2002. *Purity and Danger: An Analysis of Concepts of Pollution and Taboo.* New York: Routledge.

Duneier, Mitchell. 1999. *Sidewalk.* New York: Farrar, Straus and Giroux.

Eazy-E. 1992. *5150: Home 4 Tha Sick.* CD. Los Angeles: Ruthless Records.

Eisner, Mark D., Paul D. Blanc, Theodore A. Omachi, Edward H. Yelin, Stephen Sidney, Patricia P. Katz, Lynn M. Ackerson, Gabriela Sanchez, Irina Tolstykh, and Carlos Iribarren. 2011. "Socioeconomic Status, Race and COPD Health Outcomes." *Journal of Epidemiology & Community Health* 65 (1): 26–34.

Elliott, John O., Bo Lu, Bassel F. Shneker, J. Layne Moore, and James W. McAuley. 2009. "The Impact of 'Social Determinants of Health' on Epilepsy Prevalence and Reported Medication Use." *Epilepsy Research* 84 (2/3): 135–45.

Elliott, Ross. 2016. "Executive Director's Report: SB 1300—an Increase in Medi-Cal Rate Comes at a Cost." *Siren,* Summer 2016): 2–5. www.the-caa.org/docs/siren/CAA-Siren-16-2.pdf.

Ellis, Kathryn, Ann Davis, and Kirstein Rummery. 1999. "Needs Assessment, Street-Level Bureaucracy and the New Community Care." *Social Policy & Administration* 33 (3): 262–80.

Emerson, Robert M., Rachel I. Fretz, and Linda L. Shaw. 2011. *Writing Ethnographic Fieldnotes*, 2nd ed. Chicago: University of Chicago Press.

EMS1. 2014. "How Pittsburgh's 'Freedom House' Shaped Modern EMS Systems." *EMS1*, January 31. www.ems1.com/ems-management/articles/1977832-How-Pittsburghs-Freedom-House-shaped-modern-EMS-systems/.

Eng, Monica. 2017. "Why Send a Firetruck to Do an Ambulance's Job?" *National Public Radio*, April 11. www.npr.org/sections/health-shots/2017/04/11/523025987/why-send-a-firetruck-to-do-an-ambulances-job.

Engel, Robin Shepard, and Eric Silver. 2001. "Policing Mentally Disordered Suspects: A Reexamination of the Criminalization Hypothesis." *Criminology* 39 (2): 225–52.

Engels, Friedrich. (1885) 1993. *The Condition of the Working Class in England*. Edited by D. McLellan. Oxford: Oxford University Press.

Evans, Bryan, Ted Richmond, and John Shields. 2005. "Structuring Neoliberal Governance: The Nonprofit Sector, Emerging New Modes of Control and the Marketisation of Service Delivery." *Policy and Society* 24 (1): 73–97.

Evans, Tony. 2011. "Professionals, Managers and Discretion: Critiquing Street-Level Bureaucracy." *British Journal of Social Work* 41 (2): 368–86.

Farmer, Paul. 1996. "On Suffering and Structural Violence: A View from Below." *Daedalus* 125 (1): 261–83.

———. 2004. "An Anthropology of Structural Violence." *Current Anthropology* 45 (3): 305–25.

Feagin, Joe. 2006. *Systemic Racism: A Theory of Oppression*. New York: Routledge.

Fields, W. Wesley, Brent R. Asplin, Gregory L. Larkin, Catherine A. Marco, Loren A. Johnson, Charlotte Yeh, Keith T. Ghezzi, and Michael Rapp. 2001. "The Emergency Medical Treatment and Labor Act as a Federal Health Care Safety Net Program." *Academic Emergency Medicine* 8 (11): 1064–69.

Foucault, Michael. 1973. *The Birth of a Clinic: The Archaeology of Medical Perception*. New York: Vintage.

Fry, Lincoln J. 1990. "Counselor Reactions to Work in Prison Settings." *Journal of Offender Counseling Services Rehabilitation* 14 (1): 121–32.

Gee, Gilbert C., and Chandra L. Ford. 2011. "Structural Racism and Health Inequalities: Old Issues, New Directions." *Du Bois Review* 8 (1): 115–32.

Giglio, Rebecca E., Guohua Li, and Charles J. DiMaggio. 2015. "Effectiveness of Bystander Naloxone Administration and Overdose Education Programs: A Meta-Analysis." *Injury Epidemiology* 2 (10): 1–9.

Goffman, Erving. 1961. *Asylums: Essays on the Social Situation of Mental Patients and Other Inmates*. New York: Anchor.

Gordon, James A. 1999. "The Hospital Emergency Department as a Social Welfare Institution." *Annals of Emergency Medicine* 33 (3): 321–25.

———. 2005. "The Science of Common Sense: Integrating Health and Human Services in the Hospital Emergency Department." *Annals of Emergency Medicine* 45 (3): 251–52.

Gordon, James A., Carl R. Chudnofsky, and Rodney A. Hayward. 2001. "Where Health and Welfare Meet: Social Deprivation among Patients in the Emergency Department." *Journal of Urban Health* 78 (1): 104–11.

Gottlieb, Daniel J., Alexa S. Beiser, and George T. O'Connor. 1995. "Poverty, Race, and Medication Use Are Correlates of Asthma Hospitalization Rates: A Small Area Analysis in Boston." *CHEST* 108 (1): 28–35.

Govindarajan, Anand, and Michael Schull. 2003. "Effect of Socioeconomic Status on Out-of-Hospital Transport Delays of Patients with Chest Pain." *Annals of Emergency Medicine* 41 (4): 481–90.

Gratton, Matthew, Alex Garza, Joseph Salomone, James McElroy, and Jason Shearer. 2010. "Ambulance Staging for Potentially Dangerous Scenes: Another Hidden Component of Response Time." *Prehospital Emergency Care* 14 (3): 340–44.

Grevin, Francine. 1996. "Posttraumatic Stress Disorder, Ego Defense Mechanisms, and Empathy among Urban Paramedics." *Psychological Reports* 79 (2): 483–95.

Gross, Samantha J. 2018. "East Boston Getting by with 1 Dedicated Ambulance." *Boston Globe,* January 5. www.bostonglobe.com/metro/2018/01/05 /ambulance-response-times-rise-east-boston-waits-for-reinforcements /So6fcqgMgQgZZNgnhGg2uJ/story.html.

Hall, Mark A., Paul B. Ginsburg, Steven M. Lieberman, Loren Adler, Caitlin Brandt, and Margaret Darling. 2016. "Solving Surprise Medical Bills." *Schaeffer Initiative for Innovation in Health Policy, a Brookings Institution— USC Schaeffer Center Partnership.* http://healthpolicy.usc.edu/documents /Solving%20Surprise%20Medical%20Bills_102016.pdf.

Hansen, Helena, Philippe Bourgois, and Ernest Drucker. 2014. "Pathologizing Poverty: New Forms of Diagnosis, Disability, and Structural Stigma under Welfare Reform." *Social Science & Medicine* 103:76–83.

Hansen, Helena, and Jonathan Metzl. 2016. "Structural Competency in the U.S. Healthcare Crisis: Putting Social and Policy Interventions Into Clinical Practice." *Journal of Bioethical Inquiry* 13 (2): 179–83.

Hasenfeld, Yeheskel, and Eve Garrow. 2012. "Nonprofit Human-Service Organizations, Social Rights, and Advocacy in a Neoliberal Welfare State." *Social Service Review* 86 (2): 295–322.

Haslam, Julie. 2015. "Emergency Medical Services: Decreasing Revenue and the Regulated Healthcare Environment. Will Ambulance Transport Providers Survive?" *Journal of Health Care Finance* 42 (2): 2–16.

Hawkins, Nathaniel M., Pardeep S. Jhund, John J. V. McMurray, and Simon Capewell. 2012. "Heart Failure and Socioeconomic Status: Accumulating

Evidence of Inequality." *European Journal of Heart Failure* 14 (2): 138–46.

Hays, Sharon. 2003. *Flat Broke with Children: Women in the Age of Welfare Reform*. New York: Oxford University Press.

Hiday, Virginia Aldeigé, and Padraic J. Burns. 2010. "Mental Illness and the Criminal Justice System." In *A Handbook for the Study of Mental Health*, edited by T. L. Scheid and T. N. Brown, 478–98. Cambridge: Cambridge University Press.

Hochschild, Arlie Russell. 1983. *The Managed Heart: Commercialization of Human Feeling*. Berkeley: University of California Press.

Hock, Marcus Ong Eng, Joseph P. Ornato, Courtney Cosby, and Thomas Franck. 2005. "Should the Emergency Department Be Society's Health Safety Net?" *Journal of Public Health Policy* 26 (3): 269–81.

Hohl, Karen L. 1996. "The Effects of Flexible Work Arrangements." *Nonprofit Management and Leadership* 7 (1): 69–86.

Holmes, Seth. 2013. *Fresh Fruit, Broken Bodies: Migrant Farmworkers in the United States*. Berkeley: University of California Press.

Honberg, Ron. 2015. "Should Police Accommodate People with Mental Illness in Crisis? The Supreme Court Weights In—Kind Of." *National Alliance on Mental Illness*, May 19. www.nami.org/Blogs/NAMI-Blog/May-2015 /Should-Police-Accommodate-People-with-Mental-Illne.

Hseich, Arthur. 2014. "More Medical Calls May Lead to Fire Department Overhauls." *EMS1*, September 25. www.ems1.com/ems-management/articles /1995766-More-medical-calls-may-lead-to-fire-department-overhauls.

Hsia, Renee Y., Delphine Huang, N. Clay Mann, Christopher Colwell, Mary P. Mercer, Mengtao Dai, and Matthew J. Niedzwiecki. 2018. "A US National Study of the Association between Income and Ambulance Response Time in Cardiac Arrest." *JAMA Network Open* 1 (7): e185202.

Hupe, Peter, and Michael Hill. 2007. "Street-Level Bureaucracy and Public Accountability." *Public Administration* 85 (2): 279–99.

Iezzoni, Lisa I., Stephen C. Dorner, and Toyin Ajayi. 2016. "Community Paramedicine—Addressing Questions as Programs Expand." *New England Journal of Medicine* 374 (12): 1107–9.

Ikeler, Peter. 2016. *Hard Sell: Work and Resistance in Retail Chains*. Ithaca, NY: Cornell University Press.

Institute of Medicine. 2007. "Emergency Medical Services: At the Crossroads." www.nap.edu/catalog/11629/emergency-medical-services-at-the-crossroads.

Irwin, John. 1970. *The Felon*. Berkeley: University of California Press.

———. 1985. *The Jail: Managing the Underclass in American Society*. Berkeley: University of California Press.

———. 2004. *The Warehouse Prison: Disposal of the New Dangerous Class*. Los Angeles: Roxbury.

Jacobs, Ken, Nereida Heller, Saba Waheed, and Sam Appel. 2017. "Emergency Medical Services in California: Wages, Working Conditions, and Industry Profile." UC Berkeley Center for Labor Research and Education. http://laborcenter.berkeley.edu/pdf/2017/emergency-medical-services-in-california.pdf.

James, Doris J., and Lauren E. Glaze. 2006. *Mental Health Problems of Prison and Jail Inmates*. Washington, DC: Bureau of Justice Statistics, US Department of Justice.

Jerolmack, Colin, and Alexandra K. Murphy. 2017. "The Ethical Dilemmas and Social Scientific Trade-Offs of Masking in Ethnography." *Sociological Methods & Research*. https://doi.org/10.1177/0049124117701483.

Johnson, Jacob. 2011. "Homeless Patients Pose Unique Problems for EMS." *EMS1*, September 6. www.ems1.com/medical-clinical/articles/1119239-Homeless-patients-pose-unique-problems-for-EMS.

Jones, Camara Phyllis. 2002. "Confronting Institutionalized Racism." *Phylon* 50 (1/2): 7–22.

Kalleberg, Arne L. 2013. *Good Jobs, Bad Jobs: The Rise of Polarized and Precarious Employment Systems in the United States 1970s to 2000s*. New York: Russell Sage Foundation.

Keane, Christopher, James E. Egan, and Mary Hawk. 2018. "Effects of Naloxone Distribution to Likely Bystanders: Results of an Agent-Based Model." *International Journal of Drug Policy* 55:61–69.

Keisling, Phil. 2015. "Why We Need to Take the 'Fire' Out of 'Fire Department.'" *Governing*, July 1. www.governing.com/columns/smart-mgmt/col-fire-departments-rethink-delivery-emergency-medical-services.html.

Kelly, Brendan D. 2005. "Structural Violence and Schizophrenia." *Social Science & Medicine* 61 (3): 721–30.

Kerr, Gillian D., Peter Higgins, Matthew Walters, Sandip K. Ghosh, Fiona Wright, Peter Langhorne, and David J. Stott. 2011. "Socioeconomic Status and Transient Ischaemic Attack/Stroke: A Prospective Observational Study." *Cerebrovascular Diseases* 31 (2): 130–37.

Kisely, Stephen, Leslie Anne Campbell, Sarah Peddle, Susan Hare, Mary Pyche, Don Spicer, and Bill Moore. 2010. "A Controlled before-and-after Evaluation of a Mobile Crisis Partnership between Mental Health and Police Services in Nova Scotia." *Canadian Journal of Psychiatry* 55 (10): 662–68.

Kizer, Kenneth W., Karen Shore, and Aimee Moulin. 2013. "Community Paramedicine: A Promising Model for Integrating Emergency and Primary Care." UC Davis Institute for Population Health Improvement. www.ucdmc.ucdavis.edu/iphi/publications/reports/resources/IPHI_CommunityParamedicineReport_Final%20070913.pdf.

Kleindorfer, Dawn O., Christoper J. Lindsell, Joseph P. Broderick, Matthew L. Flaherty, Daniel Woo, Irene Ewing, Pam Schmit, Charles Moomaw,

Kathleen Alwell, Arthur Pancioli, Edward Jauch, Jane Khoury, Rosie Miller, Alexander Schneider, and Brett M. Kissela. 2006. "Community Socioeconomic Status and Prehospital Times in Acute Stroke and Transient Ischemic Attack Do Poorer Patients Have Longer Delays from 911 Call to the Emergency Department?" *Stroke* 37 (6): 1508–13.

Kleinman, Arthur, Veena Das, and Margaret M. Lock. 1997. *Social Suffering*. Berkeley: University of California Press.

Kluttz, Daniel, and Neil Fligstein. 2016. "Varieties of Sociological Field Theory." In *Handbook of Contemporary Sociological Theory*, edited by S. Abrutyn, 185–204. Cham, Switzerland: Springer International.

Korteweg, Anna. 2003. "Welfare Reform and the Subject of the Working Mother: 'Get a Job, a Better Job, Then a Career.'" *Theory and Society* 32 (4): 445–80.

Krieger, Nancy, Pamela Waterman, Jarvis T. Chen, Mah-Jabeen Soobader, S.V. Subramanian, and Rosa Carson. 2002. "Zip Code Caveat: Bias Due to Spatiotemporal Mismatches between Zip Codes and US Census–Defined Geographic Areas—the Public Health Disparities Geocoding Project." *American Journal of Public Health* 92 (7): 1100–1102.

Krumperman, Kurt. 2010. "History of Community Paramedicine." *Journal of Emergency Medical Services*, June 22. www.jems.com/articles/2010/06/history-community-paramedicine.html.

Lamb, H. Richard, Linda E. Weinberger, and Walter J. DeCuir. 2002. "The Police and Mental Health." *Psychiatric Services* 53 (10): 1266–71.

Lara-Millán, Armando. 2014. "Public Emergency Room Overcrowding in the Era of Mass Imprisonment." *American Sociological Review* 79 (5): 866–87.

———. 2017. "States as a Series of People Exchanges." In *The Many Hands of the State: Theorizing Political Authority and Social Control*, edited by K.J. Morgan and A.S. Orloff, 81–102. Cambridge: Cambridge University Press.

Larkin, Gregory Luke, Cynthia A. Claassen, Andrea J. Pelletier, and Carlos A. Camargo. 2006. "National Study of Ambulance Transports to United States Emergency Departments: Importance of Mental Health Problems." *Prehospital and Disaster Medicine* 21 (2): 82–90.

Lasser, Karen E., David U. Himmelstein, and Steffie Woolhandler. 2006. "Access to Care, Health Status, and Health Disparities in the United States and Canada: Results of a Cross-National Population-Based Survey." *American Journal of Public Health* 96 (7): 1300–1307.

Latimore, Amanda D., and Rachel S. Bergstein. 2017. "'Caught with a Body' yet Protected by Law? Calling 911 for Opioid Overdose in the Context of the Good Samaritan Law." *International Journal on Drug Policy* 50:82–89.

Leidner, Robin. 1993. *Fast Food, Fast Talk: Service Work and the Routinization of Everyday Life*. Berkeley: University of California Press.

Levy, Jonah D. 2010. "Welfare Retrenchment." In *The Oxford Handbook of the Welfare State*, edited by F.G. Castles, S. Leibfried, J. Lewis, H. Obingerand, and C. Pierson, 552–65. Oxford: Oxford University Press.

Liebling, Alison, David Price, and Guy Shefer. 2010. *The Prison Officer*. New York: Willan.

Link, Bruce G., and Jo Phelan. 1995. "Social Conditions as Fundamental Causes of Disease." *Journal of Health and Social Behavior* 35:80–94.

Lipsky, Michael. 1980. *Street-Level Bureaucracy: Dilemmas of the Individual in Public Service*. New York: Russell Sage Foundation.

Lombardo, Lucien. 1989. *Guards Imprisoned: Correctional Officers at Work*. New York: Routledge.

Lopez, German. 2017. "He Helped His Overdosing Friend by Calling 911: Police Slapped Him with a Manslaughter Charge." *Vox*, May 24. www.vox.com/policy-and-politics/2017/5/24/15684664/opioid-epidemic-manslaughter-overdose-charge.

Lopez, Steven H. 2006. "Emotional Labor and Organized Emotional Care Conceptualizing Nursing Home Care Work." *Work and Occupations* 33 (2): 133–60.

Love, David. 2014. "Opinion: Is 911 'Still a Joke' for African-Americans?" *Grio*, April 23. http://thegrio.com/2014/04/23/is-911-still-a-joke-for-african-americans.

Lucas, Liza. 2016. "Changing the Way Police Respond to Mental Illness." *CNN*, September 28. www.cnn.com/2015/07/06/health/police-mental-health-training/index.html.

Ludwig, Gary. 2010. "Public vs. Private Ambulance Service." *Firehouse*, September 29. www.firehouse.com/home/article/10466494/iafc-iaff-and-metro-chiefs-issue-advisory-on-amr-activities.

Lundberg, Olle, Monica Åberg Yngwe, Maria Kölegård Stjärne, Jon Ivar Elstad, Tommy Ferrarini, Olli Kangas, Thor Norström, Joakim Palme, and Johan Fritzell. 2008. "The Role of Welfare State Principles and Generosity in Social Policy Programmes for Public Health: An International Comparative Study." *Lancet* 372 (9650): 1633–40.

MacKenzie, Ellen J., and Anthony R. Carlini. 2008. "Configurations of EMS Systems: A Pilot Study." *U.S. Department of Transportation, National Highway Traffic Safety Administration*. www.ems.gov/pdf/research/Studies-and-Reports/Configuration_of_EMS_Systems.pdf.

Malone, Ruth E. 1998. "Whither the Almshouse? Overutilization and the Role of the Emergency Department." *Journal of Health Politics, Policy and Law* 23 (5): 795–832.

Mannon, James. 1992. *Emergency Encounters: EMTs and Their Work*. Boston: Jones and Bartlett.

Marmar, Charles R., Shannon E. McCaslin, Thomas J. Metzler, Suzanne Best, Daniel S. Weiss, Jeffery Fagan, Akiva Liberman, Nnamdi Pole, Christian Otte, Rachel Yehuda, David Mohr, and Thomas Neylan. 2006. "Predictors of Posttraumatic Stress in Police and Other First Responders." *Annals of the New York Academy of Sciences* 1071 (1): 1–18.

Marmot, Michael. 2004. *The Status Syndrome: How Social Standing Affects Our Health and Longevity.* New York: Henry Holt.

Maruca, Joe. 2015. "Factors to Consider for Fire Departments Thinking about Providing Ambulance Service." *National Volunteer Fire Council,* August 18. www.nvfc.org/factors-to-consider-for-fire-departments-thinking-about-providing-ambulance-service.

Marwell, Nicole P. 2007. *Bargaining for Brooklyn: Community Organizations in the Entrepreneurial City.* Chicago: University of Chicago Press.

Marx, Karl. (1867) 1978. "Capital, Volume One." In *The Marx-Engels Reader,* edited by Robert C. Tucker, 294–438. New York: W. W. Norton.

Marzuk, Peter M., Kenneth Tardiff, Andrew C. Leon, Charles S. Hirsch, Marina Stajic, Laura Portera, and Nancy Hartwell. 1997. "Poverty and Fatal Accidental Drug Overdoses of Cocaine and Opiates in New York City: An Ecological Study." *American Journal of Drug and Alcohol Abuse* 23 (2): 221–28.

Massey, Douglas S., and Nancy A. Denton. 1993. *American Apartheid: Segregation and the Making of the Underclass.* Cambridge, MA: Harvard University Press.

McConnel, Charles E., and Rosemary W. Wilson. 1998. "The Demand for Prehospital Emergency Services in an Aging Society." *Social Science & Medicine* 46 (8): 1027–31.

McKee, Kim. 2015. "An Introduction to the Special Issue—the Big Society, Localism and Housing Policy: Recasting State-Citizen Relations in an Age of Austerity." *Housing, Theory and Society* 32 (1): 1–8.

Mclean, Katherine. 2016. "Good Samaritans vs. Predatory Peddlers: Problematizing the War on Overdose in the United States." *Journal of Crime and Justice* 41 (1): 1–13.

McNiel, Dale E., and Renée L. Binder. 2005. "Psychiatric Emergency Service Use and Homelessness, Mental Disorder, and Violence." *Psychiatric Services* 56 (6): 699–704.

Mears, Greg, Beth Armstrong, Antonio R. Fernandez, Clay Mann, Kevin McGinnis, Cindy Raisor Mears, Nels D. Sanddal, Teri L. Sanddal, and Fraces S. Shofer. 2012. *National EMS Assessment.* Washington, DC: Federal Interagency Committee on Emergency Medical Services, US Department of Transportation, National Highway Traffic Safety Administration. www.ems.gov/pdf/2011/National_EMS_Assessment_Final_Draft_12202011.pdf.

Meisel, Zachary F., Jesse M. Pines, Daniel Polsky, Joshua P. Metlay, Mark D. Neuman, and Charles C. Branas. 2011. "Variations in Ambulance Use in the

United States: The Role of Health Insurance." *Academic Emergency Medicine* 18 (10): 1036–44.

Meléndez, Edwin, Luis Falcón, and Josh Bivens. 2003. "Community College Participation in Welfare Programs: Do State Policies Matter?" *Community College Journal of Research and Practice* 27 (3): 203–23.

Metz, Donald. 1981. *Running Hot: Structure and Stress in Ambulance Work.* Cambridge, MA: Abt.

Metzl, Jonathan M., and Helena Hansen. 2014. "Structural Competency: Theorizing a New Medical Engagement with Stigma and Inequality." *Social Science & Medicine* 103:126–33.

Milward, Brinton, and Keith Provan. 2003. "Managing the Hollow State: Collaboration and Contracting." *Public Management Review* 5 (1): 1–18.

Mistovich, Joseph J., and Keith J. Karren. 2010. *Prehospital Emergency Care.* 9th ed. Boston: Pearson.

Morabito, Melissa Schaefer. 2007. "Horizons of Context: Understanding the Police Decision to Arrest People with Mental Illness." *Psychiatric Services* 58 (12): 1582–87.

Morgan, Kimberly J., and Andrea Louise Campbell. 2011. *The Delegated Welfare State: Medicare, Markets, and the Governance of Social Policy.* Oxford: Oxford University Press.

Morgan, Kimberly J., and Ann Shola Orloff. 2017. "Introduction." In *The Many Hands of the State: Theorizing Political Authority and Social Control,* edited by K. J. Morgan and A. S. Orloff, 1–32. Cambridge: Cambridge University Press.

Moskos, Peter. 2008. *Cop in the Hood: My Year Policing Baltimore's Eastern District.* Princeton, NJ: Princeton University Press.

Muntaner, Carles, Orielle Solar, Christophe Vanroelen, José Miguel Martínez, Montserrat Vergara, Vilma Santana, Anitía Castedo, Il-Ho Kim, Joan Benach, and the EMCONET Network. 2010. "Unemployment, Informal Work, Precarious Employment, Child Labor, Slavery, and Health Inequalities: Pathways and Mechanisms." *International Journal of Health Services* 40 (2): 281–95.

Myers, Zach. 2017. "Police Urge People to Call 911 to Report Overdoses Despite Risk of Arrest." *Fox59,* May 15. http://fox59.com/2017/05/15/police-urge-911-calls-for-overdoses-despite-risk-of-arrest.

Navarro, Vicente, Carles Muntaner, Carme Borrell, Joan Benach, Águeda Quiroga, Maica Rodríguez-Sanz, Núria Vergés, and M. Isabel Pasarín. 2006. "Politics and Health Outcomes." *Lancet* 368 (9540): 1033–37.

Neff, Joshua, Kelly R. Knight, Shannon Satterwhite, Nick Nelson, Jenifer Matthews, and Seth Holmes. 2017. "Teaching Structure: A Qualitative Evaluation of a Structural Competency Training for Resident Physicians." *Journal of General Internal Medicine* 32 (4): 430–33.

Newland, Chad, Erich Barber, Monique Rose, and Amy Young. 2015. "Survey Reveals Alarming Rates of EMS Provider Stress and Thoughts of Suicide." *Journal of Emergency Medical Services,* September 28. www.jems.com /articles/print/volume-40/issue-10/features/survey-reveals-alarming-rates-of-ems-provider-stress-and-thoughts-of-suicide.html.

Nolan, Kathleen. 2011. *Police in the Hallways: Discipline in an Urban High School.* Minneapolis: University of Minnesota Press.

Novak, Kenneth J., and Robin S. Engel. 2005. "Disentangling the Influence of Suspects' Demeanor and Mental Disorder on Arrest." *Policing: An International Journal* 28 (3): 493–512.

O'Driscoll, Peter T., Jim McGough, Holly Hagan, Hanne Thiede, Cathy Critchlow, and Russell Alexander. 2001. "Predictors of Accidental Fatal Drug Overdose among a Cohort of Injection Drug Users." *American Journal of Public Health* 91 (6): 984–87.

Padgett, Deborah K., Victoria Stanhope, Ben F. Henwood, and Ana Stefancic. 2011. "Substance Use Outcomes among Homeless Clients with Serious Mental Illness: Comparing Housing First with Treatment First Programs." *Community Mental Health Journal* 47 (2): 227–32.

Palmer, Eddie. 1983. "'Trauma Junkies' and Street Work: Occupational Behavior of Paramedics and Emergency Medical Technicians." *Journal of Contemporary Ethnography* 12 (2): 162–83.

Parkinson, Gary C. 1980. "Cooperation between Police and Social Workers: Hidden Issues." *Social Work* 25 (1): 12–18.

Parsons, Talcott. 1951. "Illness and the Role of the Physician: A Sociological Perspective." *American Journal of Orthopsychiatry* 21 (3): 452–60.

Peck, Jamie. 2010. "Zombie Neoliberalism and the Ambidextrous State." *Theoretical Criminology* 14 (1): 104–10.

Phillips, Jennifer E., and William M. P. Klein. 2010. "Socioeconomic Status and Coronary Heart Disease Risk: The Role of Social Cognitive Factors." *Social and Personality Psychology Compass* 4 (9): 704–27.

Pierson, Paul. 1994. *Dismantling the Welfare State? Reagan, Thatcher, and the Politics of Retrenchment.* Cambridge: Cambridge University Press.

Piven, Frances Fox, and Richard Cloward. 1971. *Regulating the Poor: The Functions of Public Welfare.* New York: Pantheon.

Police Executive Research Forum. 2011. "Labor-Management Relations in Policing: Looking to the Future and Finding Common Ground." www .policeforum.org/assets/docs/Critical_Issues_Series/labor-management%20 relations%20in%20policing%20-%20looking%20to%20the%20future%20 and%20finding%20common%20ground%202011.pdf.

Prottas, Jeffrey. 1979. *People Processing: The Street-Level Bureaucrat in Public Service Bureaucracies.* Lexington, MA: Lexington.

Pulkingham, Jane, Sylvia Fuller, and Paul Kershaw. 2010. "Lone Motherhood, Welfare Reform and Active Citizen Subjectivity." *Critical Social Policy* 30 (2): 267–91.

Ragone, Michael G. 2012. "JEMS Surveys 200 Most Populous Cities." *Journal of Emergency Medical Services*, January 31. www.jems.com/articles/print/volume-37/issue-2/administration-and-leadership/jems-surveys-200-most-populous-cities.html.

Rasmussen, Eric, and Erin Smith. 2017. "'Someone Is Going to Die': 25 Investigates Finds Dangerous Ambulance Shortage." *Boston 25 News*, November 21. www.fox25boston.com/news/someone-is-going-to-die-25-investigates-finds-dangerous-ambulance-shortage/651046875.

Regehr, Cheryl, Gerald Goldberg, and Judy Hughes. 2002. "Exposure to Human Tragedy, Empathy, and Trauma in Ambulance Paramedics." *American Journal of Orthopsychiatry* 72 (4): 505–13.

Reyes, Victoria. 2018. "Three Models of Transparency in Ethnographic Research: Naming Places, Naming People, and Sharing Data." *Ethnography* 19 (2): 204–26.

Robinson, Ed. 2004. "Fatal Glitch in 911—Man Died amid Outage." *New York Post*, March 30. https://nypost.com/2004/03/30/fatal-glitch-in-911-man-died-amid-outage.

Rodriguez, Robert M., Jonathan Fortman, Chris Chee, Valerie Ng, and Daniel Poon. 2009. "Food, Shelter and Safety Needs Motivating Homeless Persons' Visits to an Urban Emergency Department." *Annals of Emergency Medicine* 53 (5): 598–602.e1.

Rosenthal, Elisabeth. 2013. "Think the E.R. Is Expensive? Look at How Much It Costs to Get There." *New York Times*, December 4. www.nytimes.com/2013/12/05/health/think-the-er-was-expensive-look-at-the-ambulance-bill.html.

Ross, David W., John R. Schullek, and Mark B. Homan. 2013. "EMS Triage and Transport of Intoxicated Individuals to a Detoxification Facility Instead of an Emergency Department." *Annals of Emergency Medicine* 61 (2): 175–84.

Roth, Alisa. 2018. *Insane: America's Criminal Treatment of Mental Illness*. New York: Basic.

Ruger, Jennifer Prah, Christopher J. Richter, and Lawrence M. Lewis. 2006. "Clinical and Economic Factors Associated with Ambulance Use to the Emergency Department." *Academic Emergency Medicine* 13 (8): 879–85.

Rui, P., and K. Kang. 2014. "National Hospital Ambulatory Medical Care Survey: 2014 Emergency Department Summary Tables." Center for Disease Control. www.cdc.gov/nchs/data/nhamcs/web_tables/2014_ed_web_tables.pdf.

Sallaz, Jeff. 2009. *The Labor of Luck: Casino Capitalism in the United States and South Africa*. Berkeley: University of California Press.

Salomone, Jeffrey P., and Peter T. Pons. 2011. *PHTLS: Prehospital Trauma Life Support*. 7th ed. St. Louis, Mo: Jones & Bartlett Learning.

Sampson, Robert J., William Julius Wilson, and Hanna Katz. 2018. "Reassessing 'Toward a Theory of Race, Crime, and Urban Inequality': Enduring and New Challenges in 21st Century America." *Du Bois Review* 15 (1): 13–34.

Sánchez-Jankowski, Martín. 2008. *Cracks in the Pavement: Social Change and Resilience in Poor Neighborhoods*. Berkeley: University of California Press.

Sasson, Comilla, Jason S. Haukoos, Leila Ben-Youssef, Lorenzo Ramirez, Sheana Bull, Brian Eigel, David J. Magid, and Ricardo Padila. 2015. "Barriers to Calling 911 and Learning and Performing Cardiopulmonary Resuscitation for Residents of Primarily Latino, High-Risk Neighborhoods in Denver, Colorado." *Annals of Emergency Medicine* 65 (5): 545–52.e2.

Scott, Roger L. 2000. "Evaluation of a Mobile Crisis Program: Effectiveness, Efficiency, and Consumer Satisfaction." *Psychiatric Services* 51 (9): 1153–56.

Sears, Alan. 1999. "The 'Lean' State and Capitalist Restructuring: Towards a Theoretical Account." *Studies in Political Economy* 59 (1): 91–114.

Seim, Josh. 2016. "Short-Timing: The Carceral Experience of Soon-to-be-Released Prisoners." *Punishment & Society* 18 (4): 442–58.

———. 2017. "The Ambulance: Toward a Labor Theory of Poverty Governance." *American Sociological Review* 82 (3): 451–75.

Seim, Josh, Joshua English, and Karl Sporer. 2017. "Neighborhood Poverty and 9-1-1 Ambulance Contacts." *Prehospital Emergency Care* 21 (6): 722–28.

Seim, Josh, Melody J. Glenn, Joshua English, and Karl Sporer. 2018. "Neighborhood Poverty and 9-1-1 Ambulance Response Time." *Prehospital Emergency Care* 22 (4): 436–44.

Seiter, Richard. 2002. "Prisoner Reentry and the Role of Parole Officers." *Federal Probation* 66 (3): 50–54.

Shaw, Mary. 2004. "Housing and Public Health." *Annual Review of Public Health* 25 (1): 397–418.

Sherman, Rachel. 2007. *Class Acts: Service and Inequality in Luxury Hotels*. Berkeley: University of California Press.

Slate, Risdon, and W. Wesley Johnson. 2008. *The Criminalization of Mental Illness: Crisis and Opportunity for the Justice System*. Durham, NC: Carolina Academic Press.

Smith, Steven Rathgeb, and Michael Lipsky. 1993. *Nonprofits for Hire: The Welfare State in the Age of Contracting*. Cambridge, MA: Harvard University Press.

Smith-Bernardin, Shannon, and Michelle Schneidermann. 2012. "Safe Sobering: San Francisco's Approach to Chronic Public Inebriation." *Journal of Health Care for the Poor and Underserved* 23 (3): 265–70.

Soss, Joe, Richard C. Fording, and Sanford Schram. 2011. *Disciplining the Poor: Neoliberal Paternalism and the Persistent Power of Race.* Chicago: University of Chicago Press.

Sporer, Karl, Alan Craig, Nicholas Johnson, and Clement Yeh. 2010. "Does Emergency Medical Dispatch Priority Predict Delphi Process-Derived Levels of Prehospital Intervention?" *Prehospital and Disaster Medicine* 25 (4): 309–17.

Squire, Benjamin T., Aracely Tamayo, and Joshua H. Tamayo-Sarver. 2010. "At-Risk Populations and the Critically Ill Rely Disproportionately on Ambulance Transport to Emergency Departments." *Annals of Emergency Medicine* 56 (4): 341–47.

Srebnik, Debra, Tara Connor, and Laurie Sylla. 2012. "A Pilot Study of the Impact of Housing First–Supported Housing for Intensive Users of Medical Hospitalization and Sobering Services." *American Journal of Public Health* 103 (2): 316–21.

Stanley, Ian H., Melanie A. Hom, and Thomas E. Joiner. 2016. "A Systematic Review of Suicidal Thoughts and Behaviors among Police Officers, Firefighters, EMTs, and Paramedics." *Clinical Psychology Review* 44:25–44.

Starr, Paul. 1982. *The Social Transformation of American Medicine: The Rise of a Sovereign Profession and the Making of a Vast Industry.* New York: Basic.

Steadman, Henry J., and Michelle Naples. 2005. "Assessing the Effectiveness of Jail Diversion Programs for Persons with Serious Mental Illness and Co-Occurring Substance Use Disorders." *Behavioral Sciences & the Law* 23 (2): 163–70.

Stiell, Ian, Graham Nichol, George Wells, Valerie De Maio, Lisa Nesbitt, Josée Blackburn, and Daniel Spaite. 2003. "Health-Related Quality of Life Is Better for Cardiac Arrest Survivors Who Received Citizen Cardiopulmonary Resuscitation." *Circulation* 108 (16): 1939–44.

Stuart, Forrest. 2016. *Down, Out, and Under Arrest: Policing and Everyday Life in Skid Row.* Chicago: University of Chicago Press.

Sufrin, Carolyn. 2015. "'Doctor, Why Didn't You Adopt My Baby?' Observant Participation, Care, and the Simultaneous Practice of Medicine and Anthropology." *Culture, Medicine, and Psychiatry* 39 (4): 614–33.

———. 2017. *Jailcare: Finding the Safety Net for Women behind Bars.* Oakland: University of California Press.

Suleiman, Ezra. 2003. *Dismantling Democratic States.* Princeton, NJ: Princeton University Press.

Swor, Robert, Iftikhar Khan, Robert Domeier, Linda Honeycutt, and Kevin Chu. 2008. "CPR Training and CPR Performance: Do CPR-trained Bystanders Perform CPR?" *Academic Emergency Medicine* 13 (6): 596–601.

Sykes, Gresham. 1958. *The Society of Captives: A Study of a Maximum Security Prison.* Princeton, NJ: Princeton University Press.

Tangherlini, Timothy. 1998. *Talking Trauma: A Candid Look at Paramedics through Their Tradition of Tale-Telling.* Jackson: University Press of Mississippi.

Taylor, Todd B. 2001. "Threats to the Health Care Safety Net." *Academic Emergency Medicine* 8 (11): 1080–87.

Thomas, Avis J., Lynn E. Eberly, George Davey Smith, and James D. Neaton. 2006. "ZIP-Code-Based versus Tract-Based Income Measures as Long-Term Risk-Adjusted Mortality Predictors." *American Journal of Epidemiology* 164 (6): 586–90.

Tobin, Karin E., Melissa A. Davey, and Carl A. Latkin. 2005. "Calling Emergency Medical Services during Drug Overdose: An Examination of Individual, Social and Setting Correlates." *Addiction* 100:397–404.

United States Census Bureau. 2012. "Geographic Terms and Concepts—Census Tract." www.census.gov/geo/reference/gtc/gtc_ct.html.

———. 2018. "American Community Survey (ACS)." www.census.gov/programs-surveys/acs.

Van Halen. 1986. *5150.* CD. Burbank, CA: Warner Bros. Records.

Viscelli, Steve. 2016. *The Big Rig: Trucking and the Decline of the American Dream.* Oakland: University of California Press.

Visconti, Adam J., Glenn-Milo Santos, Nikolas P. Lemos, Catherine Burke, and Phillip O. Coffin. 2015. "Opioid Overdose Deaths in the City and County of San Francisco: Prevalence, Distribution, and Disparities." *Journal of Urban Health* 92 (4): 758–72.

Wacquant, Loïc. 2009. *Punishing the Poor: The Neoliberal Government of Social Insecurity.* Durham, NC: Duke University Press.

———. 2013. "Constructing Neoliberalism: Opening Salvo." *Nexus: Newsletter of the Australian Sociological Association* 25 (1): 1–9.

Waitzkin, Howard. 1991. *The Politics of Medical Encounters: How Patients and Doctors Deal with Social Problems.* New Haven, CT: Yale University Press.

Wamhoff, Steve, and Michael Wiseman. 2005/2006. "The TANF/SSI Connection." *Social Security Administration Research, Statistics, and Policy Analysis.* www.ssa.gov/policy/docs/ssb/v66n4/v66n4p21.html.

Washko, Jonathan D. 2015. "Understanding Why EMS Systems Fail." *Journal of Emergency Medical Services,* January 26. www.jems.com/articles/print/volume-40/issue-2/administration-and-leadership/understanding-why-ems-systems-fail.html.

Watkins-Hayes, Celeste. 2009. *The New Welfare Bureaucrats: Entanglements of Race, Class, and Policy Reform.* Chicago: University of Chicago Press.

Weber, Max. (1948) 1991. "Science as a Vocation." In *From Max Weber: Essays in Sociology,* edited by H. H. Gerth and C. W. Mills, 129–56. Abingdon, VA: Routledge.

Weiskopf, Constance. 2005. "Nurses' Experience of Caring for Inmate Patients." *Journal of Advanced Nursing* 49 (4): 336–43.

Williams, David R., and Selina A. Mohammed. 2013. "Racism and Health I: Pathways and Scientific Evidence." *American Behavioral Scientist* 57 (8): 1152–73.

Wilper, Andrew P., Steffie Woolhandler, Karen E. Lasser, Danny McCormick, David H. Bor, and David U. Himmelstein. 2009. "Health Insurance and Mortality in US Adults." *American Journal of Public Health* 99 (12): 2289–95.

Wintemute, Garen J. 2015. "The Epidemiology of Firearm Violence in the Twenty-First Century United States." *Annual Review of Public Health* 36 (1): 5–19.

Western, Bruce. 2006. *Punishment and Inequality in America*. New York: Russell Sage Foundation.

Yuill, Chris. 2005. "Marx: Capitalism, Alienation and Health." *Social Theory & Health* 3 (2): 126–43.

Yuma-Guerrero, Paula, Rebecca Orsi, Ping-Tzu Lee, and Catherine Cubbin. 2018. "A Systematic Review of Socioeconomic Status Measurement in 13 Years of U.S. Injury Research." *Journal of Safety Research* 64:55–72.

Zamosky, Lisa. 2013. "Who Pays for the Ambulance?" *Los Angeles Times*, August 23. http://articles.latimes.com/2013/aug/23/business/la-fi-healthcare-watch-20130825.

Zebib, Laura, Justin Stoler, and Tanya L. Zakrison. 2017. "Geo-Demographics of Gunshot Wound Injuries in Miami-Dade County, 2002–2012." *BMC Public Health* 17 (174): 1–10.

Zekman, Pam. 2017. "Mayor Must Intervene in Ambulance Shortage, Inspector General Says." *CBS Chicago*, December 14. http://chicago.cbslocal.com/2017/12/14/mayor-must-intervene-in-ambulance-shortage-inspector-general-says.

Index

Founded in 1893,
UNIVERSITY OF CALIFORNIA PRESS
publishes bold, progressive books and journals
on topics in the arts, humanities, social sciences,
and natural sciences—with a focus on social
justice issues—that inspire thought and action
among readers worldwide.

The UC PRESS FOUNDATION
raises funds to uphold the press's vital role
as an independent, nonprofit publisher, and
receives philanthropic support from a wide
range of individuals and institutions—and from
committed readers like you. To learn more, visit
ucpress.edu/supportus.